INTRODUCTION

'It took me four years to paint like Raphael,
but a lifetime to paint like a child.'
Pablo Picasso

Those of us who look at art with real interest – that is, hopefully, most of the people who pick up this book – go around with a pantheon of artists already assembled in our heads. There are greater and lesser figures in it, of course, and it evolves over time, with some once-revered artists forfeiting their place in the glorious front row and receding into the shadows, or being excluded altogether and replaced by new idols. An early admiration for Gustave Moreau or Stanley Spencer, say, might give way to a preference for Gustav Klimt or Lucian Freud; conversely, an extensive show of Picasso's ceramics might make us question, at least momentarily, the pride of place that we have long ascribed to the master of Málaga. Aesthetic appreciation is by its very nature continually in flux, even fickle, and occasionally swayed by an inept exhibition or a dismissive review. Some movement, some minor re-evaluation, is always going on; even one's own passing mood, whether gloomy or elated, affects the nature of appreciation, casting a ray of light or a sudden shadow over the Titian or Rodin seen a dozen times before. These constant re-evaluations are no passing fancies, no mere whims, because in the process the viewer is redefined as much as the work viewed. At times, this reappraisal takes on a curious urgency, as if it affected one's whole identity to know whether Matisse's *Piano Lesson*, say, long admired but not seen for years, still holds that same enigmatic enchantment; or indeed if one continues to be immune to the graphic charms of Cy Twombly or the later work of Christian Schad, as I certainly am. But then any worthwhile pantheon can only be highly personal, even if it stays within the bounds of the accepted canons of taste. It is the result of the intricate, intimate re-evaluation that never stops taking place as one weaves between fresh discovery and lost illusion.

Over the years, a fairly stable hierarchy is established, however, with less jostling in the ranks and the top artists that one carries around – the artists who have trained one's eye and defined one's sensibilities most – having grown increasingly prominent. They sit there in a kind of parliament, reminiscent (in my mind's eye) of Francisco de Goya's *Junta of the Philippines*, with the light playing between them, debating the respective qualities of their art and the influence it has had in forming that elusive concept, part instinct, part education, known as 'taste'. So, after a time, one carries this assembly of the chosen few about wherever one goes, like a portable altar, a symbol of one's faith, referring to it constantly, above all while visiting an exhibition or museum.

Keeping this choice company and communing with it is one of the art critic's or art historian's great privileges. We choose our heroes and live with them: they are our points of reference, our touchstones. An editor of mine at the *New York Times Book Review* once told me that he began every morning, very early, by reading a favourite Greek or Latin author in the original; 'after that,' he added, 'no one can spoil your day'. I particularly liked the image of this ageing, learned classicist in solitary communion with Aeschylus or Ovid as the streets beneath his apartment in mid-town Manhattan reverberated with the clanging of garbage trucks and the wailing of police sirens. Indeed, I was so struck by it that I followed his example as best I could by starting every morning of my remaining fortnight in New York in contemplation of a favourite object or painting at the Metropolitan Museum. My friend was right, I realized on the first visit, having wandered in awe amongst its magnificent Assyrian sculptures. Once you have glimpsed the grandeur of Ashurnasirpal II's court, constructed so many, many centuries before Grand Central Station, the humdrum problems of the present-day urban round – the clogged traffic, a stray incivility, the driving sleet – cannot touch you. Communication with great art confers a certain inviolability.

Perhaps this is the inherent draw of art, its prime magnetism, the quality that brings it so close to religion. It takes you almost literally out of yourself, back in time, forward in imagination. It lifts you up and transforms you: the everyday is no longer everyday but specific, enhanced, sacred. Even if you know nothing about these larger-than-life alabaster reliefs, once painted in vivid colours and lining the walls of the

vast Northwest Palace at Nimrud eight centuries before Christ, you are aware that you are in the presence of an achievement of such might and conviction that it deserves (as much as anything does) to be called 'divine'.

My own pantheon – the pantheon from which the following selected essays have been drawn – does not have these Assyrian sculptures at its forefront, although they are certainly there in the shadows, along with dozens of other ancient artefacts, statues as well as model funerary boats from Egypt, bronze figures, and stone temples from Greece. But the front ranks are filled with artists, personal heroes, from the past century or so. If things had turned out differently, I should have been happy enough to have focused on any other great period of art, whether Minoan or medieval or nineteenth century. One reason I did not was because, as a very young man, I was too absorbed by life itself and finding my own place in it to be able to take a real interest in art.

When that interest finally came, it was not as a result of a memorable visual epiphany – the dazzling pattern of form and colour in a Poussin that suddenly illuminated a dark museum corner, or the serene organization of shapes across the sculpted facade of a Romanesque abbey set among fields of lavender – but through a chance event in everyday life. And this in turn, it occurs to me as I write, may be why my interest in art has always been rooted in a more general fascination with artists themselves, their thoughts and feelings, their lives as well as the images that they have created. The interest was awoken in fact not – as, more conventionally, it should have been – from the brush I had with formal art history as a student, but from a rather random encounter in what one might call very ordinary, if not actually low, life: in a Soho pub, smelling of spilt beer and disinfectant, shortly after opening time. It was June 1963, and I was about to have an experience that would change my life, making art as vital as a love affair, or even as urgent as a murder mystery in which you have become implicated.

Standing aimlessly in that pub, I am about to meet a man who, however distinct and haunting his art, had led a life that was more cruel, more bizarre, and in every way more extreme than the images that issued from it. I had not yet seen those images – indeed, the painter in question was barely a name to me at that time – and when I first did, I found them frightening, degenerate, and repellent. But it was too late by then:

I was already caught up in an existence so powerful that even the horrific art that it produced did nothing to diminish my fascination with his larger-than-life personality (although I remember fervently hoping that life was not about to imitate the art I had just seen).

I have often wondered, since that fateful first meeting with Francis Bacon, whether it was his example alone that made me quite as receptive to artists' lives as to their art. My brief study of art history had already convinced me that I could not aspire to being a Wind or a Wittkower or indeed a Wölfflin or a Worringer. Even my admiration for Erwin Panofsky stemmed partly from the awareness that I could never hope to emulate even the footnotes of such far-reaching, erudite investigations into art history. Mine was a lighter temperament that sought less to deduce theories than to make art more accessible and shed light on its cultural and biographical origins. Nor did I warm to those I considered lesser writers on art who focused exclusively on the work in itself, eschewing all background information in favour of a purely formal analysis, which, while enlightening from time to time, struck me as a sacrifice of the general – the bigger picture – to the particular. Dry analyses of form and composition with claims to scientific rigour have their place, for sure, serving admirably to counter ill-considered art gush. And indeed, art historians such as Rosalind Krauss and Linda Nochlin have in different ways exposed the more reductive and problematic aspects of biography-based interpretation. But while rigorous formal and iconographic analysis might sharpen the eye, it often falls short of quickening the heart, which has always been my primary interest. Concentration on minute details makes perfect sense when confronted by a fragment of an ancient frieze, since it has already been shorn of its wider context. But why deprive research on a work of its matrix and its maker if they are readily available? It should be axiomatic (as it was for Giorgio Vasari when he wrote his *Lives of the Great Artists*) that the most compelling accounts of an artist blend both life and work, case by case, in whatever proportion seems appropriate. It is also evident that many lifelong lovers of art history find their way into the field's more intellectual and sociohistorical elements via a curiosity about its great characters and their stories.

But getting to know Bacon – his aura, his background, his overall attitudes to existence – before I got to know his work in any depth (in

the early 1960s, there was precious little on public display) meant that my reactions to his canvases would always be deeply coloured by my knowledge of the man. Anyone who had met him would have been struck by the stark contrast between this seemingly suave, amiable boulevardier and the panicked violence emanating in waves from his pictures. There was total disjunction, a Jekyll-and-Hyde enigma that hit you between the eyes. How could one possibly relate to the other? The answer could only be found in what the artist himself called the 'violence of life', in his own enigmatic biography and his reactions to what had befallen him as a hypersensitive child who had witnessed both the 'Troubles' and two world wars while remaining doomed, because of his sexuality, to remain an extreme, tortured outsider throughout.

> *'Know then thyself; presume not God to scan,*
> *The proper study of mankind is Man.'*
> Alexander Pope, *Epistle II, Essay on Man* (1733)

Although the essays that follow were written in varied circumstances and for different purposes, certain leitmotivs soon make themselves felt. Many modern artists have thought of themselves or have been regarded as outsiders, and none more so than the first to appear in these selected writings. Vincent van Gogh's life reads like a nightmare from which he was never able to awake: an unrelenting round of frustration, isolation, and humiliation. In his greatest paintings, it can be felt in every sweep of the brush, embedded in the grain of the paint like memory traces. Painting is Van Gogh's triumph over his life's shortcomings, incorporating and defusing them in the sheer, exultant act of touching the blank canvas into colour, into deep whorls of observation and emotion. In Van Gogh's work, you never have to look for the life since all his life is there, in the chromatic altercation, the awkward form, the frenzied brushstrokes raining down. More graphically than any other artist, his life is his work; his work, his life: they flow freely into one another until they form a whole, and as you go from one painting to another you can almost hear his voice in the background, paraphrasing or forming the words of yet another letter to his brother Theo, creating a continuous, background commentary.

The essay that follows in this selection – on Aristide Maillol and the 'red' Count Kessler – came about for a very telling reason. I had been asked to write a preface to an exhibition of Maillol's sculpture in Barcelona, and although I was familiar with the artist's life and work, I did not find the indirect entry that I needed to grapple with the subject until I learnt about the relationship between the earthy, Catalan sculptor, a lifelong devotee of the full female form, and his refined, homosexual patron, Count Harry Kessler. The fact that the two men, with their widely differing temperaments and tastes, were joined on their shared, frequently bedevilled trip to Greece by the famously oversensitive Hugo von Hofmannsthal provided further grist to my mill, and whereas I might have produced a worthy but dull introduction to Maillol's serene forms, I felt that a more biographical approach might enable me to get closer to this spontaneous son of the soil who, once at the Acropolis (I was delighted to learn), clambered up to embrace the caryatids on the porch of the Erechtheion until he was hauled down again like a foreign satyr by the on-site guards; this anecdote alone suggested vividly how he came across to his contemporaries. If there is a light-hearted, irreverent element to this approach, it is even more apparent in 'Picasso's Trousers'. Having been commissioned by a men's fashion website to write about Picasso, it occurred to me that the great Spaniard, about whom everything appeared to have been said, had always displayed a distinct dress sense, both when he wanted to impress (as during the '*époque des duchesses*') and when he was merely clowning about in hats for the camera.

A comparative gravitas returns with one of the themes that has interested me most throughout my writing career: the cross-pollination between literature and art. In this anthology, there are not only overviews of Joan Miró and Alberto Giacometti's interaction with the poets of their time, but a portrait of a still underestimated 'painter-poet' genius, Henri Michaux, and an analysis of the way R. B. Kitaj, with his obsessively literary imagination, constructed his pictures like novels. Literature was abidingly important to many of the artists I discuss here, from Balthus and Salvador Dalí to Bacon and Freud. As Frank Auerbach, a close friend of the latter two artists, once said graphically, 'Painting is a cultured activity. It's not like spitting.' Since formal analysis can go only so far in illuminating how these intricate crossovers between art and literature

take place, a biographical background becomes totally relevant. It would be impossible to describe the imaginative cohesion achieved between Miró and Paul Éluard in their illustrated book *À Toute Epreuve* without proper mention of the way their lives interacted, just as the significance of both Surrealism and existentialism to Giacometti and his friendships with André Breton, Jean-Paul Sartre, and Jean Genet are key to an understanding of his work. Similarly, the impact of LSD and mescaline on Michaux or 'outsider' art on Jean Dubuffet – central elements of their biographies – are of prime importance in evaluating the work that absorbed and was transformed by them.

Exactly why the charismatic Russian nobleman Nicolas de Staël chose to throw himself to certain death from his eleventh-storey studio terrace in Antibes will probably never be known. But this biographical fact stands like a huge question mark over every evaluation of the impetuous artist's work, to the extent that his entire oeuvre could be interpreted as a mediation between the forces of darkness and light, exultation and despair, as well as between the apparently irreconcilable demands of abstraction and figuration. Staël's imagery was torn between harmony and chaos, and at its most poignant it remains poised on the knife's edge of these dominant contradictions in the art of mid-twentieth-century Europe – held in precarious equilibrium for a brief second before he fell. His contemporary Zoran Music, also Slav, came from the even greater darkness of a concentration camp. For decades, this survivor of Dachau persisted in composing ravishing *vedute* of Venice, boats bobbing past the Giudecca or sombre yet faintly glimmering interiors of San Marco. He then found he could suppress his memories no longer, and the horrors of mass extermination – pale, stick-thin bodies, dead and dying, piled up in heaps – erupted amid these visions of earthly paradise and replaced them with the deadly banality of hell. Music was a true witness of his century, but as an artist he would have made no lasting impact if his life had not been totally upended one day because an offer to join the SS caused him to burst out laughing right in the face of a Nazi officer – a spontaneous reaction that had him deported to Dachau instead.

Also from the Balkans, another child of the past century was the gifted, obsessive Montenegrin artist Miodrag Đurić, better known to friends and the art world alike as Dado. Dado's visions of hell ran as fluently from his

brush – which he sometimes represents as a dripping penis – as music did from Mozart's fingers. Early memories of seeing dead or dying men strung up in trees around his native Cetinje during the Second World War set the tone for his entire oeuvre. The canker was everywhere, in the legless children as much as in the putrescent elders (many of the former were modelled on Dado's children, and the latter, on his Paris and New York dealers), yet all these ingenious scenes of catastrophe took place against a beneficent blue sky. Dado's own life remained true to this vision, and he lived in spectacular squalor with his large family in a half-timbered house in the lush Normandy countryside that might have been a banker's retirement dream save for the leaking roof, the unhinged doors, and the artist's bright frescoes of doom that covered every inside and outside wall. Like Staël, like Music (or indeed like Giacometti and Bacon), Dado could not escape a vision of extremity that marked his life and his art deeply. As with those other artists, this struck a deep chord in me, and I have often wondered to what extent our understanding and our friendship were linked to the fact that we both grew up under the shadow of war.

> 'To me Art's subject is the human clay, / And landscape but a
> background to a torso; / All Cézanne's apples I would give away /
> For one small Goya or a Daumier.'
>
> W. H. Auden, *Letter to Lord Byron*, 1936

This is not one of Auden's finer poems, admittedly, but its point is well taken. I would certainly take exception to giving away all of Cézanne's apples, but much as I admire his singular still lifes, I should prefer to see them not only as spatial constructions on a table, but hanging on the tree, surrounded by branches and possibly even pecked at by birds; and (however little, admittedly, this has to do with Cézanne's unique achievement) I should rather see that tree with other trees and possibly glimpse the background, the landscape against which it grows, with some trace of the human beings that inhabit that world. In other words, I would argue once again for completeness over isolation, the whole over the detail, the big picture.

Auden's lines seem to me to sum up part of the point I have been trying to make in this brief preface-cum-curriculum-vitae. I had never

expected the following essays and catalogue introductions, some of which date back to the 1960s, to be included in an anthology. Whether long or short, written for newspapers, magazines, or exhibition catalogues, they have certain similar themes running through them. On the whole, the artists discussed are ones whom I have most admired over the years, sometimes to the extent of writing about them frequently, getting to know them personally, or even devoting a book or an exhibition to them, as I have in the case of Maillol, Schad, Bacon and Giacometti, Miró, Tàpies and Staël, Music, Dado, and Mason. Others have come about because a particular publication commissioned a text about them. Looking over the list, however, it is gratifying to note that there is not a single artist here whom I would disavow, even though the choice represents a span of nearly sixty years.

Nor was I conscious at the time that I was writing them that these 'Artists' Lives' constituted an attempt to bring both the art and the artist alive. Although I am only mildly interested in what this or that painter had for breakfast, I was fascinated to learn, for instance, that Picasso would regularly lament never finding a soup that could match those he remembered and still savoured from his childhood in Málaga, just as Giacometti's brother, Diego, enthralled me when he described the Paris that he and his brother discovered when they first moved there and found their studio in Alésia, behind Montparnasse, in the early 1920s. Sonia Delaunay recalling Apollinaire or Balthus evoking Rilke also had a mesmerizing effect on me, illuminating their lives and their works in a stimulatingly unexpected way.

Similarly, to take more contemporary artists, by going round Barcelona at night with Tàpies, I realized that the sage imbued with Oriental philosophy and quantum physics whom I had encountered in the studio was only one facet of a fascinating artist who could also let his hair down, joke, and gossip when out on the town and primed by good Catalan wine, just as Raymond Mason's sculptures, meanwhile, never released their secrets so convincingly as when he spoke to me about his upbringing in working-class Birmingham and his first years of blissful exile in Paris. Again, sitting next to Michaux at a dinner made it abundantly clear that the acerbic writer/painter, then well into his eighties, was as sharp-witted, challenging, and unpredictable in table talk as when writing and drawing.

So the life of the artist has always appeared to me not necessarily as interesting as the work (after all, my encounter with Bacon apart, it was always the work that first sparked my interest), but as an integral part of any close study of the ways images originate and evolve. The life is integral to the whole discourse about art, and the complex relationship between the two remains crucial since they react to each other in subtle, often self-reflexive ways. No doubt that was why I have never become closely involved with abstract art: its load of tactile humanity has always seemed to me too dispersed, too etherealized into a vocabulary of form and colour – in a word, too abstracted. It reminded me of the logical positivism with which I had struggled as a student until I realized that what I was looking for was a philosophy not so much of thought and language but of feeling, of being and living, that I then found in the no doubt woollier domains of existentialism. Similarly, it was no accident that the two artists who have been most central to me are Giacometti and Bacon, who more than any others were instrumental for keeping figuration alive and meaningful throughout the long dominance of abstract art. To take the point further, it is surely no accident that I, brought up in the immediate postwar period, should have been so viscerally and lastingly drawn to their stark, unforgiving imagery.

Having sketched out my trajectory through the art world and nailed my aesthetic preferences to the mast, I realize that I have omitted perhaps the most essential, and certainly the earliest, component in the origin of these essays: my parallel, literary pantheon. The lifelong interest that I have in writing about art stemmed, first and foremost, from an interest in writing itself. It surely follows that, alongside the artists who have fascinated me, I should own up to a few of the writers whose work has marked me most. There are clearly legions of writers that one has absorbed, from the Bible and Shakespeare on, but as I began to search for my own 'voice', I was drawn both to the prolix brilliance of Joyce and the sparse precision of Beckett, to the haunting despair of Eliot and the magical irony of Borges. Many others were, of course, ringing in my ears, and I could go on, citing the dark skills of the Jacobean dramatists through the sheer 'visuality' of Stendhal to the infinite subtleties of Proust (then the queer extravagance of Djuna Barnes, *e tutti quanti*). But those four writers were my 'gods' as I wrote; and, as mentioned, I remained particularly alert to the affinities

between these two pantheons of mine, such as Eliot's importance for Bacon or Beckett's closeness to Giacometti.

If the following essays are essentially portraits of the artists, at work in their times, they also create, as in a two-way mirror, a portrait of the person who wrote them at different moments of his career, which, as one after the other of these articles reveal, was spent chiefly in Paris, even if the articles concerned took him occasionally as far afield as Montenegro and São Paulo.

So all portraits are in part self-portraits, and in the end there is perhaps no more spontaneous and unselfconscious portrait to be found of oneself than through the portraits one paints of other people. I am delighted that these texts have survived their transient existences in daily newspapers or monthly magazines and filtered through several decades as dog-eared, yellowing copies – surprised to find themselves still alive, and even more astonished to be offered a crisp, new lease of life. Where necessary, they have been edited and updated, but I hope that they still carry the original mixture of enthusiasm, perplexity, and conviction that they had when first written. Certain essays share a similar theme and have been grouped accordingly.

It is a great privilege to have been read once. To be reread has to qualify as every writer's dream.

PART I

1

VINCENT VAN GOGH: BETWEEN SHADOW AND THE SUN

What better way to begin a book about artists' lives than by a tribute to Vincent van Gogh? Of all the artists I have been closely engaged with, he is the one whose life never fails to move me by its poignancy: the chasm between his lofty aspirations and the misery of his everyday existence. This comes across so vividly in his letters to his brother Theo that the artist's voice rings in one's ear, as if one had actually overheard him talking. At the same time, no other artist I know speaks so directly, so urgently, to the eye. Van Gogh's very brushstrokes communicate instantly, bypassing any meaning or narrative. His images pulsate with a near intolerable intensity, forcing themselves on to your unconscious before you have even had time to take them in consciously, like the glare of the sun, or like the first strains (for all the differences between the two creators) of a Wagnerian opera. You submit to Van Gogh, and the impact his art has had on you becomes the measure by which you will judge all subsequent pictorial sensation.

I wrote this essay at the invitation of a French academic publisher, who then had it translated into French. This is the first time it has been published in English.

No artist has communicated more powerfully and more universally than Vincent van Gogh. Whatever the museum, however distinguished the other painters on display, his pictures always stand out, demanding immediate attention. The simpler the subject – some worn-out boots, a vase of sunflowers – the more insistent the works seem to grow, as if

ARTISTS' LIVES

Front cover images: (from top left) *Lucian Freud in his studio*, 1954 (detail). Photo Paul Popper/Popperfoto via Getty Images. *Dora Maar*, 1941 (detail). Photo Rogi André; National Gallery of Art, Washington. *Salvador Dalí*, 1950s (detail). Photo Guy Gillette/Photo Researchers History/Getty Images; © Fundació Gala-Salvador Dalí. *Aristide Maillol*, Marly-Le-Roy, 1934 (detail). Photo Josef Breitenbach; © Josef and Yaye Breitenbach Charitable Foundation, courtesy Gitterman Gallery.

First published in the United Kingdom in 2023 by
Thames & Hudson Ltd, 181A High Holborn, London WC1V 7QX

First published in the United States of America in 2023 by
Thames & Hudson Inc., 500 Fifth Avenue, New York, New York 10110

This paperback edition published in 2024

Artists' Lives © 2023 Thames & Hudson Ltd, London

Text © 2023 Michael Peppiatt

Edited by Andrew Brown
Designed by Karolina Prymaka

British Library Cataloguing-in-Publication Data
A catalogue record for this book is available from the British Library

ISBN   978-0-500-29796-4

Printed in Great Britain by Bell & Bain Ltd, Glasgow

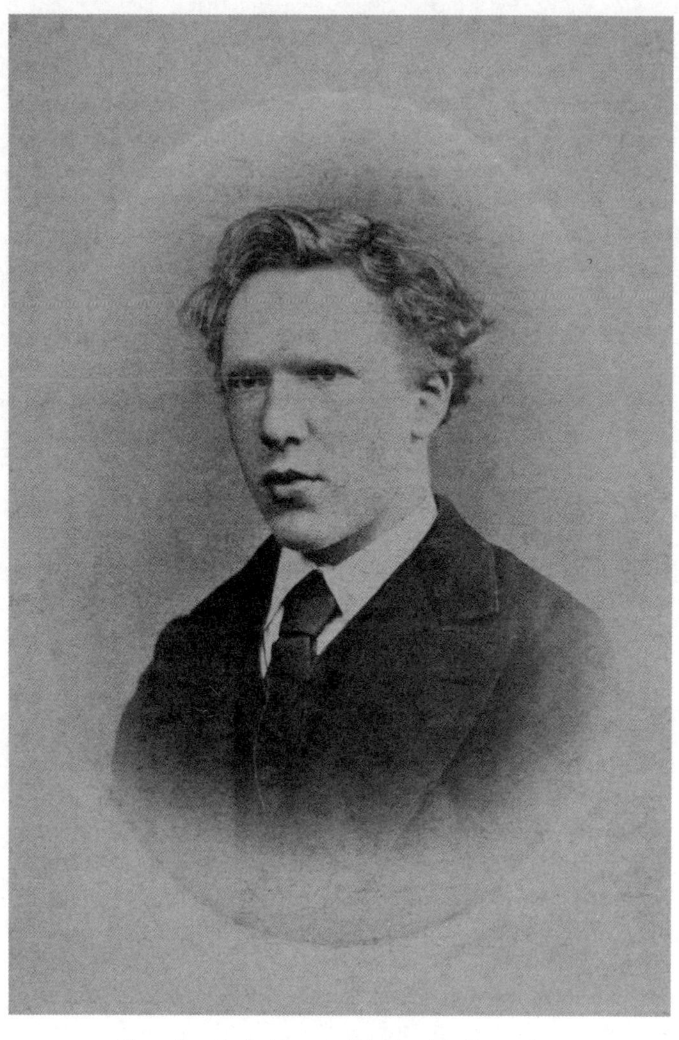

Vincent van Gogh at the age of nineteen, The Hague, 1873,
photographed by Jacobus de Louw

Van Gogh had infused the very grain of his pigment with living urgency. Never, perhaps, has there been less of a division between art and life. In looking at a Van Gogh picture, we seem to enter that specific moment in the artist's existence, sharing with an unforgettably disturbing directness its extremes of exaltation and despair.

Dramatic as Van Gogh's life was, only an artist of consummate skill could have succeeded in conveying these emotions so intensely. What sets him apart is not the human tragedy that he embodies but his unique ability to suggest the depth of his passions and forebodings. Art was the one means that he had at his disposal to attempt to deal with the rawness of his feelings. To counterweigh the scepticism that his paintings provoked and his own very real doubts, he had a manic drive and an ultimate belief in his own special powers, which allowed him to absorb whatever was most useful to him from every artist and every new movement that he encountered.

Thus, parallel to the often poignant facts of his life, there is a stylistic biography in which one sees Van Gogh's career developing in quite clear-cut stages, from his early, dark, and often clumsily painted compositions through the key influences of Japanese art, Impressionism, and pointillism to the highly personal, swirling outlines and expressionistic brushstrokes of his last period. Amazingly, these stylistic shifts all occurred within just ten years (from 1880 to his death in 1890), with many of his most famous paintings accomplished as the end drew nearer.

In Van Gogh's case, it is particularly difficult to separate the life from the work, since each illuminates and intensifies the other. His art is a high-wire act of extraordinary balance amid constant danger and threat. Van Gogh communicated this tension so directly that his pictures seem to have been snatched from the brink of disintegration. But they nevertheless form a distinct pictorial language, expressing degrees of joy and foreboding never registered before. With their startlingly modern awareness of inner turmoil, his paintings were to open new horizons for artists from Munch to Bacon by way of the Fauves and the German Expressionists. It is also this enduring legacy to the history of art that the following essay sets out to explore.

*

*'And – my plan for my life is to make paintings and drawings,
as many and as well as I can – then, when my life is over, I hope
to depart in no other way than looking back with love and
wistfulness and thinking, oh paintings that I would have made!'*

Letter 405, to Theo van Gogh, Nieuw-Amsterdam, Sunday,
11 November 1883[1]

Go into any good collection of late-nineteenth-century painting, and
the work that catches your eye most insistently is likely to be a Van Gogh.
It is not because its subject matter is more arresting – on the contrary, his
themes are among the simplest, even the most disinherited, imaginable.
Nor is it because his canvases demonstrate such obvious evidence of
stylistic innovation or technical mastery: indeed, they often look awkward
or excessive, and in the company of such polished practitioners as Degas
and Seurat, Van Gogh seems to stand out like a clumsy provincial at an
elegant reception. The quality of his work is uneven, his inspiration often
derivative, and his scope relatively limited. So one might very reasonably
wonder why, a good century after the end of his brief painting life, his
works exercise a breadth of appeal and fascination that has no equal in
the history of modern art.

There seems to be something in the very grain of Van Gogh's paint
that, once lodged in one's visual sense, never loses its power to disturb
and excite. It creates an immediate, physical sensation, far swifter and
more commanding than most aesthetic responses, as if the nerves were
alerted by a particular rawness in the pigment. His paintings appear
above all to talk not more loudly, but more urgently than any of his contemporaries' work. While Monet's vivid compositions or the structured
monumentality of Cézanne make other, more ordered claims on our
attention, Van Gogh pulls us repeatedly by the sleeve and forces us to
confront a vision of manic intensity. It is as if, having failed in his earlier
vocation as a preacher, the Dutch painter were making up for lost time:
if the world cannot be made to listen, then it must be made to see. The
magic and the abiding mystery of the images that tumbled from Van Gogh
with such extraordinary speed is their intensity. It is an intensity that was
once the preserve of religious painting but which, since the Renaissance,
had gradually lost the role that it played in art. Perhaps the greatest of

Van Gogh's achievements was that he restored fervour to art. Painting became the faith that he had sought so desperately elsewhere, and he knew instinctively how to communicate this extraordinary conviction – which endured every test and hardship – to utmost effect.

This intensity, which enabled Van Gogh to instil into a discarded boot the degree of pathos that one might traditionally associate with a Pietà, came from a life that had begun in painful confusion and which became more and more exclusively devoted to painting. One might expect, beside the potency of his images and their devouring exactions on him, that Van Gogh would have led an uneventful, colourless life. In some outward respects, it was an uneventful, colourless life. Yet because it was mirrored so closely in his paintings – as well as in his remarkable letters – the life has a relevance and a poignancy second to none. And since the myth has never ceased to grow around him since his death, the artist's life has generated quite as much interest and speculation as the work – even though, of course, Van Gogh's entire existence would have sunk without trace had it not given rise to such a haunting body of paintings.

Few artists' lives have been so inextricably intertwined with the works that they created. At every turn, in thumbnail sketches and drawings, in oil studies and fully fledged pictures, Van Gogh records his life, whether it is a glass of absinthe, a newly discovered landscape, a face that has touched the artist's deep compassion, or the joy prompted by a flowering almond branch. The works form the most complete diary, kept day by day, almost instant by instant, recording an astonishing diversity of thought and mood. Just as the work is the most complete and profound autobiography, the life was totally directed towards the accomplishment of his art. Quite early on, to his acute distress, Van Gogh realized that he would never have a normal existence, however deeply he desired it. A wife and family, and even close companionship – beyond the bond with his long-suffering brother Theo – would remain out of reach. It came as a bitter realization, but in time he gave into it, understanding that, without such hostages to fate, he was free to concentrate all his aspirations and energies on his art. Thus any account of Van Gogh would fall automatically short if it did not view the artist's life and work as an inseparable whole.

*

*'But on the road that I'm on I must continue; if I do nothing,
if I don't study, if I don't keep on trying, then I'm lost, then
woe betide me. That's how I see this, to keep on, keep on, that's
what's needed.*

*But what's your ultimate goal, you'll say. That goal will
become clearer, will take shape slowly and surely, as the croquis
becomes a sketch and the sketch a painting.'*

Letter 155, to Theo van Gogh, Cuesmes, between about
Tuesday, 22 and Thursday, 24 June 1880

Nothing in Van Gogh's early life pointed to the meteoric artistic career to
which he was destined. He was born at the presbytery in Zundert, a village
in North Brabant, on 30 March 1853 – exactly one year after the stillbirth
of his parents' first child, also named Vincent Willem van Gogh. Vincent
was the eldest of a family that eventually numbered three boys and three
girls. Neither his father, a pastor in the Dutch Reformed Church, nor his
mother showed much understanding of their son's difficult, taciturn
temperament or his later, artistic aspirations. From these early days, only
the passionate interest that he developed in nature, making detailed but
otherwise undistinguished drawings of birds, insects, and plants, was to
remain with the artist throughout his life.

At sixteen, after a fragmentary education, Vincent began an apprenticeship at The Hague office of the Paris-based art dealers Goupil & Cie,
which had taken over his uncle's gallery there. Vincent's efforts as a
fledgling dealer were well appreciated, and in 1873 he was transferred
to the firm's branch in London. Meanwhile, his younger brother Theo,
with whom he had sworn an oath of lifelong friendship, started work at
Goupil's gallery in Brussels. In London, Vincent developed an admiration
for Constable and Turner, as well for the black-and-white illustrations
he found in magazines such as *The Graphic*. He also fell unhappily in
love, and his performance at the gallery deteriorated. Against his will, he
was then transferred to Paris, where it became clear, both to him and to
his employers, that he had lost all interest in the art trade. Having been
dismissed in April 1876, Vincent returned to England, where he tried his
hand as an unpaid teacher and then as assistant to a Methodist preacher

on the outskirts of London, where, to his great satisfaction, he was occasionally allowed to preach.

Lack of any future prospects caused Van Gogh to go back to Holland in 1877 and work in a bookshop in Dordrecht. By now he was, as his sister Elisabeth commented, 'daffy with piety', attending churches of all denominations and writing sermons. He began taking courses to prepare himself for theological studies, but this proved to be another false start. After a brief training as an evangelist, he went to the Borinage coal-mining region in the south of Belgium. Over the following two years, he identified deeply with the miners and their families, voluntarily living a life of hardship, giving away all his possessions, sleeping on straw, and barely eating. His parents were in despair, and his father even talked of having him committed to a mental asylum. Meanwhile, Van Gogh had made numerous drawings, some crudely energetic, others showing the fine sense of draughtsmanship that was to become the foundation of his development as an artist. Theo had already suggested that he might become a painter, and once his religious ardour had begun to cool, Vincent moved in October 1880 to Brussels to study art, making friends with the artist Anthon van Rappard and exploring his enthusiasm for Rembrandt and the peasant paintings of Jean-François Millet.

In April 1881, Van Gogh returned to live with his parents in Etten. He concentrated on mastering perspective and anatomy, while making copies from Millet and portraits of local people. His efforts were encouraged by the painter Anton Mauve, under whose guidance he produced his first watercolours and still lifes in oil. A hopeless love affair with his widowed cousin Kee Vos ruined an otherwise peacefully productive period. At the end of the year, a bitter argument with his father led Van Gogh to break with his parents. He left for The Hague, where he rented a room and studied drawing with Mauve. From this time on, he became financially dependent on Theo, with whom he corresponded regularly and at length, ranging over a wide variety of concerns and topics, until he died. He set up house openly with one of his models, a pregnant prostitute called Sien, and made numerous drawings of her: some of them, such as *Sorrow*, are among his first truly personal works. 'I want to make drawings that *move* some people', he wrote to his brother (Letter 249, The Hague, on or about Friday, 21 July 1882).

Despite his attachment to Sien and her newborn son, the relationship proved untenable, although this turned out to be the one and only time Van Gogh was to experience any kind of domestic happiness. Having broken with Sien, he left for Drenthe, a province whose remote farmhouses and peat fields had attracted many painters, including Van Rappard and Mauve, before him. The brooding landscape moved him to make a number of eloquent paintings, but isolation and lack of materials persuaded him that he would be better off living again with his parents, who were now established in Nuenen, a village close to Eindhoven.

Relations with his parents were strained ('There's a similar reluctance about taking me into the house as there would be about having a large, shaggy dog in the house', he confided to Theo [Letter 413, on or about Saturday, 15 December 1883]), but Van Gogh set to work with a will, modelling himself on Millet and concentrating on scenes of local peasants in the fields and weavers at their looms. He continued to read widely, and in order to correlate musical harmony with Delacroix's theories of colour, he tried learning to play the piano. Towards the end of 1884, he embarked on a long series of studies of peasants' heads and hands that culminated in the masterpiece of his Dutch period, *The Potato Eaters*. Shortly before he completed this complex figure painting from memory, his father died of a stroke. Although deeply affected by the death, Van Gogh continued to work hard, and when finding models became difficult, he turned to painting landscapes, much inspired by the collections that he had seen at the recently opened Rijksmuseum in Amsterdam.

Feeling the need to widen his horizons, Van Gogh left Nuenen at the end of 1885 for the port of Antwerp. Here he explored not only the docks and the dance halls but also the museums, where Rubens's great figure paintings particularly impressed him. He enrolled at the Royal Academy of Fine Arts so he could find models cheaply, but his incisive graphic brilliance failed to find favour with the teachers there. Plagued by illness, he was diagnosed with advanced syphilis, and before leaving Antwerp he painted a strange picture featuring a skeleton smoking a cigarette. For some time, he had mooted the idea of moving to Paris to live with Theo, who was now established there as an art dealer. In March 1886, he arrived at the Gare du Nord without warning, sending his brother a note to meet him at the Louvre. Theo took him in, and not long thereafter the brothers moved into a larger apartment on the rue Lepic in Montmartre, where one room served as a studio. Vincent began studying at Fernand Cormon's atelier, where he drew and painted from live models and plaster casts, and met Émile Bernard and Henri de Toulouse-Lautrec, who later made a memorable portrait of him in pastel. He was also to get to know several other important artists during this period, including Camille Pissarro, Georges Seurat, Paul Signac, and, of course, Paul Gauguin.

The fact that Van Gogh wrote very few letters while he was staying in Paris means that we know less about this period than the other stages in his brief painting career. But there is no doubt that the experience transformed the way he thought and painted, since there, at last, he was directly confronted by the latest developments in modern art, notably the work of the Impressionists and Post-Impressionists, making him aware that the dark palette that he had cultivated in Holland was now altogether retrograde. He began consciously to lighten his range of colours by painting a series of still lifes and flowers, as well as the views over Paris that he could see from his bedroom window. He also painted portraits and landscapes, experimenting with the techniques of Impressionism and pointillism and absorbing them into a highly personal manner of his own. Japanese prints, which he had begun to collect in Antwerp, exerted another powerful influence on his emerging mature style. But contact with the big city, with its intrigues and warring factions of artists, combined with excesses of absinthe and overwork began to undermine Van Gogh's already fragile health. For some time past, he had been dreaming of the bright colours and sunlight of the South, and suddenly, much to his beleaguered brother's relief, he decided to move to Arles in Provence.

*

'I'd like you to spend some time here, you'd feel it – after some time your vision changes, you see with a more Japanese eye, you feel colour differently. I'm also convinced that it's precisely through a long stay here that I'll bring out my personality. The Japanese draws quickly, very quickly, like a flash of lightning, because his nerves are finer, his feeling simpler.'
Letter 620, to Theo van Gogh, Arles, on or about Tuesday, 5 June 1888

Van Gogh arrived in February 1888 to find Arles under snow. As soon as he had found a hotel room and bought some paints, however, he set to work. He painted several versions of the *Langlois Bridge*, and as the local orchards began to flower, he produced a series of rapturous studies of blossoming fruit trees. In May, he began renting the Yellow House but was too short of money to make it habitable until the following September. Meanwhile, he put up at the Café de la Gare; the owner's wife, Madame Ginoux, became the model for his *L'Arlésienne* portraits. During this time, Van Gogh started sketching with a reed pen, which responded to his wish to make every mark expressive and enabled him to make some of his most remarkable drawings.

In May, he sent his first consignment of paintings to Theo, with whom he had resumed a vigorous correspondence. When he went down to Saintes-Maries-de-la-Mer in the Camargue in June, for instance, he sent his brother evocative word-pictures, full of colour, such as this description of a nocturnal walk:

'I took a walk along the seashore one night, on the deserted beach. It wasn't cheerful, but not sad either, it was – beautiful. The sky, a deep blue, was flecked with clouds of a deeper blue than primary blue, an intense cobalt, and with others that were a lighter blue – like the blue whiteness of milky ways. Against the blue background stars twinkled, bright, greenish, white, light pink – brighter, more glittering, more like precious stones than at home – even in Paris. So it seems fair to talk about opals, emeralds, lapis, rubies, sapphires. The sea a very deep ultramarine – the beach a mauvish and pale reddish shade, it seemed to me – with bushes.'

Letter 499, to Theo van Gogh, Saintes-Maries-de-la-Mer, on or about Sunday, 3 or Monday, 4 June 1888

This short stay produced a number of vivid paintings and reed-pen drawings of fishing boats and fishermen's cottages.

Alongside a series devoted to harvesting scenes, including such large canvases as *Stacks of Wheat near a Farmhouse*, Van Gogh painted *The Sower*, where he returns to his earlier interest in peasant scenes but with a completely different palette of highly saturated, complementary colours. He also made several outstanding portraits, notably of Joseph Roulin, the postal agent who remained a staunch friend to Van Gogh during his subsequent breakdown, the gardener Patience Escalier, and the Belgian poet Eugène Boch. During the summer, he produced four *Sunflower* paintings as part of an extensive decorative scheme for the Yellow House, which he hoped, out of an ill-fated mixture of idealism and loneliness, he could turn into a 'Studio of the South' where like-minded artists could live and work together. Van Gogh was especially eager for Gauguin, whose work and personality he greatly admired, to join him in Arles. When at length Gauguin accepted, Van Gogh was overjoyed. While awaiting Gauguin's arrival, Van Gogh moved into the Yellow House, furnishing it with money that Theo had sent him, and continued painting hard despite bad health. Having finished the famous view of his new dwelling, Van Gogh made his *Self-Portrait as a Bonze*, which he intended to exchange with Gauguin for the latter's self-portrait, and the *Night Café*, also rendered in harshly contrasting colours, in which the troubled atmosphere and nightmarish perspective hint at the effects that excessive quantities of absinthe can have – and which Van Gogh knew all too well from drinking bouts with his friend Roulin.

When Gauguin eventually arrived, Van Gogh felt instantly better, although he remained anxious as to whether his friend would like Arles and their somewhat curious domestic arrangements sufficiently to stay. For the first few weeks, the two artists appeared to benefit from one another's company. Once the weather became unsuitable for painting out of doors, they began working together in the confines of the Yellow House. Gauguin persuaded Van Gogh, for whom working from life had become second nature, to paint from memory, which he did, producing among other pictures *Memory of the Garden in Etten*. However, Gauguin's direct influence made Van Gogh feel uneasy and vulnerable, and before long arguments began to rage between the two highly opinionated artists. For his part, Gauguin was understandably disturbed to wake up from time to time to find Van Gogh standing by his bed, silent and staring. On 23 December, two months after Gauguin's arrival, their dramatic quarrel broke out. According to Gauguin, Van Gogh first threatened him with a cut-throat razor and later turned it on himself. The following morning, having bled profusely from his partly severed ear and apparently close to death, Van Gogh was admitted to hospital, where he made a rapid recovery thanks to the care of Dr Félix Rey, whom the artist later portrayed. He also produced two haunting self-portraits with his bandaged ear. Not long thereafter, Van Gogh suffered another attack; he was convinced that he had been poisoned and he began hearing voices in his head before being hospitalized again. On his release, a group of local citizens petitioned the mayor of Arles to have Van Gogh sent back to his family or institutionalized. Conscious that he was no longer able to look after himself, Van Gogh had already decided to have himself admitted to the asylum in nearby Saint-Rémy-de-Provence.

*

'I'm struggling with a canvas begun a few days before my indisposition. A reaper, the study is all yellow, terribly thickly impasted, but the subject was beautiful and simple. I then saw in this reaper – a vague figure struggling like a devil in the full heat of the day to reach the end of his toil – I then saw the image of death in it, in this sense that humanity would be the wheat being reaped. So if you like it's the opposite of that Sower I tried before. But in this death nothing sad, it takes place in broad daylight with a sun that floods everything with a light of fine gold.'

Letter 800, to Theo van Gogh, Saint-Rémy-de-Provence,
Thursday, 5 and Friday, 6 September 1889

At Saint-Rémy, Van Gogh was provided with two cells, one for sleeping, and the other for painting. He set to work right away, painting the landscape that he could see from his window and the flowers – notably irises and lilacs – in the asylum's garden. In June 1889, barely a month after his arrival, Van Gogh produced *The Starry Night,* an ecstatic vision of white and gold spheres illuminating the firmament that arches over a Provençal village sunk in sleep. Occasionally, the artist was allowed to work under supervision outside the asylum, but the need to paint proved so strong that no amount of confinement would have deterred him. He painted cypress and olive trees writhing with such intense, flamelike energy that they irradiate from the canvas.

In July, Van Gogh was struck down by another severe attack that prevented him from working for six weeks. When he recovered, he painted some harvesting scenes from woodcuts by Millet, a Pietà inspired by Delacroix, and two haunting self-portraits. In September, with Theo's help, a couple of his pictures, *Starry Night over the Rhône* (completed in Arles) and *Irises*, were exhibited at the Société des Artistes Indépendants in Paris; and in January 1890 five of his works were shown at the annual exhibition of the artist group Les Vingt in Brussels. In the same month, the critic Albert Aurier published an outspokenly laudatory article about his work in the *Mercure de France*; Van Gogh was gratified by it, but he wrote to Aurier to tell him that Adolphe Monticelli and Gauguin were far more important artists than he was. When he learnt that Theo had become a father, he painted some almond blossoms for the child's nursery. Van Gogh completed five portraits of Marie Ginoux, 'L'Arlésienne', based on a drawing by Gauguin. He was allowed to take one of them as a present to Madame Ginoux in Arles, but was later found wandering about in a pitiful, aimless state.

A long period of illness ensued, during which Van Gogh nevertheless managed to produce numerous studies of themes dating back to his time in Nuenen, which he called 'Memories of the North'. Having recovered, he told Theo that he felt 'damaged by boredom and grief' at Saint-Rémy (Letter 868, to Theo van Gogh, Saint-Rémy-de-Provence, Sunday, 4 May 1890), and that what 'remains to me of reason and capacity for work is absolutely in danger' (Letter 866, to Theo van Gogh, Saint-Rémy-de-Provence, on or about Friday, 2 May 1890). He entreated his brother to have him moved closer to Paris. Dr Paul Gachet, who was also a collector and an amateur painter close to many artists, agreed to look after him if he came to live near to him in Auvers-sur-Oise. Before leaving the asylum, Van Gogh experienced a further burst of creativity, producing another night scene and the magnificent *Vase with Violet Irises against a Yellow Background*.

It was agreed that he should stop in Paris on his way to Auvers. Meeting him for the first time, Theo's wife, Johanna, was astonished to encounter a sturdy, broad-shouldered man who looked healthier than her own husband. Van Gogh, who was visibly heartened by the prospect of change, stayed with them for three days and was able to pass in review the huge number of works by him that had accumulated in their apartment. He also enjoyed seeing his little nephew, Vincent Willem, but the artist nevertheless found Paris too overwhelming to extend his stay.

*

'They're immense stretches of wheatfields under turbulent skies, and I made a point of trying to express sadness, extreme loneliness.'
Letter 898, to Theo van Gogh and Johanna van Gogh-Bonger, Auvers-sur-Oise, on or about Thursday, 10 July 1890

Auvers made an immediately positive impression on him. For some time, Van Gogh had yearned for a more northern atmosphere, reminiscent of his childhood in Holland, and the rustic village's thatched roofs in particular made him feel at home. Van Gogh also took to Dr Gachet, while noting that the physician seemed in quite as fragile a mental state as he was himself (later he decided that Gachet was indeed 'sicker' than he was). In early June, less than a month after his arrival, Van Gogh painted an arresting portrait of Gachet with what he called, in a letter to Gauguin, 'the deeply sad expression of our time' (Letter RM23, to Paul Gauguin, Auvers-sur-Oise, on or about Tuesday, 17 June 1890). Having taken a room in the local inn run by the Ravoux family, Van Gogh was free to come and go, paint when he liked, or visit Gachet's house, where he could admire the doctor's collection of Impressionist paintings or make himself useful in the garden. Mostly, however, he continued to devote himself to capturing his reactions to the life around him in drawings and pictures. Having painted the narrow streets of Auvers with their thatched houses, he climbed up out of the village towards the wheatfields that lay on every side, evoking their green and golden vistas under lowering, sunless skies.

On one occasion, Theo and Johanna brought little Vincent to see him. On another, Van Gogh made the journey to Paris, where Theo had invited a few friends, including Toulouse-Lautrec and Albert Aurier; but Van Gogh grew tired quickly and left. He had been particularly disturbed by his brother's admission that he had been thinking of leaving his secure job and setting up on his own as an art dealer. Wholly dependent on Theo as he was, Van Gogh went away full of concern not only for his brother's future, but also for his own. His behaviour appears to have grown increasingly unpredictable. At one point, he flew into a rage with Dr Gachet because an Armand Guillaumin picture that he owned had been left unframed. He also seems to have become excessively downcast at the news that Theo was taking his family directly to Holland for a holiday without first visiting him.

On Sunday, 27 July 1890, Van Gogh had lunch with the Gachets, then left as if to return to work. In the evening, the Ravoux family waited in vain for him to return for supper. When he did return, Arthur Ravoux followed him to his room, where Van Gogh admitted that he had shot himself in the chest. Dr Gachet and another local doctor were sent for, but they decided against any attempt to remove the bullet, which had passed beneath the heart, and simply dressed the wound. Theo arrived from Paris and tried to convince his brother that he would survive, but Vincent simply replied: 'La tristesse durera' (The sadness will last). When it became clear that his brother was dying, Theo held him in his arms. Around half-past one in the morning of 29 July, Vincent van Gogh died, aged thirty-seven.

Six months later, his brother Theo died a broken man. It was left to his widow Johanna, who had met Vincent a handful of times, to begin to build the artist's posthumous reputation with a few small exhibitions selected from the huge body of work that Vincent had left with Theo – some 550 paintings as well as hundreds of drawings. Johanna also began to read and order Vincent's vast correspondence (initially to draw closer to her late husband). The work was continued by her son, Vincent Willem, who lived long enough to preside over the opening of the Rijksmuseum van Gogh in Amsterdam in 1973. Today, the whole process has come more than full circle. From being a madman ignored by all but his faithful brother, Van Gogh has become a source of fascinated interest and inspiration for literally millions of people.

Yet the mystery of his life and work remains. For all the popular biographies, scholarly analyses, and exhibitions that the Van Gogh phenomenon has produced, the central enigma has never been explained away. How did this largely self-taught pastor's son create in a bare ten years and in such harsh conditions an oeuvre that continues to generate deep human sympathy, exaltation, and unease? What kind of conviction enabled him to live through illness, neglect, and despair to produce such a number of astonishing masterpieces, often on an almost daily basis? By what terrible symmetry was the inventor of sublime new visions of colour also the invalid who, in crisis, would ingest his own paints? Why did he really end his life, and why, with all the pictures and letters before us, can we infer so little about his state of mind in those last fateful days? The questions go on and on, with the same urgency that Van Gogh communicated in his frenzied brushstrokes, which still reverberate in the mind long after they have been absorbed by the eye.

There is no mystery, though, as to why Van Gogh still fascinates us so compulsively, since what lies at the centre of his penetrating gaze is always the human condition, our own fate, ourselves. The miracle of Van Gogh is not that he succumbed to the conflicts of his emotions and his mental instability but that he lived through them for so long and produced images remarkable not only for their pathos, but for their painterly inventiveness and knife's-edge control. In the last analysis, it is in the order that Van Gogh gave to his inner chaos that his enduring genius lies.

1 All quotations from the artist's letters come from the Van Gogh Museum's authorized English translations, available at <https://vangoghletters.org>.

Originally published as 'Vincent van Gogh: Ombres et lumières', in Jeanne Bouniort and Michael Peppiatt, *Vincent van Gogh* (Paris: SCEREN-CNDP, 2003, 'Actualité des Arts Plastiques' collection)

2

ARISTIDE MAILLOL
AND THE RED COUNT

*Or how the German diplomat and collector
Count Harry Kessler transformed the French
sculptor's career and became a significant
patron of contemporary art*

Aristide Maillol had never loomed large in my life until I began curating exhibitions for the newly founded Musée Maillol in Paris in the late 1990s (*L'École de Londres, de Bacon à Bevan* being the first of several shows that I worked on there). This institution, which occupies the ground floor of an impressive classical townhouse built round a large *cour d'honneur* on rue de Grenelle, was founded by Maillol's redoubtable model Dina Vierny, who later became a successful art dealer. A little later, I got to know the director of the Caixa Fundació Catalunya, which has exhibition spaces at Antoni Gaudí's spectacular La Pedrera in Barcelona, who was interested in Maillol not only because of his achievement as a sculptor, but also because he was a fellow Catalan and therefore of special interest to the Catalan independence movement that had long been militating throughout the province. I was delighted to work on a Maillol exhibition in one of Gaudí's masterpieces and, as I went through all the available literature on Maillol, I came across this decisive relationship in the sculptor's life that I found so curious and so revealing, in both artistic and human terms, that I took it as the subject of my essay for the catalogue.

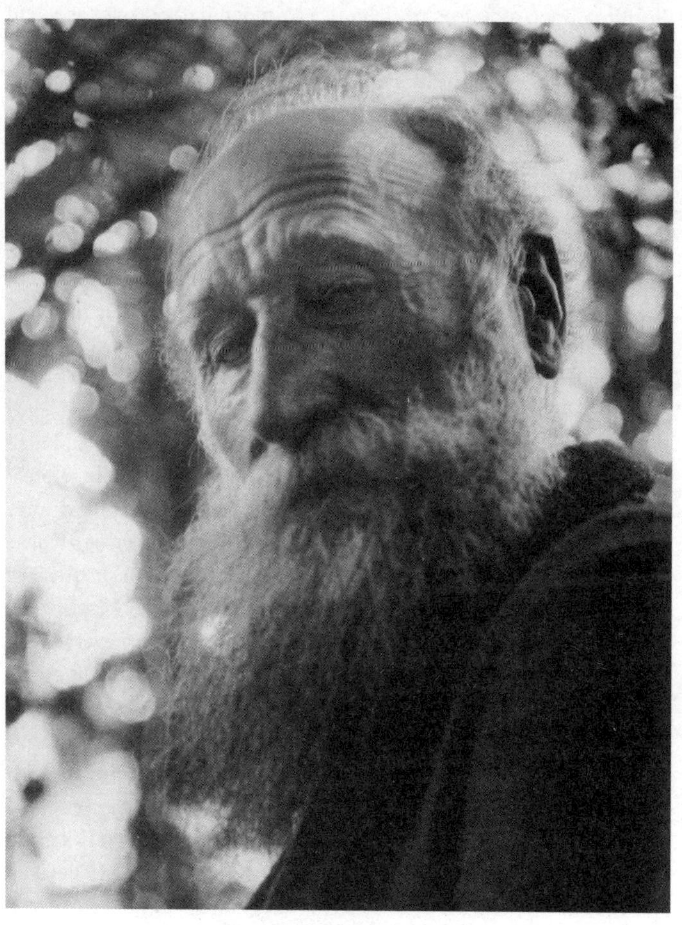

Aristide Maillol, Marly-le-Roi, 1934,
photographed by Joseph Breitenbach

They could not have been more different. One was born into a hugely wealthy, distinguished family (it was even rumoured that he was the illegitimate son of Kaiser Wilhelm I), a cosmopolitan polyglot as fluent in English and French as he was in his native German, rubbing shoulders with all the great personalities of his time, flitting from capital to capital, project to project, elegant, discreetly homosexual, and generous to a fault; the other was rooted in his native Catalan soil, as gnarled and robust as the vines his ancestors had always tended, accustomed to poverty, tight-fisted, a peasant in manners and dress, taciturn, with one big idea, endlessly dreaming of women and uniquely gifted in his ability to commemorate them as ideal, harmonious forms, not only in sculpture, but also in pencil, paint, and even tapestry. From 1904, when they first met, through the Great War, and until the late 1930s, the two men, poles apart except in their shared belief in the supreme importance of art, changed each other's lives radically and for ever.

Anyone who was anyone in the arts, politics, or international high society of the first half of the past century would have immediately recognized the name – and probably the slim silhouette and fine features – of Harry Kessler, nicknamed the 'Red Count' during the 1920s because he combined a privileged, aristocratic background with progressive socialist beliefs. Having been educated in several countries, Kessler – his first names, Harry Clément Ulrich, say it all – was at home everywhere and nowhere, travelling constantly between Weimar and Berlin, Paris and London, Rome and New York, commissioning books and works of art, organizing exhibitions, pursuing delicate diplomatic missions, speaking at key international debates and conferring in private with influential statesmen. No doubt it was this very versatility, combined with the intensity he brought to everything he undertook, that has made Kessler a less memorable figure than he might have been had he been able (like his friend Maillol) to focus his undeniable gifts and drive on a single, grand enterprise.

No one, certainly, was more keenly aware and observant than Kessler of the *grandeurs et misères* of his times, which he sought to influence repeatedly and chronicled vividly in a diary that grew so detailed and voluminous that, when fully published, it will run to several thousand pages.[1] The English poet W. H. Auden, never one to be easily impressed, called the multilingual, globetrotting Kessler 'probably the most cosmopolitan man who ever lived' and, more significantly, a 'Crown witness to his times' who seemed to have met every important contemporary except T. S. Eliot and Winston Churchill (although Kessler attended the same preparatory school just outside London as the great British statesman).[2] What would have struck anyone who came into contact with Kessler was not only how well briefed he was about the political events and personalities of his day, but also how keen a sense he had developed of what was most original in all the arts. He played both a major role in introducing modernism into the highly conservative ruling classes of Wilhelmine Germany and acted – while flitting from one capital to another – as a patron and catalyst for the new aesthetic across Europe.

Several of the individuals whom Kessler knew in Paris (notably the painter Émile Bernard and the writer André Gide) had talked to him about an unusual artist called Aristide Maillol, but in the end it was his old family friend Auguste Rodin who, having generously sung Maillol's praises as 'our strongest sculptor', convinced the count to make his acquaintance (Rodin, it should be added, was by then too internationally revered to fear competition). Kessler had in fact already acquired a small clay model by Maillol, which he carried around with him, and in his diary he described how he felt 'a curious, growing magic from its simple forms … It entrances me more and more.' From that same diary, we know that the first meeting between the two men took place on 21 August 1904 at the sculptor's house in Marly-le-Roi, not far outside Paris. Kessler recorded his first impressions carefully: '(Maillol) lives in a very primitive little country house in the middle of a big open orchard. When we knocked on the door (there was no bell), his wife came out onto a little balcony and called out "Aristide! Aristide!" towards the garden, whereupon there appeared a farmer type in a blue smock and a wide-brimmed, workman's straw hat on his head, greeting us in a very broad, rustic patois. He didn't introduce himself beyond this, and he didn't bother much about our names either. He was just Maillol: looking about 40 years old, with a full, untrimmed, black beard, very bright, expressive blue eyes, wiry, with a pronounced, noble, Spanish nose.'[3]

At that point, the French sculptor was forty-three years old and almost exactly halfway through a career that had been characterized more by hardship and obscurity than by stylistic breakthrough or public recognition. Indeed, Maillol had until then been primarily focused on tapestry and the decorative arts in general. However delicate and skilled his achievements in these had undoubtedly been, this was still Maillol before Maillol: a late developer in painstaking search of a vision that, once found, would inspire everything he drew, painted, and sculpted for the rest of his life. His beginnings as a sculptor had been timid and known mostly to a small circle of admiring fellow artists. Not long after his first encounter with Kessler, however, Maillol reached an important turning point as a sculptor by having the plaster version of his first monumental work, *La Mediterranée*, put on show at the following year's Salon d'Automne in Paris. Praise from the influential critic (and long-time Maillol enthusiast) Octave Mirbeau, as well as from the distinguished German art historian Julius Meier-Graefe, signified that, after many trials, Maillol's career had at last been launched. As Gide wrote trenchantly of *La Méditerranée*:

> *'She is beautiful. She has no meaning. This is a work of silence.*
> *I believe one must go far back in the history of art to find such*
> *a perfect disregard of everything that could distract from the*
> *manifestation of beauty.'*

Maillol's tardily begun career as a sculptor was to receive the first of many significant boosts when Kessler commissioned him to sculpt *La Méditerranée* in stone – and to render another subject he had been working on, 'Desire', in high relief. Not only did these two major commissions consolidate Maillol's burgeoning reputation, they also considerably eased his financial situation, since Kessler (whose wealth derived from international banking and vast tracts of land) was unusually open-handed with money. As Maillol recalled a year later, with elegant simplicity but obvious emotion, 'Thanks to him I was born again.'

For Kessler, it was nothing out of the ordinary to be visiting an artist in his studio, discussing projects, buying work, and recommending other pieces to friends of his. He had been an early supporter of the most radical and innovative artists in Germany, notably George Grosz and Max Beckmann, as well as the highly controversial Norwegian Edvard Munch, who over the years painted a series of portraits of the dapper count.

Meanwhile, dandy and aesthete that he was, Kessler's artistic enthusiasms were by no means limited to painting and sculpture. Fancying himself as a writer (book projects abound in his diaries), Kessler knew many of the leading literary figures of the day as well, being acquainted with poets as diverse as Rainer Maria Rilke and Jean Cocteau and developing a friendship with the then enormously influential Austrian dramatist Hugo von Hofmannsthal (whom he would invite, along with Maillol, on an epic trip to Greece). He was also deeply involved in design of all kinds, from typography and book production to architecture and interior decoration. In the latter field, he particularly admired and patronized the Belgian designer Henry van de Velde. Kessler liked to think of all the arts existing, at least potentially, in a close, symbiotic relationship; and his main residence in Weimar became a kind of elegant showcase for the combined talents of van de Velde, Maillol, and his favourite painters, notably Pierre Bonnard and Émile Bernard.

Yet with Maillol, the relationship was to prove unusually long and fruitful. Over the following decade, Kessler became not only his biggest collector by far, possessing at one point no fewer than forty of his sculptures and drawings, but also the link to several other important German art-lovers who subsequently purchased his work. As a result, Maillol's reputation stood higher in Germany than anywhere else throughout his career, his native France included (as the sculptor from Roussillon frequently complained). Moreover, Kessler would commission Maillol to produce numerous woodcuts to illustrate the luxury books, notably Virgil's *Eclogues*, that he was to produce for the small, high-quality publishing house that he set up in Weimar (called the Cranach Presse, since he himself lived, in some splendour, on Cranachstrasse).

Meanwhile, for all his jubilation at having found an artist whose work corresponded so closely to his ideal of a simple, natural, ancient beauty, Kessler had one major reservation about Maillol. For Kessler, the classical touchstone of beauty (and the focus of his carefully disguised, pent-up passion) was the male physique. Keenly aware of the discretion that a homosexual in a prominent social position needed to exercise – a public scandal involving high-ranking German officials had reinforced his wariness – Kessler kept his sexual tastes and practices top secret, even in his diaries. But he could not disguise them altogether, and parallel to his admiration for Maillol was his pressing conviction that the sculptor of pure form should turn his attention to the grace of the male, as well as the female, figure.

In his zeal to open Maillol's eyes to virile beauty (as well, no doubt, as a means of cementing their friendship), Kessler invited Maillol on a trip to London not long after their first encounter. When Kessler had asked Maillol point blank why he had never concentrated on the male form, Maillol, cannily enough, had cited the lack of models: Rodin could afford all the models he wanted, he explained, but poorer artists such as himself generally had to make do with their wives. Ostensibly, the London trip was also to develop a book project that Kessler had in mind, and for which he believed Maillol pre-eminently gifted. Thus they went to the British Museum not only to look at antique sculpture ('a revelation for me', Maillol later declared, 'I understand sculpture and art in general better'), but also to study specific typefaces. Goaded by his covert passions, Kessler then ferried Maillol down to the (traditionally both poorer and freer) East End of London to see some boxing bouts – '*Abends zum Boxen*', as Kessler notes laconically in his diary. Seated close to the ring in Whitechapel, Maillol 'sketched with unbelievable swiftness the fighters – sketches which are comparable to the finest of Delacroix's', Kessler noted with obvious satisfaction. From this trip – which included visits to the National Gallery and Dulwich Picture Gallery, as well as breakfast at the Savoy Hotel – it was clear that the boxers had made an indelible impression. 'I'll never forget it', Maillol exclaimed (presumably aware that this is what his new patron wanted to hear). 'They weren't men, they were gods.' And Kessler carefully noted down the names of some of the fighters they had seen as potential models: 'Charley Knock (for Maillol, a Greek, slim as a heroic statue) … Also for Maillol, Darkey Haley and Jack When'.

Back in France, Maillol continued to lament the lack of a model as he began work on *Desire* – where a man and a woman embrace – as well as a statue of Narcissus, the latter inspired by his recent exposure to male physiques. Kessler lost no time in finding him one – a professional cyclist and jockey named Gaston Colin. Once '*le petit* Colin' begins to pose, slender and naked, Kessler becomes an ever more assiduous visitor to the sculptor's studio, photographing the seventeen-year-old from every angle for his diary. (Meanwhile, Maillol, who was working more enthusiastically from a female model, naked save for sexy black stockings, regularly pulls open the studio door to reveal his jealous wife, Clotilde, peeping through the keyhole). From this time on, Kessler begins a passionate affair with the boy, and under pretext of employing him as his chauffeur takes him on trips to Normandy and the Channel Islands; and Maillol, sensing that what Kessler really desires is a portrait of Colin, abandons all pretence at mythology and creates a naturalistic, boyish sculpture entitled *The Cyclist*. Although the work is perfectly skilful, one senses that Maillol's interest had not been sparked by the ephebe's languid form. It remains too specific and too descriptive, far from Maillol's ideal of pure volumes in which all detail has been subsumed – like a pebble, as he once put it, rubbed smooth by the sea. This was exactly the direction that Maillol wanted to avoid: it was the way that Rodin had taken and made his own; and one of Maillol's obsessions, which recurs time and again in his recorded conversations, was the need to differentiate his sculpture as radically as possible from Rodin's, which he admired and which he seems to have absorbed precisely in order to chart his own course.[4]

Although Kessler makes no direct reference in his diary to his long-lasting relationship with Colin (one of the very few the discreet count appears to have experienced), he does digress on sexuality in general and the constraints imposed on it by society – constantly referring back to the example of Greek antiquity in which 'sensuality is the axis and pole of everything'. Admiration for Greek civilization had of course been particularly prominent in Germany since Johann Joachim Winckelmann (himself homosexual) had published his hugely influential account of ancient art in 1764. No doubt Kessler, who was steeped in classical learning, had been mulling over a trip to Greece for some time; but the encounter with Maillol (himself as simple and natural in his art as an ancient Greek, in Kessler's mind, and coming moreover from the essentially Greek land-scape of the hills around the bay of his native Banyuls) appears to have accelerated the plan.[5] To make the discovery of Greece – and *Griechentum* in general – a more profound, shared experience, Kessler decided to take with him not only Maillol but also the highly strung Hofmannsthal.

We can only guess what Kessler had in mind by taking this ill-assorted couple with him; he had at first tried to invite Maurice Denis, van de Velde, and the exotically named Hungarian painter József Rippl-Rónai along as well. As a general dilettante and would-be writer, Kessler shared the contemporary interest in creating a *Gesamtkunstwerk* or 'total art-work' (to which he clearly aspired in the carefully designed interiors of his house in Weimar); and he might well have fantasized that, as the men drank in the spirit of ancient Greece, some magnificent collaborative effort – such as a beautifully written, illustrated, and produced book – might see the light of day. No mention of such a project occurs in Kessler's carefully kept records of the trip, in which – true to his overriding admiration of the sculptor – Kessler captures as many of Maillol's comments and reactions to the changing landscape and the art and architecture that they encounter as possible.

While Maillol was generally 'like a fish in water' (as Kessler wrote to his sister), Hofmannsthal struck a gloomy note from the very moment he met up with the two other men in Athens in May 1908. The hypersensitive Austrian was soon put out not only by the light and heat of Greece, but also because he was obliged (because of Maillol) to abandon the beloved German of his writings to speak in French. All in all, Greece was a disappointment for him: 'I had expected quite falsely to find an Italy, and I found the Orient', he later confessed. Maillol, meanwhile, was in his element since he not only found so many similarities with Banyuls, but was genuinely moved by the strength and beauty of Greek art. Page after page of Kessler's diary is peppered with Maillol's reflections about the sculptures that they see and their relationship to each other, the space where they are sited, and the landscape. When they climb up to the Acropolis, Maillol is overwhelmed, simply saying: 'C'est le plus beau jour de ma vie' (It's the most beautiful day of my life). His enthusiasm knows no bounds. Indeed (in one of the rare amusing moments recorded by Kessler), the priapic French sculptor is so moved in the Erechtheion that he clambers up to embrace one of the female statues – only to be sternly reprimanded and ordered down by an attendant.

As Maillol feverishly drew the sculpture that he saw and began work on a sculpture of a Greek boy (with Kessler possibly hankering after a new juvenile conquest), disaster constantly hovered over this curious troika. Once their coach struck a child, whose fate haunted them for days as he hovered between life and death ... before finally recovering. Extreme heat (accentuated by their thick city suits), varied illnesses, personality clashes, and frayed tempers set the daily tempo, occasionally erupting into farce and fierce quarrels. At one point, feeling bored, Hofmannsthal rummaged through Kessler's luggage in search of something to read. On realizing this, the lofty Kessler was appalled by such an ungentlemanly intrusion (and perhaps anxious that Hofmannsthal might have glimpsed some homoerotic photo or other incriminating souvenir), and he upbraided his Austrian companion so severely that the latter broke down in tears. (This behaviour, Kessler later reflected with snobbish disdain, was doubtless attributable to Hofmannsthal's partly Jewish origins. Although not avowedly anti-Semitic, Kessler occasionally revealed the prejudices of his upper-class, conservative upbringing – although it is interesting to note that both men came from bourgeois families ennobled because of their wealth).

Physically and mentally tougher than his two more refined, etiolated companions, Maillol appears to be the only one to have benefited durably from this month-long rough-and-tumble through the land of Phidias. Exposure to so much antique sculpture gave him the assurance that he had drunk deep at the well of early classicism, in a way that visits to the Louvre and the British Museum never could. He perceived Greece as a larger, more exotic version of his Catalan birthplace, and if he needed further proof that his search for full, rounded form, devoid of naturalistic details and expressive devices à la Rodin, united him with the great tradition of Western sculpture, he found it in the masterpieces welded into the Greek landscape. The trip had completed his education as a sculptor, and he was able to face the future with the confidence of having studied the great primary sources of his art.

Hofmannsthal had taken himself off early, much to his own and his companions' relief. Kessler attempted bravely to live up to his ideal of gentlemanly behaviour in all circumstances, but even his well-disciplined facade, all stiff upper lip and unfailing politesse, began to crack badly towards the end of their stay. Immediately after he parted from Maillol in Naples, his health gave way and he succumbed not only to rheumatism but to a nasty bout of recriminations. Travelling and talking with Maillol had been all very well (Kessler noted in his diary), he was amusing in his picturesque way, but in the end conversation with him became impossible because he would state his own opinion and then counter anybody else's with a flat 'Enfin, moi je sens comme ça' (That's how I see things). Equally trying had been Maillol's table manners, which included eating with his fingers and spitting out fish bones and the like directly onto the carpet. Most irritating of all had been his peasant-like pleasure in getting others to pay for everything, even fares, tips, and entrance tickets. It had been a kind of '*mésalliance*', the count sighed (once again retreating into weary, patrician prejudice): Maillol belonged so inalterably to a different social class.

Such misgivings did not last long, however, and once the unwelcome intimacies of travelling to foreign lands together had been put into perspective, Kessler was once again beating a devoted path to Maillol's studio door. Of all the count's myriad projects, the idea of founding a great, private press was the one that came to obsess – and to ruin – him most. Flitting from one artistic endeavour to another (he had, to take one disastrous example, suggested himself as co-author of the libretto of *Der Rosenkavalier*, only to have Hofmannsthal disabuse him), Kessler eventually found his real calling as a uniquely demanding and sensitive publisher – and it is undoubtedly for a handful of exquisitely produced books that he will be best remembered. One of these is the edition of Virgil's *Eclogues* that, with infinite pains over many years, he struggled to produce, with lettering cut by the English typographer Eric Gill and a series of sublime woodcuts by Maillol. Due in part to his consummate familiarity with all the decorative arts, Maillol came to illustrate a wide variety of books over his long career, from *Daphnis and Chloe* and the *Georgics* to works by the Belgian Symbolist poet Émile Verhaeren. But by common assent it is the woodcuts that he produced for the *Eclogues* that constitute his finest work in this domain. Begun in 1912, they were not in fact published until 1926, because of the war and innumerable other interruptions. Maillol himself proved slow to produce these exquisite illustrations (with extraordinary single-mindedness, he appears to have avoided anything that would take him away from his central vocation as a sculptor of sublime female form), to the extent that Kessler admitted he had to go and 'stand over' Maillol (probably with the lure of a cash payment), whether in Marly or Banyuls, to get them eventually done.

Another adventure that the two, by now middle-aged, men became involved in after their return from Greece was the manufacture of a special paper for bibliophile publishing. When Kessler complained that he could not find sufficiently high-quality rag paper for his deluxe editions, he awakened Maillol's innate interest in materials. The sculptor who had studied weaving techniques and firing procedures came to life: if you wanted a good paper, first you had to find good-quality linen sheets, then add the right amount of hemp fibre, before you chewed them and chewed them.... From these humble beginnings, with the assistance of Maillol's nephew, Gaspard, the celebrated Montval paper works was set up in a little factory in the neighbouring fields. The paper produced – combining the two men's initials, MK, in its watermark – proved exceptionally successful, being used for the Cranach Presse's two most famous books, the *Eclogues* and a *Hamlet* illustrated by Gordon Craig, and later becoming a byword in bibliophile circles. Once war had broken out in 1914, however, the paper mill's days were numbered. Maillol's connections with Kessler and other German collectors were suddenly viewed with suspicion. Maillol received a telegram from Kessler, warning him that war was imminent and that he should bury his sculpture. A newspaper article entitled 'Their Artists, Spies and Secrets' appeared in the right-wing press intimating that Maillol was a German agent; the cry was further taken up by Léon Daudet under the heading *'L'art Boche'* in the far-right newspaper *Action française.* Maillol was officially called on to prove that he was not a spy. Meanwhile, the little paper mill was burnt to the ground, with Maillol nearly being killed in the incident.

Once this ugly chapter had passed and the war had ended, Maillol and Kessler did not meet again until 1922 to continue their work together on the *Eclogues* and other publications for the Cranach Presse. Kessler remarked on how the intervening years had aged the sculptor (who had feared constantly throughout the war for his son Lucien, a pilot for the French air force). The relationship between the Frenchman and the German remained very cordial, but Kessler's earlier enthusiasm as a collector and commissioner of works of art appears to have waned. The postwar years were to take a toll on both his health and his fortune. While Maillol's reputation went from strength to strength – bringing him official commissions, monumental sculptures sited in the Tuileries Gardens, and an exhibition in New York – Kessler's prospects began to dwindle. Life in Germany became increasingly fraught politically and even dangerous – Kessler noted how frequent the assassination of left-wing politicians had become. Having long made his opposition to the Nazis clear, Kessler was obliged to flee Germany the moment that Hitler took power since his own life was clearly at risk. His house and his unusually valuable collections were sold off in absentia as the harried count flitted from Paris to Mallorca and eventually to a boarding house between Lyon and Mâcon, where, with his fortune gone but his enthusiasm for new projects intact, he died in 1937.

Maillol was to live another seven years, thrust into another war during which he was once again accused of collaboration with Germany. Right up until his fatal car accident while travelling to visit Raoul Dufy in 1944, Maillol's life – in stark contrast to the solid harmony of his work – remained fraught with accidents and danger. Knowing Kessler had given his aspirations and career as an artist an incalculably important boost just as he most needed it. Maillol had rightly used this support to help him towards his steadfast aim to celebrate the female form in sculpture – an ever more fully realized quest that had effortlessly overridden Whitechapel boxing matches and the idealization of the male physique in Greek art. To his credit, Kessler had realized that the cunningly instinctive, sturdily committed Maillol was not to be diverted; and, for all his snobbish reservations about Maillol's manners, his admiration and support for the sculptor's achievement never diminished. The friendship with Maillol was, in fact, one of the very few fruitful and long-lasting relationships that the multi-talented, psychologically complex, aloof German count ever had. Together, the two men can be seen as a unique, endlessly intriguing, and changing entanglement of human opposites.

1 So far only a selection of Kessler's diaries is available in English, although a project to publish them in their entirety in German is now nearing completion. For this essay, two sources have been particularly helpful: Laird M. Easton's biography, *The Red Count: The Life and Times of Harry Kessler* (Berkeley, Los Angeles, and London: University of California Press, 2002); and James Fenton's essay 'The Secrets of Maillol', first published in the *New York Review of Books* and included in his anthology *Leonardo's Nephew: Essays on Art and Artists* (London: Viking, 1998). I should also like to thank Nathalie Houze and the late Bertrand Lorquin at the Fondation Maillol in Paris for making both their knowledge and their archives so generously accessible.

2 Auden published a tribute to Kessler entitled 'A Saint-Simon of our Time' in the *New York Review of Books*, 31 August 1972.

3 Kessler, Diaries, 21 August 1904.

4 Similar examples of hero wariness come to mind, in however different a context. Beckett could not become his own writer until he had absorbed and got rid of the influence of Joyce, a process so radical he eventually gave up writing in English and wrote for the rest of his career directly in French. But Maillol became Maillol far more easily.

5 Visits to Maillol in Banyuls convinced the impressionable Kessler of the sculptor's natural affinity to ancient Greece, which he evokes in his diaries: 'The men fish or alternatively in spring and autumn tend their vineyards. The women wash their clothes like Nausicaa in the mountain brook just before it flows into the surf. The older matrons, dark, austere women, wander in black robes and black veils like priestesses. At the well in the evening the girls stand with jars on their broad shoulders.... If Odysseus had landed here, he would have recognized a home such as his own: and this home is Maillol's.'

Originally published in the catalogue for the exhibition *Maillol*, Caixa Fundacío Catalunya, Barcelona, 2010

3

THE DARKER SIDE
OF PIERRE BONNARD

Both this and the following short essay on Aubrey Beardsley were written for the French magazine *Réalités*, in Paris, where I worked from 1966 to 1968, eventually becoming responsible for most of the articles on art and literature published in its English-language edition. I was lucky enough to be given near-complete freedom to choose not only what I wanted to write about, but also the manner in which I approached it. Bonnard attracted me partly because his work so clearly defined a particular French way of life at a time when I was desperate to adapt to a new country and its culture, and also because each picture was like a page in a meticulously kept, domestic autobiography. I had spent holidays in various houses in the French country-side, and I felt I already knew Bonnard's austerely harmonious interiors with their bowls of fruit and red-and-white chequered tablecloths; I had drunk green and yellow liqueurs under those trees and glimpsed the mysterious, overgrown recesses of their gardens. Above all, I loved the way the artist's life and his patient recording of it, scene by intimate scene, formed a whole; then, by finding a dark side to Bonnard, I made him all the more mine.

Bonnard died twenty years ago, yet already the cosy universe he created has begun to seem too safe to be true. His pictures reflect islands of bourgeois enchantment to a world that has seen so much more modern art it can hardly believe such places once existed. To like Bonnard now implies a hankering after late-nineteenth-century securities. But – since Bonnard goes deeper than many of his contemporary fans imagine – such wishful thinking tends to distort the truth about his pictures.

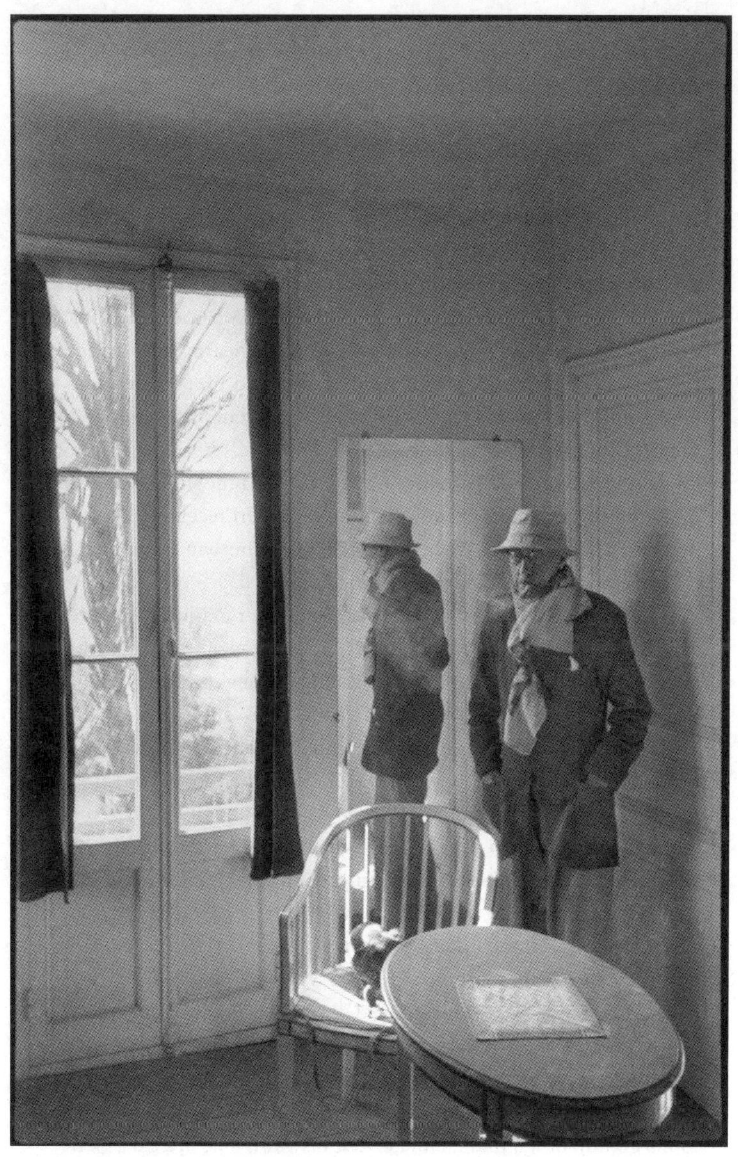

Pierre Bonnard, Le Cannet, France, 1944, photographed by Henri Cartier-Bresson

Bonnard's parentage and filial respect make welcome relief from the notion of the society-wrecked artist. His father was head of a War Ministry office, and the son, after a calm classical education, tamely began a study of law. Yet Paris held a charm that a class on torts never had, and Pierre Bonnard drifted. Writing at that time to his grandmother, he confided what fun it was to sketch people jammed up against each other in the Métro; then secretly he confirmed his pleasure by beginning art lessons at the Académie Julian.

This step brought him into contact with Édouard Vuillard, Maurice Denis, and Paul Sérusier. Sérusier, fresh from a visit to Gauguin's court in Brittany, was spreading the master's message in a nearby café: the young painters were called upon to simplify forms and proportions, and to fill them with luminously pure colours. But an event of possibly greater importance was about to swing across Bonnard's horizon. In 1891, a Rheims wine merchant paid him 100 francs for a lithograph that he had designed for a certain brand of champagne. On receiving the news, Bonnard's father danced in the garden of their suburban Paris home and gave his son the carte-blanche blessing he needed.

Somewhere along the line that led from the rue Clichy – where he shared a studio with Vuillard and Denis – to the Académie Julian, Bonnard became a Nabi (Hebrew for 'prophet'); and all thoughts he may still have had about an ordinary career fled before the Nabis' 'sublime programme'. Their members having been gathered and christened by Sérusier, Denis expounded their views. They believed, he said, 'that for every emotion, for every human thought, there existed a plastic and decorative equivalent, a corresponding beauty'. And, in vividly prophetic words, the Nabis were asked to 'remember that a picture, before being a horse, a nude, or some kind of anecdote, is essentially a flat surface covered with colours assembled in a certain order'. Yet the movement was less dogmatic than it sounds: each Nabi went forth his own way.

Bonnard himself was nicknamed 'the very Japanese Nabi', since his taste for Japanese prints had brought the planes of his early pictures up to a point-blank perspective and rippled them with decorative lines. In these, there is a deliberate playfulness, the fun in art that he had mentioned to his grandmother, that characterized his work long after the Eastern influence had faded. For, under the guise of a quiet, Orientally directed

Nabi, Bonnard was in fact discovering Bonnard. The most original and open-minded magazine in Paris of the 1890s, the *Revue Blanche*, gave Bonnard's decorative hand room to prove itself. While publishing work by Proust, Mallarmé, and the period's supreme debunker, Alfred Jarry, it carried illustrations and an occasional cover by Bonnard. In subject, these bold lithographs never wander far from above-board scenes of bourgeois life; but in style, they are akin to Henri de Toulouse-Lautrec, and between them the two artists (who were good friends) left a perfect Jekyll-and-Hyde view of Paris. While Lautrec shook out glory on whores, Bonnard established his preference for recording the intimate moments of ordinary, everyday life. Respectable pleasures had at last found their poet.

When he was twenty-eight, Bonnard met Marthe, the woman with whom he was to share his life for almost fifty years (and to marry after the first thirty). With her, Bonnard was able to explore and commemorate the ritual of day-to-day domesticity. The painter went on a microscopic safari of the house. Under his eyes, the bathroom took on another existence; a table laid for lunch was a luxuriant landscape. Nothing escaped his notice in the small but infinite realm of the home, and he learnt how to give its aspects the splendour that other painters had reserved for the gods. Signac observed this gift with admiration: 'He understands, loves, and expresses everything he sees: the tart for dessert, the eye of his dog, a ray of sunlight shafting through a window blind, the sponge in his bath.' In Bonnard's paintings, the obvious comes up for reconsideration.

With that power of transforming the ordinary, it scarcely mattered what subject he chose. Even so, like Renoir, Bonnard's special delight was painting the awkward grace of women drying themselves after washing. His wife, who had an obsession with personal cleanliness, furnished him with a thousand memories that he later crystallized into portraits. No other pictures by Bonnard contain such vibrant variations on a theme.

'We can abstract beauty out of everything' ran Bonnard's motto, and his lifelong effort to do this left him open to the charge of facility. His name has become synonymous with a gaiety and tenderness of a particular vintage, as though no other emotion had ever entered his painted sphere. *Terribilità* he did not attempt, that is true; but to say that he never touched on the darker side of life is misleading, if only because no one could have painted such apparent happiness without having experienced the shadows it cast. His nephew Claude Terrasse claims that 'he wished to paint only happy things. One will find in his work neither sadness nor suffering', but certain Bonnards are, in fact, shot through with pain.

A surprising bitterness undercuts a number of those glowing surfaces; their bright colours are worn like brave smiles. It comes as a shock – though not a disappointment – to find this poet of middle-class bliss recording Munch-like tremors of anxiety. Every now and then, despair tinges his palette. And the self-portraits, far from the expected calm of content, are echoes of an anguish that has never been explained.

Revealing though they are, these occasional examples play a minor role in Bonnard's art. His objective was to make the sense of his work available to everyone, and at one time he said that he painted with the plumber in mind. But even if modesty put a brake on his introspection, it never interfered with his desire for technical perfection. There is an inspired doggedness in the steady change and evolution of his art. He reworked his themes tirelessly and was always ready to give them some small new variation. Once, in the Musée du Luxembourg, he got his friend Vuillard to distract the guards' attention while he took out some paints and rapidly retouched a picture of his that had been hanging in the museum for years.

Fauvism, Dadaism, Cubism, and Surrealism brushed the century forward and left Bonnard virtually untouched. What formal distortions he made were either slight or unintentional. The nude that formed under his hand with two right feet remained thus: 'it makes an interesting shape', was Bonnard's explanation. And yet, in his last years, he achieved a kind of subdued résumé of what had been happening in art outside his own fragmented figuration. Just a week before his death in 1947, he put the finishing touches to the *Flowering Almond Tree*. He had said that painters should have one life to learn, then another to paint. And to judge from the explosion of colours and dramatically simplified structure of his last painting, Bonnard might have spent that other life outstripping abstract artists at their own game.

Originally published in *Réalités*, Paris, April 1967

$$4$$

AUBREY BEARDSLEY'S
BRIEF BRILLIANCE

I had always been impressed by Aubrey Beardsley's precocious talent, and took a schoolboyish delight in his elaborately obscene imagery, so I was happy to delve further into his background and his achievements, not only as an illustrator, but as a writer, when I wrote this piece in 1966 for the English-language edition of the Paris magazine *Réalités*. Having been overwhelmed by the impact of French culture, I felt a distinct relief about presenting this young English genius, so talented, elegant, and rebellious that he could almost have been ... French. Being about Beardsley's age myself at the time, I could not help but infuse my portrait of him with what I took to be a certain decadent allure.

Aubrey Beardsley's life had the acceleration given to those who know they will die young. His ambitions were quickly formed: not only would he create exactly what he wanted, but he would become famous before he died. England at the time he was working provided an ideal setting for both ambitions, for its governing classes were wrapped in an ageing dream of Victorian order and prosperity, seemingly aeons away from Beardsley's view of life. For them, fantasy was a wastrel to be kept underground (whence it secretly inflamed their respectability), or at least out of sight. Since Beardsley's drawings sprang from just that kind of fantasy – whereby vice offers more interesting alternatives to virtue – that made society shudder most, they won him instant notoriety, as well as a little real fame. For, by the age of twenty-one, Aubrey Beardsley had turned Victorian inhibitions into a strange new beauty.

Precociousness was, of course, one of his greatest gifts. Stories are told of how the child, born in Brighton in 1872, entertained family and friends with his premature skill at the piano. Occasionally, he even gave concerts at the Pavilion, and there was perhaps some nostalgia in his later habit of seating a human skeleton beside him as he played; those musical evenings in Brighton remained among the highlights of his life. His mother Ellen – a local beauty, née Pitt, renowned for her slenderness as the 'bottomless Pitt' – was a tender and lasting influence over his childhood; and it is doubtful that, apart from himself, Beardsley ever loved anyone more. At school, he was lucky enough to have a housemaster who encouraged his tastes in literature and art to the extent that, when he left, he had a solid trust in his own abilities.

For a short time thereafter, Beardsley worked in an architect's office. The training it gave him was the only one ever to affect his style, and many of his later drawings have the cold spatial precision of architectural designs. What other influences there were – Greek vases, kakemonos, the Pre-Raphaelites – were fairly current then, and less lasting. To begin with, though, Beardsley did absorb a great deal from the masters of the quattrocento – especially Mantegna, Botticelli, and Pollaiuolo.

It was while the quattrocento influence dominated and Beardsley was still only twenty that Dent, the London publishers, commissioned him to illustrate an edition of the *Morte d'Arthur*. Beardsley eased his impatience with Thomas Malory's style by doing drawings of extraordinary technical skill. They tend to be fussy and overwrought, but for sheer ingenuity of line they are hardly equalled. The subject for each of these drawings became a pretext for Beardsley to show his own uncanny powers: his lines trace as much decorative fantasy as a single sheet of paper can hold.

The emphasis soon changed. In the following year, 1893, came the commission that helped Beardsley find his true style. He was asked to do some drawings for *Salome*, Oscar Wilde's play. The results were magnificent departures from the text. Wilde (who once described Beardsley as possessing 'a face like a silver hatchet, with grass-green hair') was at first irritated by the young artist's wayward interpretation; it misrepresented, he quite reasonably thought, the nature of the play's characters. For a short time, however, the success of that edition brought the two men together.

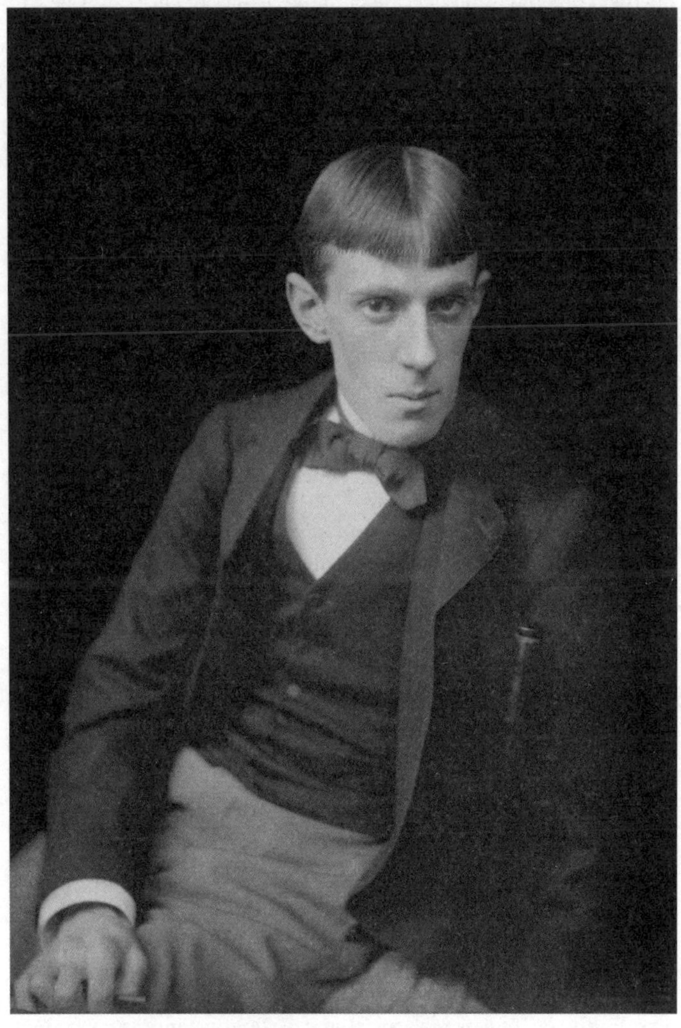

Aubrey Beardsley, c. 1890, photographed by Frederick Hollyer

Between the *Morte d'Arthur* commission and the illustrations for *Salome*, Beardsley radically reduced and simplified his drawings, clearing them of a thousand delicate but unnecessary details – as if he had brushed a cobweb off his eyes. Thenceforth, economy was to gain him his most memorable effects: his subsequent drawings are remarkable for what they have skilfully omitted. *The Black Cape*, for instance, is only an early example of Beardsley's simplified style, but it has a boldness of design that overawes its essential frivolity. The cape itself – a wild parody of the period's fashion – swirls up out of all recognition, yet the tiny white rosettes and stars just save it from being too massive a creation to exist.

The autumn of 1893 was to be a season of immense productivity for Beardsley. Alongside the *Salome* illustrations and the increasingly burdensome task of decorating the *Morte d'Arthur* came requests for book covers, title pages, and posters. Whatever the work in hand, Beardsley's style made no concessions – not even to the lady golfers of Mitcham, whose score card showed a few refined Amazons possessed of no very obvious taste for outdoor sports. Prompted by Beardsley's versatility, the publisher John Lane invited him to become art editor of a new literary quarterly. Beardsley accepted, and in the spring of 1894, the first issue of *The Yellow Book* appeared.

The Yellow Book vaguely persists as a symbol for all that was new and naughty in 1890s London. Yet its repute as a testament of decadence had less to do with its contents than with a few unforeseen incidents. When, for instance, Wilde stepped into the witness box at his trial, the court was not slow to notice an issue of *The Yellow Book* tucked beneath his arm. Thus the legend grew, even though most of the quarterly's contributors – Henry James, Arthur Waugh, Arnold Bennett – never published anything even faintly immoral. Yet the art editor made his mark, and one glance at the Beardsley cover was enough to convince the public of the review's inner depravity.

Much that has remained of this metaphorical 'yellowness' is due to Beardsley's disturbing illustrations. According to Richard Le Gallienne, the review's publisher 'had a rather nerve-wracking time with Beardsley, who, for the fun of it, was always trying to slip some indecency into his covers, not apparent without close scrutiny, so that Lane used to go over them with a microscope and submit them to a jury of his friends before he ventured to publish'. But Lane's efforts could never have ironed out Beardsley's intuitive sense for corruption. Whatever the subject, it signalled either devilry or decay. Who but Beardsley could have made Cinderella look like Lady Macbeth applying for Elysium?

At the same time, Beardsley began on a new and equally curious project. He had long held literary ambitions, having planned a history of the Spanish Armada while at school and, later, a book on Rousseau and an essay on *Les Liaisons dangereuses*. None of these materialized, but in their place came an exotic romance – never completed – called *Under the Hill*. It is as decadent a document as the *fin de siècle* produced, and for that reason it remains little known. Beardsley wrote it at intervals between 1894 and 1896, mostly in the casino at Dieppe, a home from home for many of London's new artists.

Beardsley's prose has the inventiveness and the cold frivolity of his drawings, but it lacks their coherence. In *Under the Hill*, sentences are composed as exquisite units sufficient unto themselves, and often they fit uneasily into paragraphs. Thus, his verbal technique is less assured than his draughtsmanship, but the story's descriptive passages are wonderful and they provide an invaluable insight into the young artist's obsessions.

When the fragment was published in expurgated form in 1904, it was ill received – even by some of Beardsley's admirers. One, Haldane Macfall, called it a 'laboured literary indecency … bent only on satisfying every lust in a dandified way that casts but a handsome garment over the basest and most filthy licence'. If rather less ambiguous, *Under the Hill* purveys a similar sensation – 'the unhealthy bloom upon wax fruit' – as the drawings, and it reaches those same sublime heights of artificiality. In the story – a parody of the Venus and Tannhäuser legend – Venus and her court have prepared a supper in honour of the noble visitor Tannhäuser. Beardsley took immense pleasure in studying and drawing costumes, and in the following passage his delight can hardly keep pace with his invention:

> *'As for the rest of the company, it boasted some very noticeable dresses, and whole tables of quite delightful coiffures. There were spotted veils that seemed to stain the skin with some exquisite and august disease, fans with eye-slits in them, through which*

*the bearers peeped and peered; fans painted with figures and
covered with the sonnets of Sporion and the short stories of
Scaramouch; and fans of big, living moths stuck upon mounts
of silver sticks. There were masks of green velvet that make
the face look trebly powdered; masks of heads of birds, of apes,
of serpents, of dolphins, of men and women, of little embryos
and of cats; masks like the faces of gods; masks of coloured
glass, and masks of thin talc and India rubber. There were wigs
of black and scarlet wools, of peacocks' feathers, of gold and
silver threads, of swans' down, of the tendrils of the vine, and
of human hair; huge collars of stiff muslin rising high above the
head; whole dresses of ostrich feathers curling inwards; tunics
of panthers' skins that looked beautiful over pink tights; capotes
of crimson satin trimmed with the wings of owls; sleeves cut
into the shapes of apocryphal animals; drawers flounced down
to the ankles, and necked with tiny red roses; stockings clocked
with fêtes galantes, and curious designs; and petticoats cut like
artificial flowers. Some of the women had put on delightful little
moustaches dyed in purples and bright greens, twisted and
waxed with absolute skill; and some wore great white beards,
after the manner of St Wilgeforte.'*

Beardsley's desire to refine human sensations is seldom more explicit
than in that description. It echoes the nervous despair felt all over Europe
at the time: life itself was simply not sumptuous enough to satisfy her
artists. For all the difference in rhetoric, Beardsley's plea is close to that
of Charles Baudelaire.

In the panic that followed Wilde's trial, Beardsley was dismissed from
The Yellow Book. His connections with the fallen idol, though never very
close, made him a dangerous man to employ. Yet Arthur Symons asked
him to help launch *The Savoy*, which aimed at replacing *The Yellow
Book*; and another publisher commissioned him to decorate some new
editions of Aristophanes and Juvenal. The drawings for Aristophanes are
astonishingly obscene, and they have only ever dwelt in privately circulated editions. It is curious that eroticism – the very spring of Beardsley's
creativity – was to cause him intense remorse in the last days of his life.

From his deathbed, he begged his publisher 'by all that is holy' to destroy '*all* obscene drawings'.

In the late spring of 1896, Beardsley's health – long threatened by tuberculosis – rapidly began to fail. The following spring saw him received into the Roman Catholic Church, and for a short time his health revived. He visited Dieppe once more, then Paris, but finally the cold weather drove him down to Menton. It was there, in a room specially prepared for him by his mother, that he eventually died, aged twenty-five and a half.

Beardsley's life was as brief and unexpected as his best drawings, and not even he, in his most arrogant moments, could have imagined the influence he would have after his death. For those around him, his art remained the most satisfying expression of the period's desire for new sensations in new forms. His drawings represent an absolute refusal to take anything but beauty seriously. The area of beauty he chose is narrow, but he showed it to unsurpassable advantage. It could never appeal to all tastes, yet even those it offends recognize the artist's strangely complete talent. For there is one undeniable fact about his achievement: while reaching the limitations of his vision, he rendered it visually perfect ... all in five years.

Originally published in *Réalités*, Paris, 1966

5

PICASSO'S TROUSERS

When the online men's clothing store Mr Porter asked me to write an essay for their magazine about the way that Picasso dressed, my first reaction was that the subject was too frivolous to engage with. Then I looked at the photos they had sent me of Picasso in a formal suit or playing up to the camera in a Native American headdress, and I realized there might be more there than first met the eye, and also that I would have fun delving into the way that artists, like most of us, present and reveal themselves through their clothes.

Were they bright red breaking on two-tone shoes or criss-crossed in loud golfer's check? Were they unexpectedly formal, hind parts of a bespoke suit, or baggy plus fours with Argyle socks? Were they ever tuxedo pants before they metamorphized into summer slacks or shrank into jaunty pre-war Riviera swimsuits?

They were all of these and many more, since Picasso changed the way that he dressed as often and as radically as he changed the way that he painted. He was as instinctive a dresser as he was an artist, replacing one look by another every time something in his life or his fantasy prompted it. Many of the artists around him dressed quite conventionally, above all when success caught up with them. There was Braque in his cool white scarf, Matisse plumply avuncular in a waistcoat while sketching a nude, and Kandinsky as formally attired as an old-school banker. Dalí, it is true, deliberately put on a show, with the twirled mustachios, the fur coats, and silver-topped canes. But Picasso was not putting on a show as such. Whether dressed for the opera, disguised for a *bal masqué* or simply clowning about, he was always himself – or one of his many selves.

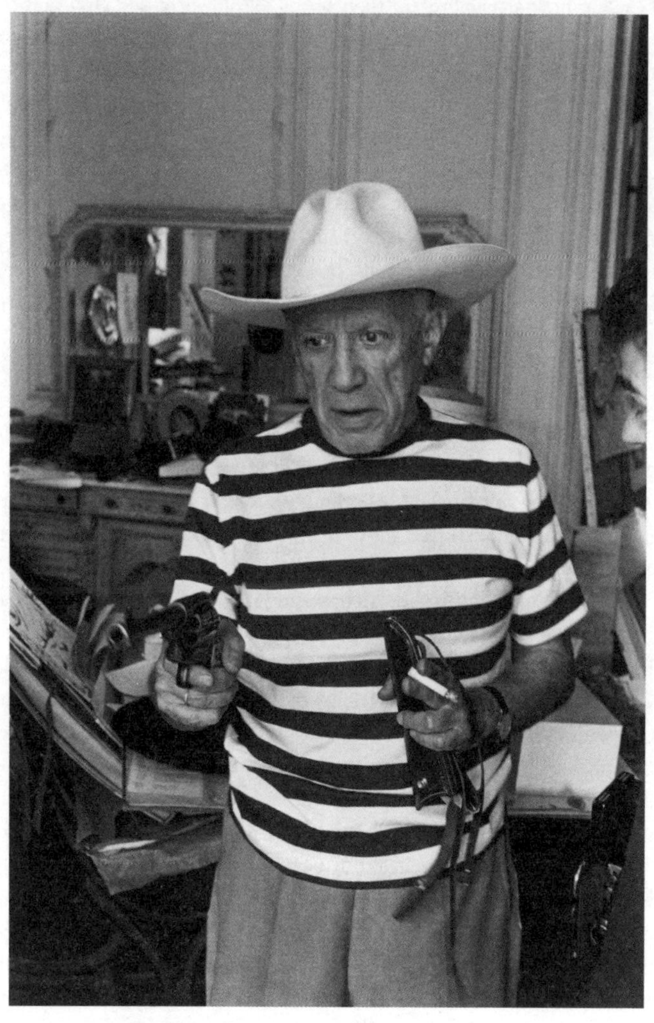

Pablo Picasso with a hat and holster given to him by the American actor Gary Cooper, Villa La Californie, Cannes, 1957, photographed by René Burri

'Only superficial people do not judge by appearances', said Oscar Wilde – bless him! And I look forward one day to reading some learned thesis on how artists present themselves to the world and why. Francis Bacon dressed in later life like a successful gangster, an upper-class English Al Capone, in tight, perfectly cut double-breasted suits with subtle stripes and threatening black leather coats, also tight, with epaulettes. Frivolous? I'm not sure. Everything he wore had its meaning for Bacon, and you can even find the clothes he loved – particularly rainbow-hued silk shirts and desert boots – in his pictures. Alberto Giacometti invariably worked in a tweed jacket and tie, however caked in plaster, paint, and clay they became. Anecdotal? I don't think so. Challenging accepted vision every day in his Montparnasse hovel, Giacometti clung to whatever shreds or threads of normality he could find.

The last time I bumped into David Hockney, he had just stepped out of his West End tailors. They were making him a new suit, he explained amiably, and the scales fell from my eyes. That immediately recognizable look that Hockney had so cleverly crafted over the years, from bright caps and stripy shirts to odd socks and comfortably baggy suits, was part of a carefully orchestrated show, mirroring his unstoppable rise from Pop art icon to cultural grandee.

Style, they say, is the man. So how did Picasso, the master artificer of the twentieth century, choose to project himself? Did he limit himself to this look or that? Did he decide at a certain point to wear his trousers wide with a crease so sharp (like his friend, the poet Jean Cocteau) it could cut a camembert in half? Of course not. He was a creature of infinite fantasy and infinite change. And having just looked through a few score photos of the *maître* at different moments in his long career, I can attest that he virtually never appeared before the camera in the same garb twice. Catch him if you can. Here he is during his early years in Paris in vaguely artisanal dress, dark overalls and donkey jackets, occasionally spruced up by a broad-brimmed hat or Romantic lavaliere. Then, without warning, he appears in clunky gaiters or, bizarrely, in an army uniform that he had borrowed from his co-Cubist, Georges Braque. These were early days, but it was already clear that Picasso enjoyed not just dressing but dressing up.

At this point, Picasso was still seeking recognition. But as he outraged then entranced the rich by his challenging imagery, he transformed his own appearance from dangerous iconoclast to cuddly lounge lizard. Out went any trace of dungaree and sweater and in came the perfect suit and tie, hatted and hankied, with just a hint of waistcoat and cufflinked sleeve. This was Picasso's so-called 'Duchess Period', when all the aristocratic and moneyed doors opened for him and he, totally self-aware and totally self-promotional, dressed for his new role in life.

But once Picasso had given proof of his ability to look – more or less – like the nobs who paid high prices for his pictures, he realized he no longer needed to reassure them. After all, he was now sufficiently wealthy and well established to lounge at the back of his chauffeured Hispano-Suiza in his underwear if he cared to. 'I want to be rich enough', he once declared, 'to live like someone who's poor.' To him that meant messing around freely and eating in shorts in the kitchen and not giving a toss if an important dealer or collector dropped by. In a trice, he went happily from top hat to beret and espadrilles, from three-piece to no-piece (or almost), since his life was now focused on either the studio, the bed, or the beach.

Even so, the love of dressing up remained. Picasso always found something to clown around in before the camera, whether it was a huge false nose, a lugubrious deerstalker or the magnificent Native American headdress that Gary Cooper had given him. As Picasso grew older, he wore less and less, often sporting no more than a Mediterranean tan and swimming trunks. But by then he was the most famous and most photographed artist in the world, and so instantly recognizable that it barely mattered what he wore.

Originally published in *The Journal*, Mr Porter, London, 9 October 2012

6

JOAN MIRÓ:
A PAINTER AMONG POETS

Since art and literature have been the two dominant interests in my intellectual life, the points at which they intersect and influence each other exert an unusual fascination, whether it is Manet illustrating Edgar Allan Poe, Picasso punctuating Pierre Reverdy's *Le Chant des Morts* with his inspired strokes of blood red, or Hockney's sensual evocations of Constantine Cavafy's world. Not surprisingly then, given the chance to write about Miró for a travelling exhibition that I had curated, it was the painter's unusually close involvement with literature that attracted me most, and above all the incomparable books that he made with some of the finest poets of his generation. In a handful of these rare volumes, such as the work that he published with Paul Éluard, *À Toute Epreuve*, image and text attain a degree of mutual relevance and harmonious interdependence perhaps never achieved before.

In memoriam Jacques Dupin (1927–2012)[1]

Throughout his long life as a painter, Joan Miró repeatedly affirmed how essential literature was to his own artistic creativity. He insisted that poetry in particular stimulated his imagination even more than the work of other painters and sculptors who interested him. One might suppose that in this he differs little from the many other twentieth-century artists who read passionately and regarded literature as a prime source of inspiration – from Picasso and Giacometti to Bacon and Tàpies. But Miró remained under the spell of poetry to a unique degree, using it as a soundboard and medium, an *ut poesis pictura*, through which he broke new pictorial

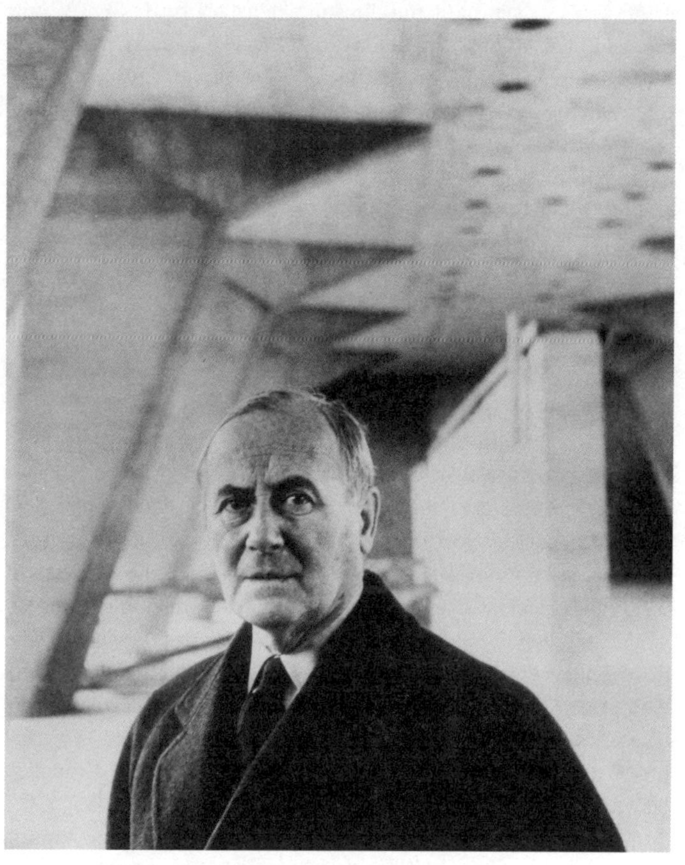

Joan Miró in 1958, photographer unknown

ground and discovered his own highly original, visual vocabulary. Avidly literate, Miró explored all kinds of experimental writing as well as the great classics, eventually building an extensive private library, now housed in the various Miró foundations. He also wrote poetry himself, called numerous paintings 'tableau-poème' or 'peinture-poème' – as we can see in the present exhibition – and created titles that are haiku-like poems in themselves. They are so evocative that it would be tempting to quote them all, because they illustrate perfectly how closely Miró's verbal and pictorial fantasy was entwined. Here are just three: *A Drop of Dew Falling from a Bird's Wing Awakens Rosalie Sleeping in the Shadow of a Spider's Web*; *Figures in the Night Guided by the Phosphorescent Tracks of Snails*; and *The Pink Dusk Fondles the Sex of Women and Birds*. In this context, it is worth remembering that Miró insisted that, 'For me the title is an exact reality.'

At the very beginning of his career, whilst chafing against the provincially hidebound atmosphere of Barcelona, Miró was already looking to literature as an ideal way to break pictorial convention and forge a new language in paint. As a Catalan first and foremost, he had begun to read the great poets of his own tongue,[2] both ancient[3] and contemporary, from an early age, becoming keenly aware that language was the very basis of identity, both personal and political. But it was the dual impact in 1917 of an exhibition of modern French art at the Galeries Dalmau and the discovery, via Francis Picabia, of Guillaume Apollinaire's *Calligrammes* that set Miró on his unusual course as a painter among poets – an artist whose visual imagination was most powerfully stimulated by verbal imagery, to the extent that he was later to state: 'I make no distinction between painting and poetry.'[4]

When Miró first moved to Paris in the early 1920s, he found himself, more by chance than by design, in a community dominated by writers; he soon realized that he found both their company and their work more stimulating than those of most of the artists he met. Thenceforth, like Picasso, Miró's most important friendships would be with poets rather than painters. His next-door neighbour at 43 rue Blomet, the painter André Masson, shared his interest in the surge of literary excitement that had begun to grip Paris.[5] 'Masson was a great reader and full of ideas', Miró later recounted. 'Among his friends were virtually all the young poets of the day. Through Masson, I met them – through them, I heard poetry discussed. The poets Masson introduced me to interested me more than the painters I met in Paris. I was carried away by the ideas they brought and especially the poetry they discussed. I gorged myself on it all night long – poetry principally in the tradition of Jarry's *Surmâle*.' As well as Alfred Jarry, whom Miró idolized and reinterpreted in several series of exuberantly grotesque images (which he reinvented later as a critique of Franco), the young painter might have mentioned his fervent admiration for Rimbaud, Lautréamont, and Mallarmé, each of whom had overturned poetic convention and invented a new form of writing. Though generally timid and withdrawn in company, Miró soon established a circle of highly gifted friends ranging from Tristan Tzara and Pierre Reverdy to Georges Limbour, Antonin Artaud, and Michel Leiris – many of whose writings later inspired him, as we shall see, to create whole series of images for specially conceived and finely produced *livres d'artiste*.

More importantly, at the time of his extended stays at the rue Blomet – where the Catalan sculptor Pablo Gargallo had sublet him a makeshift studio – Miró found that the conversations with his new poet friends helped him to break new ground in his own artistic endeavours. Writing to Leiris in August 1924, he tells the writer: 'I am working furiously; you and all my other writer friends have given me much help and improved my understanding of many things. I think about our conversation, when you told me how you started with a word and watched to see where it would take you. I have done a series of small things on wood, in which I take off from some form in the wood. Using an artificial thing as a point of departure like this, I feel, is parallel to what writers can obtain with an arbitrary sound.' And, with a subversive flourish, he ends the letter: 'This is hardly painting, but I don't give a damn.'

Being already in contact with some of the leading experimental writers in Paris inevitably led Miró to meet the Surrealist poets, notably André Breton, Paul Éluard, and Louis Aragon, shortly before the First Surrealist Manifesto was published in November 1924. They, too, were to make a lasting impression on the young Catalan painter, encouraging him to join them in allowing dreams and the unconscious free rein over everyday rational thought. Miró needed little persuasion. He was at the most crucial moment in his development, having just made the transition from the realism of *Ear of Grain* (1923) to the sign language that appears first in *The Kiss* (1924), thus going in one bound from representation to a pictorial metaphor or ideogram. In Surrealism, Miró found the ideal vehicle for exploring the unknown and transcending what he thought of as the limitations of visual art. 'I went about a great deal with poets', he said later, with characteristic modesty, 'because I thought one must go beyond form to achieve poetry.' This quiet but incredibly daring foray into uncharted territory brought an outpouring of images so spontaneous and strange that no less an authority than Breton himself was impelled to concede that, 'Miró is the most Surrealist of us all.'

In many ways, Miró was a Surrealist *avant la lettre*, before the term (originally coined by Apollinaire) had become common currency. He had not waited, for instance, for the Surrealists to announce that they had eliminated the word 'like' from their imaginative vocabulary – in the sense that 'your eyes are like stars' would thenceforth be 'your eyes are stars'. Eyes had floated enigmatically through Miró's firmament ever since his sudden break with representational imagery: nothing was 'like' because there was nothing to compare it to: his universe was too new and unique for analogy. Nevertheless, Miró was considerably reassured by the interest his work had aroused, and even more by the fact that the Surrealist Galerie Pierre gave him his first one-man show in June 1925.

Much though Miró had gained from Surrealism's approval and its boldly radical attitudes, which seeped deeply into his painterly imagination, he nevertheless resisted calls to associate himself more closely with the movement, since he foresaw that it would encroach on his creative freedom and end in disaster. Giacometti, for instance, had been kicked out of the Surrealist fold for deciding to return to the human figure as the focus of his art. Having managed to escape Breton's wrath by keeping a low profile, Miró was able (unlike Giacometti) to keep all the literary friendships that he had made, out of innate loyalty and a continued passion for poetry. 'What really counts is to strip the soul naked', he declared with fervour. 'Painting or poetry is made as we make love; a total embrace, prudence thrown to the winds, nothing held back.' This abiding fascination prompted Miró not only to go on devouring his friends' new work and letting it permeate his pictorial inventiveness but eventually collaborating with them, on often lengthy and costly projects, to illustrate it.

The origins of this kind of 'illustration' (for want of a better word),[6] which was to become a central and essential activity for Miró, lay in his learning the techniques of drypoint, engraving, and etching from the Cubist painter Louis Marcoussis and using them to produce some of his earliest collaborations with poets, such as the etchings he made for the publication of Georges Hugnet's poem 'Enfance' in 1933.[7] Miró's talents for this type of parallel creativity were immediately apparent, but even he could not have imagined how large a place the *livres d'artiste* were going to assume in his work. Thanks to the importance that he accorded to literature and the very many friendships he had made with poets, Miró ultimately provided images for no fewer than 260 books, some of them quite modest but many of exceptional quality, including several that extended and redefined what the *livre d'artiste* could actually achieve. But, as he himself knew, Miró could never have set his sights so high had a rich tradition not existed, above all in France, of artists and writers working closely together to create exceptional publications.

At this point, it would be worth outlining how the relatively modern concept of the *livre d'artiste* had come about. Many artists before Miró had of course been drawn powerfully to literature as a source of pleasure and inspiration to the extent that the frontiers between the two tradition-ally very separate forms of expression – painting and writing – gradually became so permeable as almost to dissolve. That moment was reached towards the end of the nineteenth century when some of the most inno-vative painters began to consider illustrating literary texts as a desirable and challenging artistic undertaking – turning the two disciplines, as it were, into one. There were notable earlier examples, such as William Blake illustrating his own *Songs of Innocence and Experience* or Eugène Delacroix producing vivid imagery in 1828 for the ageing Goethe's *Faust*; there was also Édouard Manet's lithographs for the French edition of Poe's poem 'The Raven' (translated by Stéphane Mallarmé) or Aubrey Beardsley's sinuously suggestive drawings for Aristophanes' *Lysistrata* (considered so scandalous that they were confined to a privately circulated edition).

But the high point of achievement in artist's books begins with the charismatic art dealer Ambroise Vollard persuading his circle of artists – notably Pierre Bonnard, Odilon Redon, Georges Rouault, and Marc Chagall – to focus their creative energies on illustrating a variety of classical texts and modern poetry, which were then published as limited-edition, luxury books in which only the most advanced techniques and finest materials were employed. For his first project – Paul Verlaine's poem 'Parallèlement', illustrated by Bonnard in 1900 – Vollard chose a medium-heavy Dutch wove paper (*'vélin de Hollande'*) and a Renaissance font designed by Claude Garamond, then commissioned the best lithographer in Paris to print Bonnard's delicately erotic sketches in a rose-sanguine ink. Passionate about every aspect of these *éditions de luxe*, Vollard went on to plough most of his picture-sale profits into some of the greatest *livres d'artiste* ever produced. He set the bar very high, and subsequently only a handful of art publishers rose to meet the challenge. The Greek-born publisher Tériade continued in the same tradition, enabling Henri Matisse to produce his marvellous *Jazz*, for instance, and Picasso to enhance Reverdy's *Le Chant des Morts* with a series of simple but starkly eloquent red marks. Similarly, Albert Skira, who founded the Surrealist magazine *Minotaure*, produced a number of fine artists' books, among them Ovid's *Metamorphoses* illustrated by Picasso.

Picasso, who illustrated a range of poets from Ovid and Luis de Góngora to his friend Max Jacob, would have been the artist Miró instinctively wanted to match (and indeed, at the time of his death, Miró was working on illustrating Góngora himself). Here the Catalan may in fact have surpassed the genius of Málaga, not so much because of the vast range of texts that he enhanced but by the unusual sensitivity that he brought to literary works. While Picasso tends to remain brilliantly and unmistakably Picasso in his illustrations, Miró blends more subtly with the written word, creating images in counterpoint to it; rarely do his illustrations overwhelm the poetry that inspired them. It would be false to pretend that the quality of Miró's work in this domain is not uneven, growing sometimes repetitive or mechanical. But, taken over all, what is extraordinary about his illustrated books is the sense of fecundity they convey: of images tumbling over each other in an unstoppable flood from an apparently inexhaustible source. In many of the books that he illustrated, one feels, Miró is exactly like a talented child at play, endlessly inventive and never tiring. At the same time, he shows the judgment and discretion of a highly trained adult, knowing when to stop before the page is overloaded and its hair's-breadth balance lost.

To give a quick overview of this significant aspect of Miró's oeuvre, one might point first of all to the astonishing number of contemporary poets whose work he illustrated. This includes not only virtually all the writers already mentioned here as his friends and colleagues – from Tzara and Leiris to Éluard and Breton – but many others, some of them considerably younger,[8] whom he met in his long career or others he admired from afar. Since the two poles of his existence were Catalonia and Paris, most of the writers are French, Catalan, or Spanish. But there were also numerous foreign poets, notably Pablo Neruda and Octavio Paz, as well as the odd Englishman (Stephen Spender), American (James Johnson Sweeney), and even Japanese (Shuzo Takiguchi).[9] A few texts were from previous centuries, notably the medieval treatise in Catalan by several anonymous hands on the properties of various stones, entitled *Lapidari*, or St Francis of Assisi's evocative song 'Canticle of the Sun'. Each time one can sense how the mood of the painter has changed, from frenzied to calm, simple to intricate, exuberant to dark with foreboding.

In these magnificent productions, painter and poet are clearly the stars, the uncontested protagonists. As with the production of films, however, there is a large cast of lesser but essential participants who craft the specially woven paper, choose the typeface and the page layout, prepare the lithographs, woodcuts, or engravings and oversee the printing, and fashion the slipcase in which the finished volume is stored, as well as the publisher who attempts to sell the limited-edition copies, some of them enhanced with additional suites of illustrations on various fine papers, and so recoup some of the considerable expenditure involved. Here we are transported to the world of bibliophilia, and without being a bibliophile myself, I cannot read the descriptions of these volumes without a mounting sense of concupiscence. Snatches of the descriptions will give some idea why, if we take an example at random, say, the suite of etchings to René Crevel's *La Bague d'aurore*, the Ring of Dawn. Here we have, 'loose in a cover of Rives wove with four folded flaps and the first etching printed on the front in a grey-beige cloth box with two grey labels printed in red glued to front and spine respectively: 1 etching with aquatint printed in colours on Rives wove, for the cover, unsigned. 22 etchings with aquatint printed in colours. 1 etching dated and signed in the copperplate and pencil.' And so on, with an edition of eighty-nine copies broken up into such imponderables as the two copies marked 'Japon nacré', with the twenty-three etchings on japon nacré paper inscribed 'épreuve d'artiste' and numbered 1/2 and 2/2. As for the printing in 1957, there is the following bald summary: 'Fequet et Baudier, Paris', for the text and typography; 'Robert Dutrou et Atelier A. Crommelynck, Paris', for the etchings.

This has to be poetry to book collectors' ears, and I think it has an undeniable appeal even to those who are not hooked. It is in itself a poetic language evoking considerable specialist skills and a rare – not to say rarefied – concern for maintaining the highest levels of technique and materials. Poet and painter undertook these projects as a labour of love, and they would have been remunerated at most by a certain number of copies of these deluxe editions once published. The publishers themselves would have underwritten the costs mainly for the prestige that such high-quality enterprises confer, since they were not commercially profitable in the short term – even though, nowadays, some of Miró's most famous books, like *Parler Seul*, which he did around the poem by Tristan Tzara, can fetch anything between $50 and $100,000. Miró's publishers ranged from art dealers – such as his own in Paris, Aimé Maeght – to art-book specialists such as XXe Siècle and Pierre-André Benoît in Paris or Ediciones Polígrafa in Barcelona. Since these books were always expensive and endlessly time-consuming, many more mainstream publishers would have shied away from such an exacting task. One Swiss publisher, Gérald Cramer, showed unusual commitment, however, and it is worth taking a detailed look at what he achieved, not only because it took him more than ten years to bring a single book out, but also because it is by far the most famous book that Miró ever did and it is widely considered one of the greatest *livres d'art* of all time, inspired by Paul Éluard's poems entitled *À Toute Epreuve*.

Sometimes known as the 'people's poet', Éluard is one of the most engaging characters of twentieth-century literature and, more specifically, of the Surrealist movement. Although he was one of Breton's most trusty lieutenants and thus obliged to some extent both to toe and to enforce the 'party line', Éluard was intensely involved with many of the leading artists of his day, from Salvador Dalí and Max Ernst to Picasso: he wrote about their work and collected it, as well as earning a precarious living

– like Breton – from dealing in it. His warmth and brilliance as a poet endeared him to the artists in a way that Breton's trenchant authoritarianism never could. Given his innate reserve, Miró would have found the amiable Éluard the least threatening of the movement's big guns. The two men first met, as we have seen, in 1924, just as Miró was finding his feet in Paris, and two years later Éluard wrote a poem entitled 'Joan Miró', in part inspired by the latter's recent painting *La Naissance du Monde*, whose airy weightlessness is celebrated as, 'Away with the hill. Away with the forest. The sky is more gorgeous than ever.'

Cramer's very first illustrated book, published in 1945, was Éluard's eulogy *À Pablo Picasso*, and his cordial relations with the French poet prompted him to come up with another project for them to work on together. As Éluard's marriage to the Russian adventuress Gala had unravelled (she was to leave him to live with Dalí), he had written a sequence of lyrical poems entitled *À Toute Epreuve*, originally published in 1930.[10] Éluard and Cramer quickly agreed that Miró would be the ideal person to illustrate the book, not only because they both admired Miró's work but because *À Toute Epreuve* was partly inspired by his native Catalonia, where Éluard and Gala had gone to stay with Dalí. Miró accepted the commission enthusiastically, even though he was about to embark on another important project, illustrating Tzara's *Parler Seul*. Possibly because of this, Miró decided to make woodcuts for *À Toute Epreuve* rather than etchings or lithography – the techniques he chose for most of his artists' books. The woodblocks came to include everything from bits and pieces found in forests and on beaches to plywood from Miró's brother-in-law's furniture factory. All such gleaning and experimentation, including much whittling and gluing, took time, but by then Miró was totally identified with the project. 'I am completely absorbed by this damn book', he wrote to Cramer. 'I hope to create something sensational, the most important achievement in engraving since Gauguin.'[11]

Producing an outstanding artist's book required not only the intense collaboration of the three men (although Éluard died of a heart attack in November 1952), but also the skills and devotion of various specialists for the typography, layout, and printing. Jacques Frélaut had been entrusted with printing the woodcuts, and this master printer was not above using an old toothbrush, moulded to fit his hand, in order to achieve the exact texture and tone that Miró required. To give some idea of the magnitude of the task – to make a book that, in Miró's words, had 'all the dignity of a sculpture carved in marble' – suffice it to say that the 233 woodblocks, collaged with everything from wire to old engravings, required no fewer than 42,000 passes through the press to create the finished book. The layout had been inspired from the beginning by Stéphane Mallarmé's revolutionary 'Un coup de dés', but in a significantly modernized form, just as the format and look of the book were comparatively simple – a clear demarcation from Vollard's voluminous, ornate *éditions de luxe*. When the edition of 130 copies on Arches wove paper came out eventually in 1958, Miró was not even midway in his long career as a creator of artists' books, but *À Toute Epreuve* represented a peak of achievement – a unique fusion of image and word – that would never be surpassed.

Miró's attachment to literature never weakened. It was one of the anchors that allowed this prodigiously imaginative artist to remain rooted in the world. It was also one of the ladders that enabled him to escape the constrictions and conventions of visual art. Miró could not have been a painter without poetry, but for him poetry was always to hand because in his mind there was no fundamental difference between the two and he had lived at a time when – a sign of high culture that we perhaps have lost – each could be seen as a vital complement and stimulus to the other.

1 The French poet Jacques Dupin, a leading authority on Miró and Giacometti
   (see the interview on pp. 152–63), was a friend of mine whose poetry and art writings
   I also admired.
2 Catalan is spoken right through north-eastern Spain down to Valencia, as well
   as in the Balearic Islands.
3 Like all Catalans with literary interests, Miró held the poet and philosopher
   Ramon Llull (1232–*c.*1315) in special esteem. He was also marked by the writings
   of the two great Spanish mystics St Teresa of Avila and St John of the Cross, as well
   as by the sonnets of Francisco de Quevedo.
4 'I make no distinction between painting and poetry. I have sometimes illustrated
   my canvases with poetic phrases, and vice versa. The Chinese, those great lords of
   the spirit, isn't that what they did?', interview with Georges Duthuit, 'Où allez-vous
   Miro?', *Cahiers d'Art*, Paris, nos 8–10, 1936).
5 Miró talked about his experiences of the time to his biographer, Jacques Dupin,
   who recorded them as *Joan Miró: Memories of the Rue Blomet*.
6 'Illustration' brings to mind what Gustave Doré or 'Phiz' or John Tenniel produced
   to enliven stories by Honoré de Balzac, Charles Dickens, or Lewis Carroll. From the
   late nineteenth century, when some of the greatest creative artists began making
   images for books, the results were less 'illustrations' than parallel inventions.
   By the time we come to Miró, it is clear that in his *livres d'artiste* the text stimulates

the imagery but is often no more than a point of departure for flights of independent visual invention.

7   From then on, Miró experimented tirelessly with the techniques of print-making, which he regarded as an art form in its own right. While he was in New York in 1947, for instance, he spent time at Stanley William Hayter's famous workshop, Studio 17 (originally established in Paris), extending and refining his technical range.

8   The doyen of Miró scholars, Jacques Dupin, was one of the younger poets whose work Miró illustrated on several occasions.

9   Among Miró's meticulously preserved papers one can find evidence of all kinds of unsuspected relationships with yet other writers, such as a correspondence with Ezra Pound as well as with the long-term Parisian resident Henry Miller.

10 The poem begins: 'Une femme chaque nuit / Voyage en grand secret' (A woman each night / Travels in total secrecy). Éluard's *Letters to Gala* chronicle the poet's love and despair in his relationship with his wife.

11 Miró and Cramer's involvement in *À Toute Epreuve* can be followed in a fascinating exchange of letters so detailed and numerous that they make up a whole book: *Joan Miró – Gérald Cramer: Une correspondance à toute épreuve* (Geneva: Patrick Cramer, 2002).

Originally published as 'Joan Miró: A Painter Among Poets', in *Miró: Malerei als Poesie*, exhibition catalogue (Hamburg and Düsseldorf: Bucerius Kunst Forum, Kunstsammlung Nordrhein-Westfalen and Hirmer Verlag, 2015)

7

TALKING TO
SONIA DELAUNAY

I remember feeling distinctly daunted when, some fifty years ago, I made my way over the Seine to the discreetly elegant rue de Saint-Simon, just off Boulevard Saint-Germain, where Sonia Delaunay lived and worked. Not only did the street bear the lofty name of the great memoirist-duke of Louis XIV's Versailles, but Madame Delaunay herself had come across as imperious on the telephone, dictating what we might and might not talk about in the interview she had accorded me. She was also old enough to be my grandmother, and she had been surrounded by the 'tout Paris des arts et des lettres' from Apollinaire and Kandinsky onwards, which to me at the time seemed as unlikely as counting Dante and Giotto among one's friends. I had good reason to feel apprehensive.

A photograph taken of us during the interview rather bears the point out: it shows a sternly benign Delaunay, perfectly coiffed and dressed as if for tea at the Crillon, and a hirsute young man who looked as if he had just come off the barricades of May 1968. Yet the difference between us was sufficiently large for neither of us to take sides. She overlooked my street scruffiness, talking freely about her art and her life, while leaving no one in any doubt about the uniqueness of her experiences and the superiority of her views.[1] In retrospect, I realize that if she had not been so convinced of her talents, she could never have held her own in the male-dominated art world of the time (clearly reflected in these pages) in which she aspired to excel. As she accepted me, I forgave her bourgeois certainties and comforts, quite warming to the autocratic old lady as she revived long-forgotten worlds that I had only read about.

78

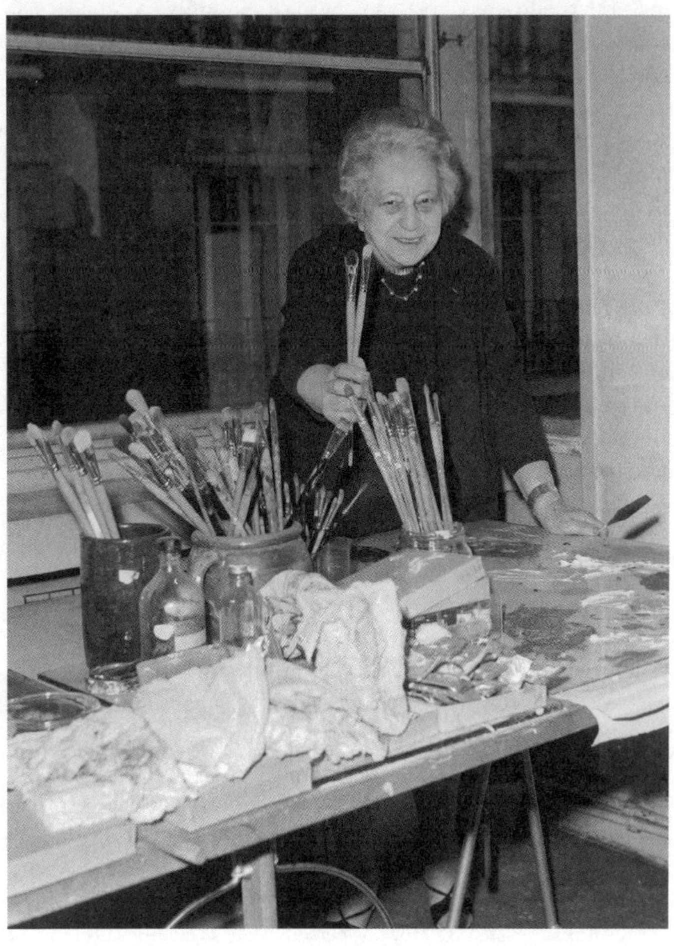

Sonia Delaunay in her Paris studio, 1965, photographer unknown

Talking to Sonia Delaunay takes you back beyond the turn of the century, past names and events solidly famous or half-forgotten, to a mansion in St Petersburg whose ease and opulence still stir her to wonder. She was born, in 1885, into a world of high-bourgeois privilege where everyone, children included, had their personal servants and moved in a way that screened them from contact with the less fortunate classes. Before going to a school that was staffed exclusively with university professors, Sonia herself was plied with governesses who made her fluent in German, French, and English. Between reading, drawing, and sitting down to heavily elaborate meals (the family cook was reputed to be second only to the tsar's), she set off on energetic, chaperoned walks, 'come rain or snow', she says, 'and that's been one of the reasons for my sound health'. Her upbringing has left her nostalgic for a certain kind of grandeur, not for the stuffiness of bourgeois salons from which she was so glad to escape, but for the kind of vision and drive that drove a city like St Petersburg forward. 'They were giants, those people', she says. And later: 'Even Catherine, for all her faults, was a really extraordinary person.' Now, from the height of her eighty-eight years, she looks round at certain aspects of contemporary life with stoic dismay. She equates socialism with mediocrity, and suggests that if people rush around so much today it is because they have no 'inner life'. Though Madame Delaunay concedes that some of the artists younger than herself 'have begun to understand colour', she sees no one of outstanding interest. Once we come to talk about those whom she knew, a number of reputations find themselves smartly reduced. A staunch supporter of former friends, such as Blaise Cendrars (whom she believes vastly underrated), and respectful of Henri Matisse ('a great man'), she nevertheless considers Georges Braque's work as 'peu de chose, vu d'aujourd'hui' (little to it, from today's perspective), and Pablo Picasso's as 'surtout du bluff' (mostly bluff). Even Piet Mondrian, whose influence she acknowledges, she regards as 'limited'. But the one person to whose memory she remains unwaveringly faithful, of course, is Robert Delaunay.

Sonia, née Terk,[2] arrived in Paris in 1905, after two years studying drawing with Ludwig Schmidt-Reutter in Karlsruhe. She enrolled at the Académie de la Palette, where her fellow pupils included André Dunoyer de Segonzac and Amédée Ozenfant, and later began to paint portraits that owed a great deal to Paul Gauguin. In 1909, she married the collector and dealer Wilhelm Uhde (who had begun exhibiting the Douanier Rousseau, Picasso, and Braque in his gallery in the rue Notre-Dame-des-Champs), and so came more and more into contact with the new artists of the day. Among these was Robert Delaunay, with whom she talked passionately about art and married, after her divorce from Uhde, in 1910.

'The Delaunays wake up talking about painting', reported Guillaume Apollinaire, who was sheltered by them in their studio on the rue des Grands-Augustins while he was waiting to be cleared of a charge of having stolen the *Mona Lisa*! (Uppermost in Sonia's memory of the poet is the hearty appetite he displayed – 'a pleasure to watch'.) It was here, in 1911, that she made her first totally abstract work: a bedcover, composed of patches of different materials, for her newborn son. This proved to be the beginning of a whole series of objects that she decorated with abstract designs, and which in time included everything from book covers and posters to dinner plates.

The Delaunays' theory of colour, partly based on Michel-Eugène Chevreul's thesis on 'simultaneous contrast', was given fresh impetus by their study of the halos produced by the Paris boulevards' recently installed electric lamps and by the moon. For Sonia, the major result of this research was her *Prismes electriques* of 1914, a highly complex patterning of colours into disc- and rainbow-like shapes. In the meantime, other capital works had come into being: the two marvellously rhythmical studies of the Bal Bullier (notorious for its tangos, and other new, loose ways – including, later, Sonia's 'simultaneous dresses', which moved Cendrars to write a poem called 'sur la robe elle a un corps' – 'she wears a body on her dress'); and the painting-cum-maquette she did for Cendrars's *Prose du transsibérien*, the whole forming a delightful, exquisitely coloured picture-poem two metres long. Although she could not have foreseen it, these works brought Sonia Delaunay's first Paris period to an abrupt end.

War broke out while the Delaunays were on holiday in Spain. They decided to stay there, and over the next six years divided their time between Spain and Portugal. The clearer, brighter light confirmed them in their conviction about the primacy of colour and provided an excellent atmosphere in which to work. 'The very quality of the light', Sonia wrote after her return, 'allowed us to go beyond Chevreul and find, not only harmonies based on contrasts, but disharmonies, that's to say rapid vibrations that exalt colour even further by placing certain warm and cold tones in close contact.' Of the many paintings she made during this happy exile, one should mention the series of *Portugaises, Chanteurs flamencos, Disques*, and, above all, the *Marché au Minho* suite, which records most fully her excitement at the prodigality of Mediterranean light. At the same time, she turned her hand to interior decorating (her private income having come to an end with the 1917 Revolution) and designing costumes for Sergei Diaghilev's production of *Cléopâtre*.

The Delaunays returned to a Paris drained to a residue of fury and disgust that was to wrench art off its nineteenth-century pedestal and shake it inside out. The mixture of revolutionary purpose, pataphysicism, and simple high jinks of the times is wonderfully illustrated in a programme note to a ball billed as the 'Transmental' and organized by the Union des artistes russes in 1923 – during which Sonia Delaunay exhibited her latest dresses: 'This will be a wonderful fun-fair by night with floats, packed streets, beauty pageants for gigolos and gigolettes, bearded women, piggyback rides, Aunt Sallies, foetuses with four heads, mermaids and mythological dances, eccentrics in flesh and blood and in unbreakable wire.... Delaunay and his troupe of transatlantic pickpockets ... Tristan Tzara and his fat birds ... Iliazd and his forty-one degree fevers, and other attractions of all kinds.'

Although she continued to live rather in her husband's shadow as a painter and was best known for her work as a decorator and designer (her clothes were worn by such women of fashion as Gloria Swanson and Nancy Cunard), Sonia Delaunay had by now developed her own pictorial style. Clearly, it owed an enormous debt to her husband's research; and, since his death in 1941, it has continued to pay homage to his discoveries. But as she herself defines it, the difference has been that whereas 'for Delaunay, movement in colour was all, I felt the need for an architecture in my compositions'. Their joint importance lies principally in the fact that, with a small number of other artists, they created a painting of pure colour, disconnected from anything but colour's own conflicts and harmonies.

Over the last thirty years, Sonia Delaunay's paintings have grown in simplicity and sureness. A very long lifetime's experience has enabled her to compose increasingly by instinct, with one colour calling forth another until – as a result of numerous gouache sketches – a complete, independent system of tones evolves. Nothing is allowed to interfere with the directness and the autonomy of this language of colour, whose rhythmic combinations are significantly extended and enriched with each new major work. In whatever direction Sonia Delaunay has developed this huge vocabulary, the result has always remained an immediately approachable experience – a universal invitation to the inner laws of the great, refreshing world of colour.

The popularity of her work has never been more evident. Last winter, some of her new tapestries, woven from specially conceived designs at the Manufacture des Gobelins, were exhibited in Paris at the Musée d'art moderne de la ville. They had all the tonal and rhythmic vigour of her best works: and the texture of the wool gave the dazzling but always firmly controlled play of colour a new resonance. Having been to the French provinces this summer, various editions of these tapestries will be on show both in Milan and New York this autumn. Meanwhile, a large Sonia Delaunay retrospective is being organized at the Musée de Grenoble, while plans are well advanced for a Robert and Sonia Delaunay Foundation, currently expected to be housed 'somewhere opposite the Louvre'.

Madame Delaunay herself, freed from many of the organizational worries by her friend and dealer Jacques Damase, has been making a series of illustrations for a new edition of Arthur Rimbaud's *Illuminations*. Even now, she spends most mornings at work on a new gouache, and is even trying to find a way of resuming large-scale painting without over-straining herself physically. Her vitality and her devotion to her art are heartening and humbling. As she enters her eighty-ninth year this month, we send her our warmest congratulations and cordially hope that she will find every facility to help her continue in her resplendent, open universe of colour.

1 Delaunay was sufficiently free in her opinions as to be quite indiscreet, even cruel. She told me that her relationship with Jacques Damase, her dealer, who was present during our interview, had begun when she 'found him in the gutter'.
2 She was actually born Sara Stern, but she took on her wealthy uncle's name, Terk (changing her first name in the process), after she went as a small child to live with him and his wife in St Petersburg.

Originally published in *Art International*, Lugano, December 1973

8

CHRISTIAN SCHAD'S PORTRAITS OF THE 1920s

I would never have had the chance to explore the seductively decadent atmosphere of Christian Schad if Jill Lloyd, art historian, German Expressionism expert, and my wife, had not succeeded in putting on the artist's first exhibition in France at the Musée Maillol in Paris in 2002, followed by his first showing in the United States at the Neue Galerie, New York. This chance encounter illustrates how unexpectedly some artists come into your life. A couple of Schad's paintings had lodged themselves in my memory as perfect portrayals of decadence and impending doom, but I knew nothing of his background or career. For the essay that I was invited to write for the exhibition catalogue, I delved into his unusual destiny and the handful of haunting images he left behind to try to find out how, sometimes despite themselves, certain artists are driven to prophesy. Schad has remained in my 'pantheon' ever since because he encapsulated an exotic, louche world seemingly seconds before it toppled into extinction.

Christian Schad's great portraits of the late 1920s slip into our consciousness like half-remembered dreams. We never feel we understand fully what they mean or why, with their luminous clarity, they seem so familiar; and part of their power to fascinate us stems from this elusiveness. Yet the characters the portraits make so memorable belong to a time and place we recognize instantly. It is the Europe of our parents and grandparents, not yet recovered from the trauma of a first world war and about to slide towards another, even mightier conflagration. Immaculate in evening dress or transparent gowns, Schad's characters sleepwalk towards destruction.

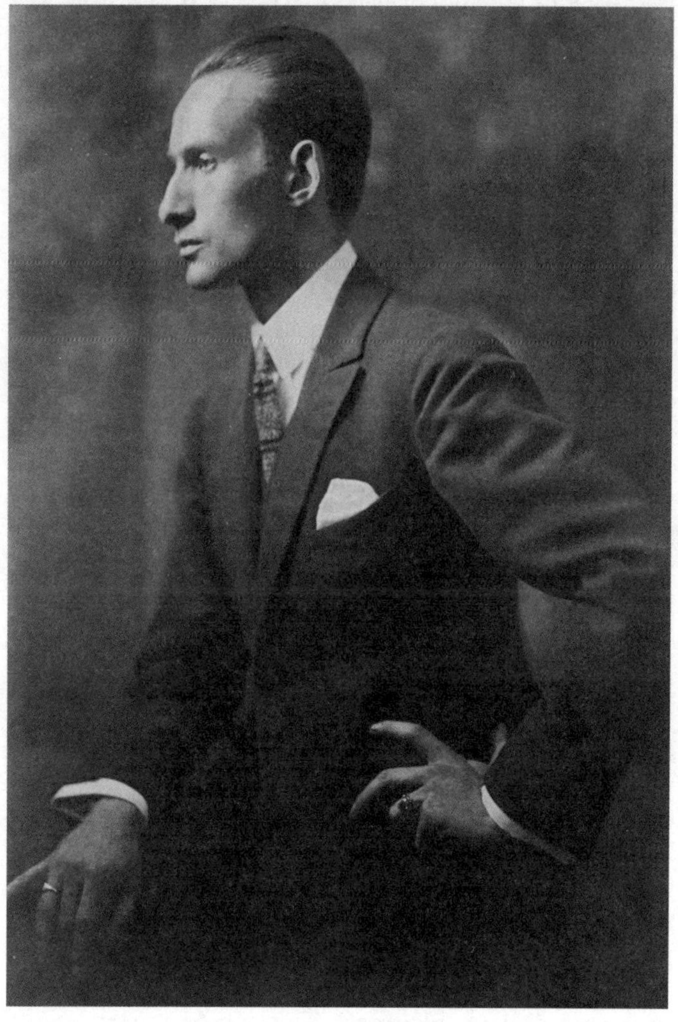

Christian Schad, Munich, c.1930, photographed by Franz Grainer

This critical moment in a civilization doomed to disappear still speaks to us with a prophetic urgency. By searching beneath the highly polished, enigmatic surface of Schad's portraits, we sense that we might come closer to understanding our own immediate past.

Nineteen twenty-seven was in several respects a momentous year in Schad's life. Several of his greatest paintings were executed during this time: not only the *Self-Portrait* and the *Count St Genois d'Anneaucourt*, but the precise, psychologically penetrating portraits of Baroness Vera Wassilko, the composer Josef Matthias Hauer, and the writer Ludwig Bäumer. After several years living in Naples and Rome, Schad had moved with his Italian wife, Marcella, to an impressive studio in Vienna, and his latest works were exhibited there at the Galerie Würthle. He made numerous drawings, including a delightfully impudent *Narcissus*, inspired by the collected stories of his friend Walter Serner, and the first book on his art, written by the prominent critic Max Osborn, came out with a selection of his portraits. In the same year, he also divorced from Marcella (after a four-year marriage) and went to live temporarily in Berlin, where he participated in a Neue Sachlichkeit group show and had a solo exhibition at the Galerie Neumann-Nierendorf. Thus, in the course of that annus mirabilis, Schad had changed cities, begun a new private life, and established his signature style in several masterpieces.

This is the Christian Schad who stares out at us from the *Self-Portrait*, a remarkably concise summary of his life and aesthetic credo to that date. The artist has just turned thirty-three. Poised and attentive, Schad seems confident of the poetic quality and force of this painting that presents his ascetic good looks and his undoubted talents to the world. To his signature, neatly inscribed in the sheet rumpled by love, he might have followed Jan van Eyck and added '*Als ich kan*' – ([As good] as I can). A little earlier, Schad had declared in a catalogue foreword that, after studying the Old Masters in Italy, it was clear that he painted well – anyone could see that; the question that remained was whether he was also a 'good painter' since good painters were born not made.[1] The steady brown gaze, scrutinizing itself as in a mirror, does not appear to have any doubts on the second score either.

'Painting a picture is not an intellectual but an instinctive activity', Schad cautions in a text he later wrote about the *Self-Portrait*,[2] and the most revealing reactions to painting are also instinctive rather than intellectual. The instinctive reaction to this enigmatic scene is to look for clues that will help elucidate it. The narcissus that looms between the two clearly provides a lead. Both lovers are immured in their own thoughts, their own worlds; their physical contact now over, they could not be further apart. Certainly, the circumstances hardly encourage prolonged intimacy since only a curtain separates them from the night sky outside. The chimneys in the background, Schad suggests in his explanatory note, may denote 'a vague longing for Paris' (although the artist never lived there, it was to remain his ideal city). But they also evoke something far less picturesque, such as an industrial landscape at night, with a sinister building, like a watchtower, rising on the left.

This painting, Schad tells us in his note, is part reminiscence, part symbol. He painted it, as he painted most of his portraits, entirely from memory, without direct reference to a model – although he did occasionally make preparatory drawings. The artist was very proud of his unusually strong, recapitulative powers – 'I have a good memory for things and people that interest me', he once observed; and for the woman's delicate hand with its black ribbon (and intriguingly dirt-rimmed fingernails), Schad called to mind the hand of a girl he had seen at a shooting booth in the Prater amusement park in Vienna. The woman herself is not a single identifiable person, but more a composite of women Schad had known or noticed. The fact that she is fairer in body than in face, and that Schad resolutely turns his own face away, may refer to the artist's own marital break-up and the problems he felt he had in maintaining a relationship. The ugly scar on the woman's face is clearly documented in Schad's writings and can be traced to a practice that had struck him in Naples, where lovers would scar their mistresses to demonstrate their passionate sense of exclusive ownership.

Not the least curious attribute in this painting is Schad's diaphanous lime-green shirt. The artist dismissed it laconically, saying that he thought that having a veiled nudity might generate a greater painterly interest ('And I suppose', he wrote in his note on the *Self-Portrait*, 'I found it more pleasing as a painter to show my naked body through a shirt of the kind woven in ancient times on the island of Kos, rather than painting one nude in front of another'). Although Schad could not have been persuaded to be more explicit, he clearly enjoyed jolting conventional sensibilities and would have subscribed to a definition Charles Baudelaire gave to dandyism: 'It is the pleasure of astonishing and the proud satisfaction of never being astonished.'[3] Offhand though his subsequent reaction was, Schad certainly knew how provocative the introduction of this transparent garment would be, and he had clearly pondered the most effective way of blending it into the picture; one notes, for instance, that the delicate lacing at the throat of the shirt recalls the stitches on his companion's cheek. It may be that the gauze-like garment represents a protective layer, a subtle barrier that the artist has erected between himself and any binding contact with his lover – a second skin that keeps his narcissism intact. Schad was also a great admirer of Édouard Manet, who clearly influenced both the way he composed his figures and the boldly frontal, melancholic gaze that characterizes them. And in the contrast Schad makes between clothed and naked flesh one might well see a subtle paraphrase of the French master's *Le Déjeuner sur l'herbe*.

The fine shirt also gives the artist a magnificent chance to show off his pictorial skills; and of course the garment would be less disturbing if it were not so exquisitely rendered. Schad wanted to paint, he once said, 'like all those who are now considered masters'.[4] This guiding ambition was pre-eminent in Schad's mind as he painted, and it is expressed with masterly confidence in his self-portrait. Not long before, Schad had completed a lengthy apprenticeship to the Old Masters in the Italian museums, and from Mantegna and Carpaccio through the High Renaissance to its decline in Bronzino and Pontormo there was little the young German artist had not absorbed and drawn on. A particular love was Raphael's *La Fornarina* and *La Donna Velata*, and certainly the paintings he admired abounded in magnificently rendered transparent costumes and other gauzy materials. Thus, the green shirt is both the affirmation of a personal style anchored in the learned techniques of the past and a tribute to those all but forgotten traditional skills.

Schad's enthusiasm for the Old Masters was by no means confined to Italy. He was also a great admirer of his own country's outstanding masters; and later in his career his technical mastery won him a commission to make a copy in tempera on panel of Matthias Grünewald's *Stuppacher Madonna* for the Stiftskirche in Aschaffenburg (the original having been removed to a museum). Grünewald had been an early influence, and Schad was particularly struck by the clarity of contour that the master of the Isenheim Altarpiece had achieved. Already apparent in the *Self-Portrait*, the graphic outline is accentuated even further in the *Count St Genois d'Anneaucourt*. In a diary entry dated April 1926, Schad's near-contemporary, the painter and theatre designer Oskar Schlemmer, summed up the desire felt by many of Germany's most promising new painters for a heightened clarity: 'If today's arts … aspire to precision and reject anything vague and dreamy, this implies an instinctive repudiation of chaos and a longing to find the form appropriate to our times.' The slim, elegant count himself has been given so pronounced an outline in his severe, somewhat constricting black-and-white evening clothes that he juts out of the picture plane, leaving his two companions to recede into the Parisian background; as in the *Self-Portrait*, there is no doubt as to who is the protagonist in this ambiguous scene.

Count St Genois typified the kind of rootless aristocrat whose wealth and status had been lost during the 1914–18 war and who could now only exist in a cosmopolitan metropolis like Vienna or Berlin where, Schad notes, anyone with 'a name, money, influence or "fame"' was accepted into society. St Genois glided between the old Austro-Hungarian nobility, now mostly dispossessed of all but their sonorous titles, and the new, moneyed bourgeoisie as easily as he did between the sophisticated salon and the demi-monde of the nightclubs and cabarets that had become such a feature of postwar life – especially in Berlin, the city of Otto Dix's *Metropolis* triptych and Alfred Döblin's pungent, Joycean evocation *Berlin Alexanderplatz*. The somewhat disturbing apparition looming over the count's left shoulder was in fact a well-known transvestite whose main habitat was just such a club in Berlin known as the 'Eldorado'.

At any other period, a painter who lovingly portrayed transvestites in transparent dresses, with rouged cheeks and an unhealthily inflamed beauty spot, might be accused of deliberate sensationalism. But the new sexual freedom, with its acceptance, not to say encouragement, of every known shade of homosexuality and erotic persuasion, was (along with social unrest and economic turbulence) a prominent feature of the Germanic capital; and people from all over the world – Schad included – travelled to witness the phenomenon at first hand. Specialized brothels and nightclubs proliferated, rejoicing in names like the 'Mikado' or the 'Voo-Doo'. In this 'Babylon of the modern world', Viennese writer Stefan Zweig noted, 'the German introduced all their vehemence and methodical organization into perversion. Along the entire Kurfürstendamm sauntered powdered and rouged young men, and they were not all professionals; every high-school boy wanted to earn some money, and in the dimly lit bars one might see government officials and financiers tenderly courting drunken sailors without shame. Even the Rome of Suetonius had never known such orgies as the pervert balls of Berlin, where hundreds of men costumed as women and hundreds of women as men danced under the benevolent eyes of the police.'[5] In a word, as the English poet W. H. Auden put it after a visit there, Berlin was 'a bugger's daydream'.

It was this fascinating daydream, tinged with its attendant nightmares, that Schad brings under scrutiny in his portrait of St Genois, implicitly incorporating the freely accepted excesses of Berlin's nightlife into his picture. Despite the more tolerant moral climate, St Genois had never openly admitted to his sexual tastes, and for his frequent forays into Viennese society he chose to be seen as the *chevalier servant* of Baroness Glasen, depicted on the left of Schad's portrait. This 'manly' woman (as Schad calls her in his note on the picture) appears to be looking daggers at the transvestite, as if both were competing for the affections of the diminutive, dapper count, just as both are shown similarly attired in transparent gowns. The Baroness holds a white feather in her ringed hand (interestingly, the same delicate white hand as Schad's mistress in the *Self-Portrait*). Does it signify cowardice, as it did during the First World War? St Genois himself certainly appears irresolute, caught between his socially acceptable persona and an unmentionable passion for a drag queen, just as he is caught between the bright lights of a room we cannot see and the ambiguous murkiness of the night outside.

Once again, Schad has chosen Paris as the backdrop to his picture, although here it is specifically Montmartre that he has taken as an appropriate milieu for his unconventional trio. Paris, which he first visited in 1925, forms the setting for many of his most important portraits. The artist kept a collection of postcards of the city and also took numerous photographs of the rooftops and the views of Montmartre that appear in his paintings. Even though Schad made only occasional visits there,

Paris remained an ideal location, and when he came to paint his friend Josef Matthias Hauer, for instance, he placed the innovative composer beneath a vast arc of another great imaginative feat, the Eiffel Tower. But Berlin, where the artist settled in 1928, provided the natural setting for two of his finest portraits of women, *Lotte* (1927) and *Sonja* (1928). Although Lotte was a milliner in a hat shop and Sonja worked as a secretary, their good looks and independence enabled them to mix freely in the same circles as Schad, who had a keen eye for female beauty and believed that the prettiest women in the world were to be found at that time in Berlin. While visiting Berlin in 1927, Schad had stayed in a small pension above the shop where Lotte worked, and when he got down to painting her portrait, he set it in one of Berlin's more upmarket dancing clubs.

Schad portrayed only people who in some way touched him, and in Lotte it was not just her arresting pale eyes and flawless complexion, but also her courageous stance as a young woman determined to live life on her own terms, without the support of a male companion. Thus Schad portrays her flawlessly coiffed and dressed, her severe black jacket softened only by a silk shirt and a bootlace tie, sitting alone. Lotte's show of self-sufficiency is nevertheless belied by the bra she has chosen for the evening, which suffuses her shirt with crimson; and the reflection behind her of the empty dance floor seems to echo her own isolation. Her situation reveals an inner conflict and a poignancy not dissimilar to the one Schad sensed in Count St Genois's predicament. While the aristocrat was torn between public opinion and private passion, Lotte has to pay the price of her independence by spending her evenings in an immaculate solitude while the lights of the nightclub turn to mad jazz rhythms in the fragmented mirrors around her and the champagne glass remains within reach yet empty.

Paradoxically, by maintaining a distant, apparently emotionless approach to his model, Schad draws us closer to Lotte. The precisely descriptive painting and the cool veneer that appears to conceal the image from the spectator's indiscreet gaze excites, on the contrary, further prying. It is as though Schad were allowing us to scrutinize the people and milieu that fascinated him through an unusually bright, powerful lens. The voyeuristic curiosity that Schad's dandyish, ironic attitude stimulates becomes more and more the real subject of his paintings, particularly in

Sonja, whose steadily mournful gaze invites a wide variety of conjectures. Like Lotte, Sonja is shown in a clearly identifiable landmark in Berlin, the Romanisches Café, and although she seems more at ease, she is also apparently alone. Again, like Lotte, she is a model of independent chic, with her impeccable make-up, stylishly simple black dress, and long cigarette holder. She is also less obviously feminine than Lotte: the Eton crop and full, handsomely virile features give her an almost androgynous air. Her stare recalls the wide-eyed gaze of the heroines of the silent screen, except that Sonja's, disillusioned and lost in the middle distance, invites no contact. Of all the friends and acquaintances who make up Schad's portrait gallery, Sonja is the most solitary; she might have walked directly out of *Nightwood*, Djuna Barnes's evocation of cosmopolitan rootlessness and despairing lesbian love in the 1920s.[6]

Once she had finished her working day in the office, Sonja was clearly drawn to a more sophisticated milieu. Here she is shown sitting at her ease in one of Berlin's best-known literary cafés, as modern as you please, with her American cigarettes within reach and a bottle of champagne cooling in its silver bucket. All the elements that make up the picture – the chiffon flower, the smouldering Camel, the powder compact – seem to have been attributed exactly the same significance, or lack of significance. Unlike the facial scar or the transparent dresses of the previous portraits we have discussed, no descriptive detail is allowed to dominate in this picture, which is held together entirely by the sitter's hypnotic stare. Nevertheless, like a roman-à-clef, the painting clearly refers to a couple of well-known figures of the time. Behind Sonja, recognizable by his curiously shaped ear, sits the poet Max Hermann-Neisse, whose frail, bent, and bespectacled form George Grosz captured so memorably. To the right, one can make out the bulky silhouette of Schad's close friend, the journalist and entomologist Felix Bryk, who was renowned for his jollity and who described himself as Schad's 'Leporello'. Schad had in fact met Sonja through Bryk, who rightly thought she might prove to be an interesting model for the artist. As one delves more deeply into this picture, it becomes apparent how closely intertwined Schad's life and his portraits were. Hermann-Neisse, for instance, had known Schad since the latter's early Dada years in Zürich. Bryk, of whom Schad made a penetrating portrait in the same year, 1928, comes back again in the artist's work as the patient whose abdomen the surgeons have opened in *Operation*. The way Schad's life impacted on his portraits is demonstrated by the number of times one suddenly comes across Maika, his girlfriend of the time. She appears not only as the subject of a couple of fine portraits but also as the devoted nurse who holds Bryk's head during the *Operation*.

In little more than two years, Schad succeeded in creating a portrait gallery of the times by recording a small number of people who struck him by their beauty, their brilliance, or their vulnerability. With his gift for presenting the bizarre as ordinary and the ordinary as bizarre, one suspects that Schad found all three qualities in the couple of circus performers he portrayed in Berlin in 1929. Agosta, the winged man, and Rasha, the black dove, were two performers at a circus known as 'Uncle Pelle' in a working-class district in north Berlin, which Schad, forever in search of unusual sights and out-of-the-ordinary people, visited with the equally inquisitive Bryk. Schad became fascinated by them and, breaking with his usual practice of painting from memory, he invited both to come and sit to him for large preparatory drawings in his studio on Hardenbergstrasse in the centre of Berlin. During these sessions, which Schad described laconically as 'more interesting than what I would have heard having five o'clock tea with someone', the artist got to know his sitters well and described their lives in the notes he later wrote about each of his main paintings.

With his spectacularly deformed chest, Agosta was displayed not only to circus crowds but also to medical students. He confessed to Schad that women in search of new erotic thrills regularly pursued him and that, being happily married, he did not know how to deal with them. Rasha's circus act consisted of entwining a boa constrictor round her body. Originally from Madagascar, she was married to a German whose speciality was lifting weights with a hook inserted into his tongue. The couple lived quietly with the snake and a small son in a caravan, Schad adds. When he came to paint them, however, Schad did nothing to accentuate their strangeness. Given the already bizarre nature of its subject, this portrait could be seen as markedly more naturalistic than its predecessors – an objective presentation of a curious human fact. What moved Schad to devote a large, carefully planned painting to the two performers was the twist of nature and fate that had set them apart from the common run of humanity. They touched a nerve, making the artist keenly aware, as he wrote in his notes about another portrait (*Baroness Vera Wassilko*) of 'how beautiful deviation or abnormality can be'.

To structure his composition, the artist placed Agosta on a favourite antique armchair that he kept in his studio. From that eminence, the winged man assumes an almost regal, if not pontifical, presence, with a cruel mouth and a challenging gaze. Rasha, meanwhile, sits meekly at his feet, conventionally dressed and freed from the embrace of her boa. Well accustomed to being put on display, both performers stare back at the spectator with equanimity and even a touch of pride. Once again, in the close-up frontality as well as in the stark contrast here between white and black skin, one is reminded of Manet. But, unlike the previous portraits, which abound with secret clues and symbols, this arresting image is presented as a statement of fact, shorn of allusion or exaggeration, with the result that it becomes all the more disturbing.

Some seventy years later, one can look back on the cycle of portraits that Schad undertook in the 1920s and read them as an extraordinarily penetrating and lucid diary of the times. Few pictures of the period plunge us so completely into the feverish modernity and brittle gaiety of that moment poised exactly between the two wars. Crucial to Schad's ability to conjure up the uneasy conscience of the age was his portrayal of the world around him without any discernible involvement. From his near contemporary, the English novelist Christopher Isherwood, also recording life in Berlin at that time, he might have borrowed the prophetic phrase, 'I am a Camera'. But the lens that he employed was necessarily his own sensibility, with its very particular affection for contemporary strangeness conveyed with a Renaissance technique. However 'objective' his portraits appear, they do far more than record: they create a whole society, full of human diversity and truth. The count, Sonja, Rasha, and Schad himself belong to the most unforgettable characters of the age, not least because one can see in their marble pallor and fatalistic gaze that their world is about to disappear for ever.

1　In the catalogue introduction to his exhibition at the Galerie Würthle in Vienna in late 1926, Schad wrote: 'That I paint well (there's no point in being shy) is beyond doubt. The only question is whether I am a good artist, and whether I was born as one.'
'Dass ich gut male, ist (das zu behaupten muss man erst nicht bescheiden sein) über

jeden Zweifel erhaben. Es fragt sich nur, ob ich auch ein guter Maler bin. Ob ich als solcher geboren wurde.'

2 Towards the end of his career, Schad provided explanatory notes to all his most important paintings.

3 'C'est le plaisir d'étonner et la satisfaction orgueilleuse de ne jamais être étonné.' Charles Baudelaire: 'Le peintre de la vie moderne', *Oeuvres complètes* (Paris: Laffont, 1980), p. 807. 'The pleasure of astonishing and the arrogant satisfaction of never being astonished oneself.'

4 'So zu malen, wie alle malten, die noch heute als Meister gelten.' 'To paint like all those who are still regarded today as masters.' Christian Schad, 'Mein Lebensweg', foreword to the exhibition catalogue *Christian Schad* (Vienna: Galerie Würthle, 1927) and reproduced in *Christian Schad* (Basel: Editions Panderma Carl Laszlo, 1972).

5 Quoted in Anton Gill, *A Dance Between Flames: Berlin Between the Wars* (London: John Murray, 1993), p. 46.

6 Conversely, *Nightwood*'s main characters might all have stepped out of Schad. Barnes pictures her Jewish-Austrian baron, Felix Volkbein, and the company he kept thus: 'Early in life Felix had insinuated himself into the pageantry of the circus and the theatre. In some way they linked his emotions to the higher and unattainable pageantry of kings and queens. The more amiable actresses of Prague, Vienna, Hungary, Germany, France and Italy, the acrobats and sword-swallowers, had at one time and another allowed him their dressing rooms…. The people of this world, with desires utterly divergent from his own, had also seized on titles for a purpose. There was a Princess Nadja, a Baron von Tink, a Principessa Stasera y Stasero, a King Buffo and a Duchess of Broadback.' Djuna Barnes, *Nightwood* (London: Faber and Faber, 1936).

Originally published as 'Christian Schad: Portraits of the 1920s', in Jill Lloyd and Michael Peppiatt (eds), *Christian Schad and the Neue Sachlichkeit*, exhibition catalogue (New York: Neue Galerie and W. W. Norton & Company, 2003)

PART II

9

A TRIBUTE TO DORA MAAR

I don't know why the *Independent* asked me to write Dora Maar's obituary unless they thought I might have come across her in the many years I lived in France. I did in fact meet her in Ménerbes, the Provençal village where she lived out the latter part of her life as a virtual religious recluse, while I was staying with John and Alice Rewald in the summer of 1969. Having encountered Alice and me first on her way to church, then again while shopping in the local market, Dora felt obliged to invite us in for a drink at the gloomy, cavernous house that Picasso had bought for her (Nicolas de Staël also acquired an ancient property for his family nearby). Inside it was cool, dark, and bare, like the interior of a convent; and in my memory at least the floors were of beaten earth. Dora shook several ancient, dusty bottles that were standing on a kitchen table but nothing came out until one of them eventually released a sticky, black trickle. Conversation proved similarly slow, and having dutifully raised our glass of what tasted like a semi-solidified walnut liqueur, we thanked her and took our leave.

Since her death, Dora has slowly 'emerged from the shadows' where she had lingered as Picasso's muse, mistress, and, most famously, his 'Weeping Woman'. There has been a growing interest both in her life at the centre of the great artistic flowering in Paris on either side of the war and in the work that she left behind. She has now been celebrated as a significant artist in her own right, with a large retrospective of her photographs and her paintings that opened in Paris in 2019 before travelling to London and Los Angeles. There is also a growing literature about her, but when I wrote the obituary below there was scant information available about her life outside her relationship with Picasso, and even less about her work. It may

96

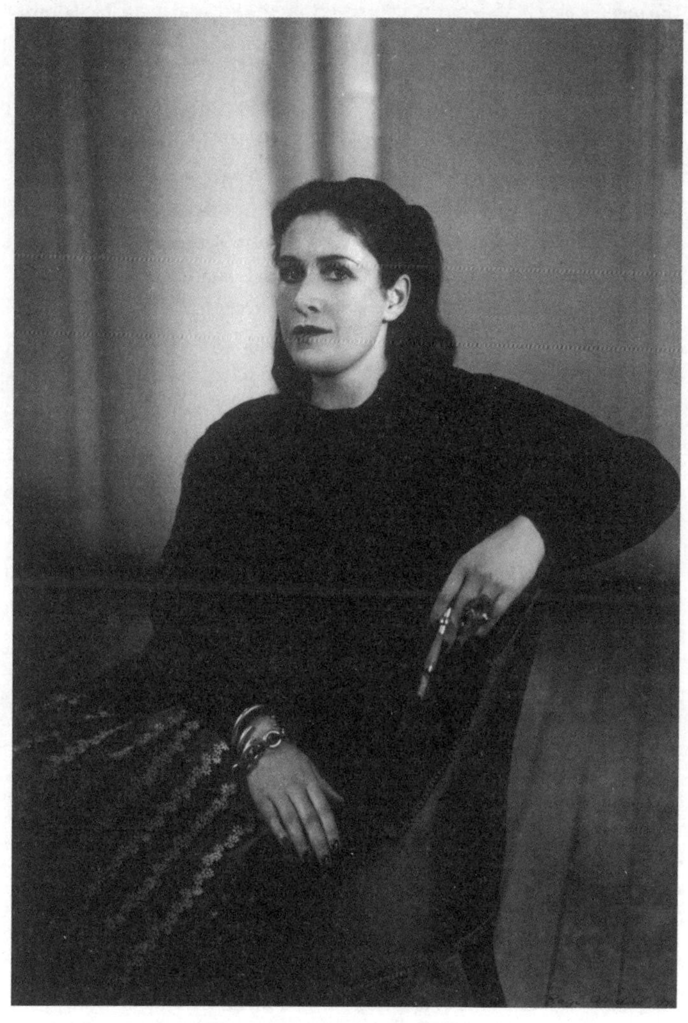

Dora Maar, 1941, photographed by Rogi André

take years before Dora Maar is sufficiently disentangled from the potent Picasso 'myth' for her achievement to be evaluated on its own merits alone. The reverse side of the coin, of course, is that the Picasso myth itself draws much of its potency from the remarkable women who were close to him.

Dora Maar, who has died within months of her ninetieth birthday, will be remembered as the most poignant of Picasso's mistresses. When she came into his life, early in 1936, she was twenty-eight and he, fifty-four. He noticed her at a nearby table at the café Les Deux Magots in Paris and was immediately drawn to her dark beauty. Although it was public knowledge in Saint-Germain-des-Prés that Picasso had left his wife Olga to live with Marie-Thérèse Walter, many young women in the quartier were at pains to attract his attention. Dora was wearing black gloves embroidered with pink flowers. Under Picasso's fascinated stare, she peeled off the gloves and began a game stabbing a knife rhythmically between her fingers. Every now and then, she came too close and drew a little blood.

This incident accurately foreshadowed the stormy and tortured love affair between them, which began in the summer of that year when they met at a friend's house near Saint-Tropez. Although generally reserved and self-willed, Dora had nothing of the innocent about her. She had trained as a painter, come into contact with Henri Cartier-Bresson and Man Ray, and her career as a photographer who had done experimental work as well as reportage was already well under way. As the mistress of the dissident Surrealist writer Georges Bataille, she was familiar not only with the avant-garde circles of Paris but also with the further limits of sexual exploration.

Born in 1907 in Tours to a French mother and a Slovenian father whose work as an architect involved long stays abroad, Dora had been brought up partly in Argentina. When she returned to Paris, she spoke fluent Spanish (a skill that Picasso especially prized) and felt socially and morally freer than her French contemporaries. In keeping with her cosmopolitan modernity and her ambition as an artist, she decided to shorten her given name of Henriette Theodora Markovitch to Dora Maar.

But nothing could have prepared her adequately for the impact of an extended relationship with Picasso. From the start, her need to commit to an absolute belief, already heralded in a deep interest in religion, clashed with the Spaniard's mercurial and wilful temperament. Her independence and the coolness of her intellectual judgment came as a challenge to Picasso, who had begun to tire of Marie-Thérèse's soothing passivity. With Dora, he was able to discuss the complexities of his work and, under her guidance, he even experimented with a technique using the shadows of objects thrown onto sensitized paper. She also proved helpful in more practical matters, finding Picasso the studio in the rue des Grands-Augustins where he painted *Guernica*. As the work progressed, Dora photographed each of its key stages, thus providing an invaluable record of its development. These photographs were included in the special issue on Picasso that the magazine *Cahiers d'Art* brought out later in 1937.

Dora also made a durable impact on Picasso's political attitudes, which became more radical under her influence. But their liaison was plagued by outbursts of jealousy and violence from the start. Picasso, whose relationship with Marie-Thérèse had continued as before, could not resist pushing the delicate situation to its limits. He fanned the animosity between the two women with an almost feminine intuition of their vulnerability, portraying the one in the other's favourite clothes, dividing to conquer down to the last detail. At one point, the two women literally came to blows in the studio, while Picasso went about his work as if nothing were amiss.

The constant shifts of emotion in their turbulent affair fuelled the brilliant and frequently cruel portraits that Picasso began to produce of Dora immediately after meeting her. She first appears, in a drawing that reflects the artist's awareness of the age gap between them, opening a door to find a bearded patriarch in wait for her on the other side. There are tender sketches that catch the distant, quizzical charm of her face, and the whimsical portraits showing her as a bird or sporting the cigarette holder she liked to brandish between her elegant fingers. Her presence in *Guernica* is unmistakable, and the image of the woman in tears that she inspired there was explored with a more personal, caustic intent in the famous 'Weeping Woman' series that Picasso started to paint a few months thereafter.

Once war had broken out and their love had been soured by too many unforgiving fights, Picasso's paintings of Dora grew in savage distortion, with formal brilliance degenerating at times into crude venom.

No doubt there was an obdurate, unyielding side to Dora's nature that whipped the domineering artist into a fury when he gave free rein to his feelings on canvas. Although he was clearly motivated by a range of other sensations and impulses when he portrayed her, Picasso nevertheless came to regard Dora above all as an object of suffering. 'For me she's the weeping woman', he confided to Françoise Gilot. 'For years I've painted her in tortured forms, not through sadism, and not with pleasure, either.'

By 1945, their affair was completely over, with Gilot having replaced Dora as Picasso's model and the mistress *en titre*. Just as nothing had prepared Dora for life with Picasso, nothing prepared her for the greater shock of life without him. Prone to mood swings at the best of times, she sank into a depression for which she was treated first with electro-shock therapy in a hospital and then, at the insistence of her friend and admirer Paul Éluard, by the psychoanalyst most reputed in the Parisian avant-garde, Jacques Lacan. Dora survived both the break-up and the therapies, but her life was drastically changed. She began going out less frequently and concentrated with admirable single-mindedness on her own painting. After producing numerous still lifes redolent of the grim simplicity that touched much postwar painting in Paris, she embarked on a series of large abstract compositions.

Dora also grew increasingly devout, leading a near-monastic existence in her flat in the rue de Savoie, just round the corner from the studio that she had found for Picasso. Later, she began spending longer periods of time in the house the artist had bought her in Ménerbes, the fortified hill village in Provence. Living alone in the comfortless gloom of this large house, she continued to paint with undiminished confidence in her own talent, but she made it virtually impossible for anyone to see her work, let alone exhibit it. Consequently, although she longed for recognition, neither her paintings nor her photographs have ever been adequately shown. With age, Dora Maar became a virtual recluse and a mystery even to the villagers of Ménerbes, who knew of her past but rarely caught a glimpse of her except on her way to Mass.

Originally published in the *Independent*, London, 2 August 1997

10

ALICE BELLONY-REWALD: PORTRAIT OF A MUSE

Alice Bellony-Rewald has been a well-known presence in the international art world for many years. Strikingly attractive and vivacious, she got to know many of the outstanding artists of the twentieth century in Paris and New York, writing about or interviewing some of them while being portrayed by others. We met, appropriately enough, first at a party in Paris, then in a museum, discovering that we shared an admiration for many of the artists who feature in this book and whom she had known personally. Bellony-Rewald has also written widely on modern art, notably memoirs of her encounters with Duchamp, Balthus, and Giacometti. I went to her apartment in the Marais in 1996 and came up with the following portrait of her.

Pablo Picasso wanted to do it, Francis Bacon thought about doing it, but Alberto Giacometti, Balthus, Oskar Kokoschka, and Hans Bellmer actually did do portraits of Alice Bellony-Rewald. Ranging from rapid sketches to fully worked paintings, most of them now hang in the stylish, loftlike apartment where Madame Bellony-Rewald, herself a painter and critic, lives in Paris. Many of the works are inscribed '*À ma chère Alice*', and a look round the walls makes it clear that this sprightly lady was at the centre of the art world, in Paris and New York, through the 1950s and 1960s.

Talking to her, it is also obvious that nothing in her background, apart from its exotic oddness, predisposed her to becoming the confidante and model of such a range of outstanding artists. Alice, as she insists on being called ('Bellony-Rewald is such a mouthful'), was born in West Africa. Her mother was Indonesian and her father, a black Frenchman from Martinique who had been posted to Dahomey as a circuit judge. But Alice has few memories of Africa, beyond the terror of hearing animals prowling round the house and crying out in the night. Her mother died when she was still a baby and she was whisked away to a totally different environment: a dour village called Ambleny in northern France where she was entrusted to a distant relation who brought her up. However unwelcoming the village seemed at first, it was almost unique in France in the 1920s in having a black bourgeoisie. All the notables, including the doctor and the lawyer, were from Martinique. Some of their names and their deeds are still very alive in Alice's mind; she recalls the doctor, Septimus Agricole, for instance, who, making the most of his calls to lonely farmhouses, was reputed to have sired most of the local population. Alice, meanwhile, was seen as a rather rebellious child, and she was entrusted for her education to the local nuns, whose simple-minded and persistent indoctrination she recalls all these years later with a distinct shudder.

— As soon as she could, Alice escaped the nuns and the bleak fields of Ambleny for Paris. She enrolled at the Sorbonne to study law, but the gaunt amphitheatres and dry theoretical teaching served only to remind her of the convent that she had so recently left. She was, on the other hand, drawn as if by a magnet to Saint-Germain-des-Prés, with its sexy mix of the new existentialist philosophy, glamorous people, and fashionable cafés. 'The war had just finished, and everybody was out on the street at that time', Alice recalls. 'There was a real feeling of relief and jubilation. Nobody wanted to stay at home because it was too uncomfortable, with next to no heating and a bathtub still filled, as it had been throughout the war, with coal or potatoes. And, of course, television was unheard of. So people flocked to Saint-Germain-des-Prés, and there was a marvellous atmosphere, because you could talk to everybody, and if you waited in the cafés you were bound to see some of your heroes. And if you didn't see them there, you'd find them late at night in one of the nightclubs, like La Rose Rouge, which were all the rage. And the famous people weren't at all stuck up. It was very easy to go over to Sartre or Picasso at the Café de Flore or Les Deux Magots and say hello, even for someone like me who had just arrived and was rather dumbstruck with admiration.'

The admiration grew and the law studies dwindled from that moment on. Alice had found her real home, both spiritually and physically, since

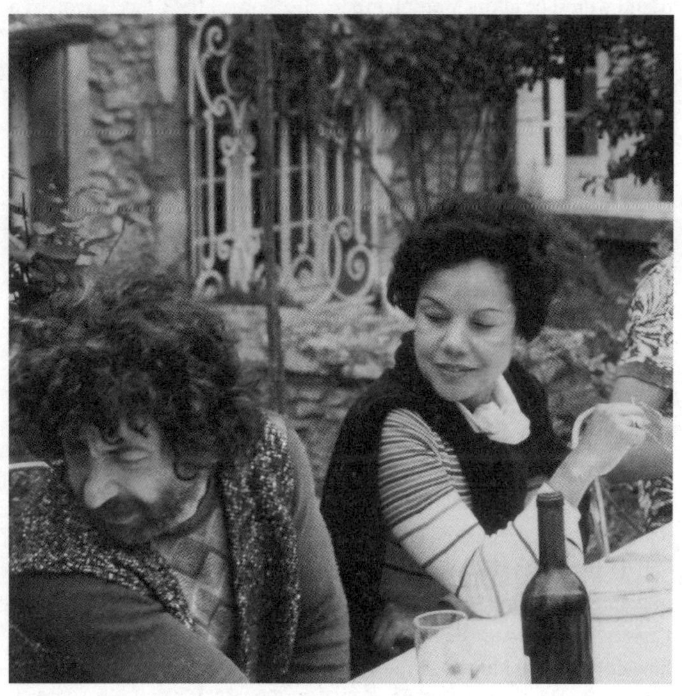

Dado and **Alice Bellony-Rewald** at Dado's home in Hérouval,
Normandy, *c.* 1975, photographer unknown

she then moved into one of the numerous hotels in Saint-Germain that catered specially to students. 'Nobody had much money then, which made contact between people much easier', she says. 'Almost everybody seemed to live in a small room somewhere, and dinner usually consisted of pasta cooked over a Primus stove. But our real homes were the cafés. You've no idea how important they were. You knew that this or that friend would be at the Montalambert, the Flore or the Deux Magots at a particular time of day, so you never really needed a rendezvous. You just turned up, and while you were waiting you might see some of the "stars", like Juliette Greco or Albert Camus, go by. Nobody had a telephone, so if you were looking for someone you'd leave a message with one of the café waiters. They were like postboxes: you could carry on a whole love affair through the waiters.'

Having by now abandoned her studies, Alice needed a job, and since she was pretty and brimming with enthusiasm, she soon landed one as an assistant in a prominent Left Bank art gallery. Her canny employer made sure that she sat in full view of passers-by, and her looks and infectious laughter soon proved as big a draw as the Renoirs and Matisses on the gallery's walls. One visitor, a German-born art historian called John Rewald, became a particularly assiduous visitor, along with personalities of the period like the Russian painter Serge Poliakoff, who would regularly bring his guitar and serenade the petite assistant. Rewald, who had already accomplished much of his pioneering work on Cézanne and had begun what would become the standard history of the Impressionist movement, became Alice's most persistent suitor. Since he had lived in Paris before the war (fleeing to New York to escape Nazi persecution), Rewald was well known in the capital's art circles. Through him, Alice began to meet a new range of artists, dealers, and collectors and establish more of an equal footing with them. After frequent stays in Paris, Rewald persuaded Alice to leave the cherished pastures of Saint-Germain for the no less heady but more alarming prospect of New York.

'All my ideas about America had come from the cinema – cowboy films and thrillers', Alice remembers. 'When I got to New York, I was plunged into a world of highly sophisticated Jewish art collectors, and it took me a long time to reconcile my mental picture of speakeasies and the Wild West with people who spoke five languages fluently and lived surrounded by period furniture, Meissen china, and Old Masters. For a long time I felt I hadn't really arrived – the real America was still out there, and I had not found it.'

Some time later, she and Rewald married and settled in a comfortable apartment on Park Avenue, surrounded by the exquisite collection of late nineteenth- and early twentieth-century drawings that Rewald had been building up since his earliest research on the Impressionists. As a couple, they made a considerable hit in the New York art world. John was respected for his scholarship and commitment, and Alice was liked for her gaiety and charm – but, more durably, for her ability to bring people out, listen to them intelligently, and discuss anything under the sun. Since her love of art had grown stronger and more informed, Alice went to all the openings and began to meet the American painters who interested her most. By the late 1950s, there was barely an Abstract Expressionist of note whose studio or loft she had not visited. There was no question, obviously, of Pollock or Rothko doing her portrait, but several of the figurative artists of the time, like Raphael Soyer, did ask her to sit for them.

Alice had also begun to write art reviews for the French-language newspaper *La Gazette de Lausanne*, and this provided her with an extra opportunity to spend time with New York artists, many of whom were by then moving downtown or out to Long Island in search of bigger, cheaper working spaces. 'The late 1950s and early 1960s were a great moment to be in New York', Alice says. 'The artistic activity and the general effervescence were quite different from what was going on in Saint-Germain. The atmosphere was more innocent, more naive perhaps, but for that reason the impact was more direct and terrifically powerful. Everything seemed possible, you know, with that American sense of optimism. Not only did people want to do new things, they also had the financial means to do them – something which was often sorely lacking in postwar France.'

Meanwhile, Alice had never lost touch with Paris, regularly plying to and fro over the Atlantic on the luxury liners, like the fabled *France*, which she adored ('All the normal rules and conventions were suspended for the five days you were at sea', she recalls with evident relish). Both she and her husband were writing about art in the press and adding to their collection, so they had two good reasons for being able to call on any of the great artists in France. They made several visits to Picasso, who received them sometimes reluctantly, sometimes cordially. Alice remembers a detailed discussion of bull-fighting with the great Spaniard before he left them to attend a corrida, but clearest in her mind was a simple lunch she shared with him in the kitchen at La Californie, his villa near Cannes. 'He was dressed only in a pair of shorts, and although he was an old man I kept noticing how beautiful his skin looked. He exuded a kind of animal energy. He was in a good mood that day, and he told me all about his favourite foods. What he liked best, he said, was soup, but the kind of soup he'd had as a boy in Spain and had never been able to find after he left. He was very easy and natural, talking as if he had all the time in the world, and of course I was overjoyed when he suddenly said he wanted to do my portrait. But in the end we never hit on the right moment, when he would have just got down to it without more ado.'

Much later, Alice formed a lively friendship with Bacon, who made a point of seeing her on his frequent trips to Paris. But the artist who made the deepest impression on her was Giacometti, whom she met in 1960 when he was at the height of his fame. Giacometti asked both Alice and her husband to his famously chaotic little studio behind Montparnasse, and he eventually agreed to make some drawings of them. 'We'd go into this sort of cave full of half-finished sculpture, tools and rags, with piles of dust everywhere', Alice recalls. 'It was extraordinary, because whenever you sat down a great cloud of dust went up, and whenever Giacometti moved, there was another great cloud. It felt as if the tiny studio was constantly dissolving. The sittings would go on for a long time, and they always followed the same pattern. Giacometti would fidget for a bit, muttering to himself and sighing very heavily. Then he would make a few marks on paper, and the mutterings and sighs would grow worse and he'd begin to say out aloud, "It's impossible, it's just impossible. How can I ever do what I want to do, how can I ever do a nose as I see it?" The grumblings went on for a while longer, and he would suddenly look at me and burst out with a phrase like: "But a head is like a landscape! How can I get a whole landscape in the space of a head?" After that he would calm down and start work in earnest. Whenever he'd finished a drawing, or rather felt he could do no more to it, he'd let it fall on the floor, saying, "It's worthless – there's no point in your having it", and to emphasize his point he'd trample over it. That was Giacometti's way. In the end he might give it to you, pretending to be amazed you'd want such a miserable thing. But it was very difficult to buy anything from him. If he really wanted to sell anything, there were always droves of American collectors queuing up, because he was even better known in the States than in Europe.'

'It became a kind of game between us', Alice continues, taking down a small ink portrait of herself by Giacometti. 'He was an attractive man, and oddly elegant even though he was often covered from head to foot in plaster dust. I went back to see him because I hoped to buy another drawing or two, but I'd always get caught up in his strange ways of doing things. Often he asked me to meet him at his local café and he'd arrive, with that great head of hair full of plaster, and just talk – about politics, often, or anything that had caught his imagination. Whenever I tried to get him to name a price for a drawing, he'd go off at a tangent. "But I don't need money", he'd say. "I've got my studio, and I don't want to move. I can't imagine being anywhere else. My wife found it too uncomfortable, so I bought her an apartment. But for myself I've got everything I need. I leave all my money with my dealer." So I used to play along with him, and I'd say, "Well, if you have all this money, why don't you give it away? Why don't you give it to someone who wants to do something like make a film?" And he thought for a while and said: "I would give it away, but nobody ever asks me." Later I said to him, "Why do you complain the whole time while you're working?" He looked genuinely surprised and said, "Do I really complain?" And then I realized his complaining was almost unconscious, like an incantation, to get himself going. One of Giacometti's great pleasures was to walk for hours on end across Paris. Often he spent the whole night out, eating late and going to a few bars and then trailing endlessly through the streets. One evening, after we'd had dinner in Saint-Germain, he walked me all the way back to where I was staying in Montmartre. It was very late. I asked him in for a drink. Once we were inside, he said, "When I was young, it was so difficult to find a woman. Now there are so many around me I don't know what to do with them." I didn't answer. Then, after a while, he said: "Give me a pen." And he drew this marvellous little head of me, there and then, before disappearing back into the night.'

Originally published in the *Guardian*, 30 December 1996

11

JOHN RICHARDSON:
THE SORCERER'S APPRENTICE

Having first met John Richardson in New York in the mid-1970s, I saw him casually on and off for years before he came up with the idea, not long after this review was published, that we might curate a Bacon / Picasso exhibition together, particularly in light of our respective roles as the artists' biographers. John also thought I might assist him directly on his monumental Picasso project, and despite misgivings about embarking on a major collaboration with him where I could never be more than an assistant, I was fascinated enough to go along with the idea and to observe John's chaotic but inspired working methods at first hand. We met frequently for a couple of years thereafter and, although we never actually succeeded in getting any kind of project off the ground, we shared numerous agreeable evenings, often in his palatial, painting- and curio-stuffed apartment downtown on Park Avenue, where he regaled me with indiscreet stories about the artists and writers, society hostesses and prominent collectors, swindlers and eccentrics he had known during his long, colourful existence. The following is a review of the memoirs about his early days, which left me regretting that Richardson had not left behind more outrageous sketches of his life and times.

Pausing midway in his mammoth biography of Picasso, John Richardson has written a concise account of the first half of his own life, and notably of his long relationship as a young man with the Cubist art historian and collector Douglas Cooper. The account concentrates on the dozen years, from early 1949 to the end of 1960, that Richardson lived with

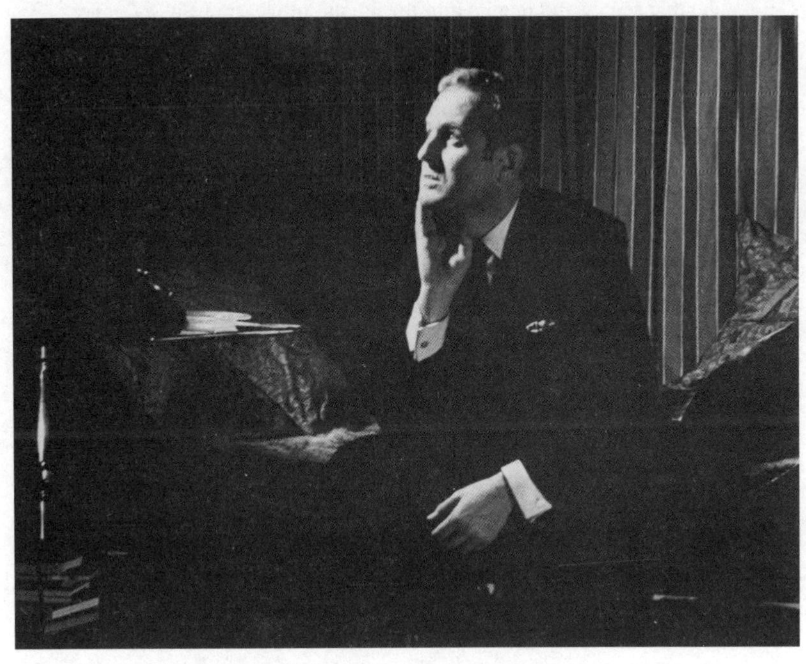

John Richardson, at his home in New York, 1965,
photographed by Leopold Joseph

Cooper, visiting museums and monuments all over Europe, meeting the great artists and other personalities of the day, and restoring the colonnaded Château de Castille in the south of France, where the two men set themselves up in some grandeur, surrounded by Cooper's outstanding collection of twentieth-century art.

Having escaped the drabness of postwar London, where they were both living when they first met, Richardson and Cooper threw their considerable energy and talents into the pursuit of pleasure. Since Cooper had come into a sizeable family fortune, he could afford to indulge both his and his younger friend's taste for amusement and luxury. When they were not looking at or acquiring the art they most admired, they were entertaining old friends or cultivating new ones. Concerts and madly social house parties alternated with lazy days on unspoilt Mediterranean beaches or trips to the corrida in the company of Jean Cocteau and Picasso. Long-suffering servants and powerful cars, driven by Cooper at breakneck speed, made such gadding about the Midi all the more agreeable, while plenty of local delicacies, from ortolans to truffles, served to blot out miserable English memories of Spam and powdered eggs.

Idyllic as this existence sounds – and indeed in many ways was, to judge from Richardson's crisply factual account – there was always a large fly in the ointment. More than for his expertise in Cubism, Cooper was known throughout the art world for his aggressively expressed opinions and his vindictiveness, which ran the gamut from casual malice to full-blown vendettas. Of the latter, the most famous was the war that Cooper waged for years against Sir John Rothenstein, while the latter was director of the Tate Gallery, and which culminated in an undignified scuffle during an exhibition opening. The fact that such attacks backfired, as Richardson notes, in no way deterred Cooper. He turned vehemently against several artists whose work he had previously championed, and he meted out passionate scorn on fellow art historians, curators, and collectors, excoriating them in print and in private, and generally behaving as if modern art were exclusively his domain.

No one who met Cooper was left in doubt as to his potential spite. In person, he looked every bit as cantankerous as his reputation suggested. I remember, before I even knew what he looked like, spotting him at a crowded reception for an auction sale in Paris in the early 1970s: with his apoplectic complexion and his corpulent frame swathed in loud tweeds, he looked like an angry gentleman farmer who had wandered into the effete pastures of art. When we were introduced, he seemed affable enough but there was a triumphant glint in his eye, as if he were a gamekeeper collaring a poacher, and before I was out of earshot, I heard him make some shrill remark about 'the impertinent Peppiatt'. I don't think he had taken exception to something I had written, but rather to the fact that I wrote about art at all.

As Cooper's close companion, with an instinctive and increasingly informed sense of art, Richardson was bound in the long run to incur his mentor's worst wrath. Like flashes of lightning, warning signs came early on in their ménage, especially when Richardson decided, despite strenuous objections from his lover, to write a study of Georges Braque; perversely enough, Cooper wanted his pupil to learn everything from him but never put what he knew to any purpose. And although Richardson only hints at the strains of living day by day with such an obstreperous, manipulative character, everything in his account seems to lead ominously to the couple's final quarrel.

When the break occurs, it is prompted by a difference in aesthetic judgment. Questions of attribution might not draw blood in most households, but this took place at the Château de Castille, sanctuary of Cubism, with its high priest present. Richardson had ventured an opinion about two paintings, supposedly by Fernand Léger, that a collector friend was thinking of buying. 'How could he have been taken in by such inert daubs?' asks Richardson, very much the sorcerer's apprentice anxious to show his expertise. 'There was a terrible silence, during which Douglas's pink face turned the colour of a summer pudding. "What a little expert we've become." And then came a shriek like calico ripping – comical but also alarming. "How dare you pontificate to me about Léger!" he yelled. "Those paintings are absolutely authentic. Get out, get out...." And then he took another look at the photographs, and I knew that he realized I was right and he was wrong. Things would never be the same again.'

From then on, their relationship unravels swiftly, with neither protagonist coming out well at the end. Richardson makes his first trips to New York, far from Cooper's clutches, and realizes, at the not too early age of thirty-six, that he might be able to earn his own living. On his return to

France, more quarrels and recriminations follow. Having burnt his former lover's personal effects, Cooper then deliberately withholds works of art that Picasso, Braque, Nicolas de Staël, and Graham Sutherland had given to Richardson. The latter retaliates by making an early morning raid on his former home to reclaim his possessions, then finds that Cooper has put the police on his trail. The twelve-year idyll tails off into farce and bitterness, even though, much later, the two men did achieve some kind of reconciliation before Cooper died in 1984.

Richardson recounts the rise and fall of Cooper in his life without much apparent animosity in a brisk narrative filled with incisive sketches of the many other personalities whom he came to know; he conjures up Marie-Laure de Noailles, Cyril Connolly, and Dora Maar in a few lines, and every description of Picasso brings the artist alive. The one person who remains mysteriously missing from this vivid picture is Richardson himself. After a brief portrait of his childhood and student days, the author turns into the detached narrator, deftly recording the whole chain of external events but giving only the most superficial account of his own thoughts and reactions. It never becomes clear, in particular, why Richardson was so seduced by Cooper, or what his feelings for him during their long liaison really were. It was certainly not sexual attraction, since Richardson found to his alarm on their first night together that Cooper was 'as rubbery as a Dalí biomorph'; and the physical side of their relationship is not mentioned again. To an extent, as Richardson suggests, the two men were obviously drawn together by a passion for art and a certain kind of father-son kinship (Cooper was thirteen years Richardson's senior). But that hardly accounts for the emotional staying power that would have been required to share so much of one's youth with (in Richardson's phrase) 'this hugely gifted, hugely flawed old buffo'.

No doubt Cooper had his saving graces and Richardson was fonder of him than his memoir conveys; the author did, one notes, dedicate the first volume of his Picasso biography to Cooper. But since neither the writer nor his lover is brought out in any psychological depth, the enduring basis of their relationship remains hard to fathom. A clue can be found perhaps in Richardson's description of his own 'upstairs-downstairs' background: his father, a distinguished soldier and successful entrepreneur, had died when Richardson was five, leaving his mother, who had been a modest employee, to bring the family up on a dwindling fortune – not enough, the author says, 'to give us much of a start in life'. When Cooper turns up (like Toad of Toad Hall, honking the horn of a brightly coloured Rolls-Royce), his wealth and, perhaps even more, his sophistication and social connections must have made him considerably more palatable to the younger, strikingly handsome, and presumably ambitious Richardson. Had Richardson revealed more about his own personality and inner drives, it would have done much to give this engaging, witty account of a not so misspent youth the resonance of a truly memorable memoir.

Originally published as a review of John Richardson's *The Sorcerer's Apprentice: Picasso, Provence and Douglas Cooper* (New York: Knopf, 1999), in the *New York Times Book Review*, New York, 12 December 1999

12

HENRI MICHAUX:
PAINTER-POET

I came across Michaux's writings first in the early 1960s when I translated several texts of his for a Tamil poetry editor in London called Tambimuttu, who founded both *Poetry London* and Lyrebird Press. I immediately identified with Michaux's strange world and tried my hand at a few short stories in a vaguely comparable vein, secure in the knowledge that he was so little known in London that no one would ever guess whose style I was imitating. I also knew a little about his drawings because Francis Bacon used to talk about them and in fact owned one that I saw in his studio in Reece Mews.

Later, when I moved to Paris, I read most of Michaux and went to every exhibition of his work I could. He had become part of my life and a singular presence in my personal pantheon, not only because I loved the savagery of his writing and the extraordinary inventiveness of the drawings, but above all because Michaux straddled both – an achievement I particularly admire. In fact, I admired him so much that when, in the mid-1970s, I was invited to dinner with him and seated by his side I continually blushed and could find nothing to say that I imagined he would not find stupid. But that is another story. What follows here in slightly condensed form is the tribute that I wanted to pay Michaux, which Jim Fitzsimmons, then my editor at *Art International*, kindly agreed to publish.

Having been for most of his life something of a special taste, Henri Michaux now finds himself high on the scale of international recognition. Consecration came no doubt when *Les Cahiers de l'Herne* devoted one of

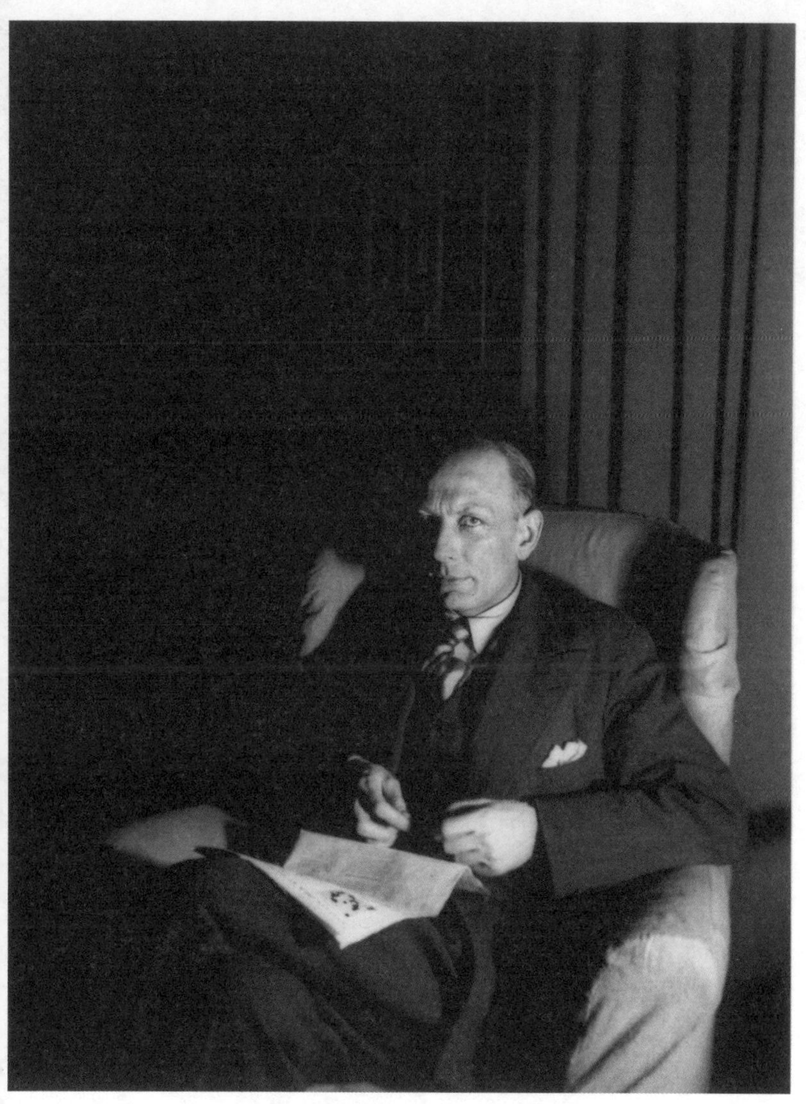

Henri Michaux, 1937, photographed by Claude Cahun

their bulky monographs to him and with the Musée de l'art moderne's retrospective – in 1965, and the first in France[1] – of his paintings. This year has continued the upward swing, and the hand of Michaux has been more in public evidence than ever. There has been a new book, a brief, curtly admonitory set of maxims called *Poteaux d'angle*; a highly successful dramatization – put on for the Festival du Marais – of a large number of short extracts of his work (above all, to the audience's huge delight, some of the best bits of his early metaphysical slapstick); a one-man and a shared show at Le Point Cardinal; and a new retrospective that opened in Charleroi in mid-November and will tour Belgium by way of Ghent and Brussels until February 1972.

The new paintings shown at Le Point Cardinal were a development on what one might call the 'blobs-in-flight' theme that has already served Michaux's imagination so well, allowing the apparently non-representational to body forth and then disappear in a constant flux between form and formlessness. *Poteaux d'angle* constitutes a string of harsh moralities thrown into occasional relief by flashes of a kind of last-ditch optimism (for example, 'Faute de soleil, sache mûrir dans la glace' [For lack of sun, know how to ripen in ice]). Neither is likely to change much in one's view of Michaux's art, but there is at the very least something immensely encouraging in seeing such clarity and suppleness of mind still in unimpaired action after seventy-two years of what he himself has always considered a vastly unequal struggle.

Venerable age, singleness of purpose and pursuit, and the fact that he echoes a whole generation of writers now dead while remaining irreducibly a man apart: these are some of the surface reasons for Michaux's bound into the diffuse limelight of late recognition. Another, less usual one is, quite simply, his activity as a painter, which, though it was under way as early as the mid-1920s,[2] has taken much longer than his writings to find a following. And here, of course, the important point is not merely that Michaux paints – lots of writers have a go at it – but that he paints so well, well enough to be approached exclusively as an innovator in plastic form, that is, as a painter, and not as a writer who happens also to paint.

In an interview published during his one-man show at Le Point Cardinal, Michaux made it clear that the two activities were never allowed to get in each other's way, that he concentrated exclusively on one or the other for longish stretches of time.[3] For him, painting is entirely independent of his writing, a totally different attempt to create a totally different language. And one may reflect that, had the painted work always been shown under another name, it would have taken the most ingenious and allusion-conscious critic a long time to imagine any connection between them. On the other hand, it often seems unnecessary and even impoverishing to implement such a rigid distinction between the two. For however exclusive each search and the vocabulary that is both its conveyance and its aim may seem, the one does broaden and highlight the other at many points. Perhaps their most important singularity is that both translate Michaux's preoccupations while offering him a means of setting his entangled imagination free: both constitute what one might call 'ways out'.

They are ways out towards another reality in which gravity has been suspended and all the rules of creation are there to be reinvented; a do-it-yourself reality, provided you have the desire and the ability to think everything (and above all the very basis of your own thinking) anew. Michaux's search for an exit from day-to-day discontent has always led him to transform. Out of his terrible sensitivity to the ridicule and futility of everyday existence he has managed to create an escape route: a capacity for recasting appearance to his own whimsical, or desperate, requirements.

Beyond a certain point in this venture, however, language lets him down, not only because it cannot transmute everything but because it is not in itself susceptible of more than a certain degree of transmutation. (In *Poteaux d'angle*, standing by themselves, are the two words '*Paroles. Paroles*'; one can almost hear him sigh.) His experiments with a language purely of his own invention have been limited, it seems, to an occasional foray – such as in poems like *Saoûls* or *L'Avenir*.[4] And it is precisely here that painting, with its infinite mobility and constant invitation to the effects of chance, has proved particularly attractive to him. Within the realm of painting, Michaux has felt himself able to devise an entirely personal language, sets of restlessly changing notations of which none has ever quite existed before. Words he could shake into new and arresting patterns; he could inform them with his wonderfully quick, subtle, and subversive spirit, but short of gibberish or another source of comparative imponderability like *Finnegans Wake*, he could not produce a hitherto unused language. With paint, and above all with watercolour, however, he could. Painting set a side of him free.

It would be quite misleading, though, to look at the paintings as though they filled in gaps in the written work or in any way existed in counterpoint to it, just as the texts themselves hardly prepare one for such an onslaught of strange imagery. Yet echoes are struck between the two. Certain early texts prefigure the chaos of the India-ink painting (or 'blobs-in-flight') just as the latter adds another dimension to the writings. The process tends on the whole to go from the written work to the painted, partly for the simple reason that most of Michaux's admirers have discovered his paintings after having read some of his texts. But it is also no doubt because his paintings admit of so little verbal definition, with the result that one is often drawn to recall sensations similar to those Michaux has already evoked in words.

What one finds above all (and it is not that surprising, even if one accepts that each activity exists separately) is that they have a common denominator. It is readily definable, even though it continually shifts out of focus, because it is the single main source of all Michaux's inspiration: suffering, in one of the many forms – degradation, sickness, panic, anguish – he has explored and given it.

Whimsical or black-humoured, suffocated with bitterness or totally guileless and laid open by the candour of despair, a sense of the inescapability of suffering moves like a sun over Michaux's universe. In a text in *La Vie dans les plis*, he says: 'Quand je ne souffre pas, me trouvant entre deux périodes de souffrance, je vis comme si je ne vivais pas' (When I am not suffering, finding myself between two periods of suffering, I live as if I were not living).[5] Suffering has him marked out at birth, an aspect of the poet that one critic, Georges Poulet, has examined at some length: 'What Henri Michaux therefore perceives in himself when he questions himself and becomes aware of himself is his ontological weakness. To make himself exist, he discovers himself without strength. This experience is nothing special. In an obvious or concealed way, it is at the heart of all the *Cogitos*, starting with that of Descartes. "I think, therefore I am" means "I think that I am not by myself, I think that if I exist, it depends only on me." So I'm weak! My weakness is to be an obviously contingent creature, to whom existence is given only in dribs and drabs. [...] Enough to breathe, yes! enough to exist, yes still, but just and without guarantee! Enough to be strong, happy, equal to the conditions required by existence? no, definitely, no! [...] It sounds like the story of an unfortunate being who, from birth – why? does he scream too much? – would be deprived of most of the gifts that are indispensable to the children of men. Deprived and aware of this deprivation.'[6]

Yet his original and enduring state of deprivation is countered, however insufficiently and at whatever cost, by a power of poetic fantasy allied to a sense of the absurd that is as ferocious as it is tonic. To put it in other words and bring it nearer home, the whole of Michaux's work is a battlefield for the elements of his suffering, for his contradictions, his loathing, his violence, and his fears. His approach to art has been directed by a search for catharsis, for a means of throwing into relief the private pain of living, the suffering that runs in the 'sang des souvenirs, du percement de l'âme, de la fragile chambre centrale' (blood of memories, of the piercing of the soul, of the fragile central chamber).[7]

But his ambition also went far beyond catharsis. He wanted to replace the life he found, and decidedly did not care for, by one that he would be continually reinventing. At first it seemed to him that such a transformation on paper was not enough; it had to take place within life itself. 'Il serait bien écrivain', he explains with doleful exactitude in an early text, *Portrait d'homme* (1936), 'car il a de continuelles inventions, mais il voudrait les voir, non écrites, mais réalisées, et que nos conditions d'existence changent du tout au tout, suivant elles' (He would like to be a good writer because he has continual inventions, but he would like to see them, not written, but realized, and our conditions of existence changed completely accordingly by them).

Forty years of tenacious infiltration into the minds of his readers have to some extent brought this about: just as in Jorge Luis Borges's terrifying and delightful story *Tlön, Uqbar, Orbis Tertius*, the texts of reality have been slowly changing. Real acquaintanceship with Michaux's work brings with it a certain Michauxization of the world, a process in which the foundations of appearance begin to crumble, the laws of cause and effect expire, and the floods of poetic chaos do away with the flimsy barriers of everyday reality. In Michaux's rebellious view, and this holds for both his writing and painting, nothing *has* to be the way it is; the outside world allows of every conceivable interpretation, it is as though it awaits the application of fantasy (after all, as Borges has pointed out, we do not know whether the world can be classed as belonging to fact or fiction[8]). Gravity, for instance, can be seen as a convention that the imaginative eye effortlessly transcends; conversely, chance can be supplied with its own curious logic. The early stories, to give more specific examples, are full of the achievements of fantasy over an irritating and hostile world: if you do not like someone's face, your mind's eye can change it – can easily unhook the offending ears and throw them away; if the presence of a mountain opposite your hotel bedroom grows too overbearing, you can bring yourself to a pitch of concentration and send it toppling.[9] Fantasy is all-powerful, and in the books up until the mescaline experiment and in most of the paintings, this elegant and summary meddling with the accepted facts of existence provides a source for the most astonishing acts of creation. There is one story about the writer's genealogy that constitutes such a powerful instance of his capacity for the strangest transformations that it is worth quoting the beginning in full:

> *'Pon was born from an egg, then he was born from a cod,*
> *and in being born he burst it, then he was born from a shoe;*
> *by bipartition, the smaller shoe on the left, and he on the right,*
> *then he was born from a rhubarb leaf, at the same time as a fox;*
> *he and the fox looked at each other for a moment, then went*
> *their separate ways. Then he was born from a cockroach, from*
> *the eye of a lobster, from a carafe; from a sea lion and he came*
> *out of her by the whiskers, from a tadpole and he came out of*
> *her behind, from a mare and he came out of her by the nostrils,*
> *then he shed tears looking for the breasts, for he came into the*
> *world only to suckle. Then he was born from a trombone and*
> *the trombone fed him for thirteen months, then he was weaned*
> *and entrusted to the sand that lay everywhere because it was*
> *the desert. And only the son of the trombone can feed himself*
> *in the desert, alone with the camel, then he was born of a woman*
> *and he was greatly astonished.'*[10]

*

In meddling with the world and the effects of chance, Michaux also echoes the world, especially in his watercolours and his paintings in India ink. The images in question hover so disconcertingly between a number of identities and the purest formlessness that they evoke comparisons in all kinds of places beyond themselves: in the whorls that turn into heads in a piece of wallpaper or the bark of a tree, in the worn surface of a road or a pitted wall, in the strange higgledy-piggledy of shorthand or a disjointed script racing across the page, or in the mirror images of words sunk into blotting paper. It is an '*écriture*' that parallels the world and the books in the most unexpected and precise ways.

But it is also distinctly other. When he abandons writing for painting, Michaux tells us in *Passages*, his outlook is quite different: 'We change marshalling yards when we start painting. The factory of words – word-thoughts, word-images, word-emotions – disappears, drowns dizzily and so simply. [...] No more desire, appetite to speak. The part of the head that found itself most interested in that cools.'[11] Words fade out to make way for signs and gestures, for the spontaneity and play of chance that Michaux makes prerequisites of painting. Discovered some time after his literary revelation (a reading of the Comte de Lautréamont, thenceforth the 'copain de génie'), painting came as a new kind of release. Here indeed was the ease of transformation, the fluidity, the immediacy of transcription, thought and gesture becoming one, that had formed a background of longing to all his written work.

In this fresh venture, watercolour was the first and abiding love, a medium to which Michaux has returned again and again, notably over the last few years (the 1970 watercolours shown this spring at Le Point Cardinal have a *painful* vitality). With its cloudings and suspensions, its ambiguous relationship vis-à-vis the paper, allowing itself to be soaked up yet leaving its stain to spread with growing paleness over vast areas of the surrounding white, watercolour proved the ideal substance.

As he tried his hand in it, Michaux became haunted by a 'perpétuelle fièvre de visages' (perpetual fever of faces), and he used watercolour to make a terrible, tenderly coloured record of the human head. Here, the restless, ingenious, and grating black humour of texts such as *Plume* was complemented by subtly haunting evidence of the perishability of all flesh, caught and as though drowned in its own contradictions. Water-colour could evoke everything, including, of course, things one had not imagined, awakening a sense of exploration that Michaux has described: 'The colours that spin like fish on the sheet of water where I put them, that's what I like in watercolour. The little heap of colouring that disintegrates into tiny particles, these passages, and not the final stop, the painting. [...] Water of watercolour, as immense as a lake, water, omnivore demon, scraper of islets, maker of mirages, breaker of dykes, overflow of worlds.'[12]

Like delicately tinted wounds, these heads float hopelessly beneath the weight of their own colour, in sorrow, terror, or anger, as though engaged still in some half-remembered struggle. Heads decomposing in the water that painted them, heads like those that run up and out of a flame, heads that are also ears or oysters, never quite definable emanations of sights grown unfamiliar, heads always about to signify, oracle heads gagged with confusion, their message flattened back on their face. In their half-pathetic, half-humorous ungainliness, there is a little Dubuffet; in their vulnerability, a little Bacon. They are often so pale in colour that one is put in mind of an X-ray or a photograph still developing beneath a layer of water. In their attitude, they range from an almost clownlike resignation to a half-conscious, half-deadened horror at what is happening to them. They stare up out of the floundering contours of their own flesh with an intensity to keep one midway between tears and acid laughter. But overall, as in the comparably battered and besieged figures of Bacon, there is also a sense of grandeur, of dignity in the face of insuperable odds.

This quality is born of Michaux's extreme awareness of the contradictions and impossibilities of life joined to a heroic determination to resist – a 'dur désir de durer'. These difficulties are apparent in all Michaux's work, where they have been deeply and brilliantly explored, but rarely resolved; beneath them is an instinctive stubbornness, a will to hold out even in the subtly corrosive, apparently serene yet mortal wash of watercolour. The essential part of the grandeur of this battle is that it will be lost. Michaux realizes this so keenly that at times he makes no attempt to dissemble his exasperation:

Were we born to be dross
Were we born, fingers broken,
To devote life to a bad problem?[13]

But at least there *has* been a struggle, and the traces remain.

Though only momentarily, Michaux then abandoned the use of water-colour to try his hand in the very different medium of India ink. From this there came the discovery of a totally new theme, in some ways even more personal and more inventive than the watercolours. I have already referred to this new theme as the 'blobs-in-flight' – those astonishing generators of panic and fantasy born of the controlled chance effects of ink on paper. More even than the heads, they have their being in the middle ground between the realms of the identifiable and the flux of formlessness. They hold this ground by their constant ambiguity, by their capacity for swinging from one area into the other, from falling, sprawling figures plucked out of oblivion into a half-articulated rush of black marks across a white surface. Like the creature in Michaux's poem 'L'Attente', they are 'êtres qui voudraient être' (beings that would like to be); created fortuitously out of a spray of ink, they are left to struggle towards some kind of further delineation. Or again, they are like the 'Meidosem', the strange tribe of beings that Michaux describes in *La Vie dans les plis*, for each of them could be well described as 'une peine qui court' (a running sentence). On another level, they are also quite simply acts of savage creation, whipped up out of nothingness, the products of a spite and impatience that their author once clarified in their regard: 'To marks now. [...] Well, I hate them. I like water, but they don't. [...] So I fight with them, I whip them, I would like to be immediately rid of their collapsed stupidity, and to galvanize them, to make them bewildered, exasperated, to combine them monstrously in spite of themselves with everything that moves, with the innumerable crowd of beings, non-beings, furies of being [...]. Quick. You have to act quickly, with these big soft ones, capable of spreading themselves out everywhere. It's right away, before they extend their domain of abjections and vomiting. Unbearable marks.'[14]

These 'big soft ones' ('*grandes molles*') are never given the first oppor-tunity to follow their supine nature. Alarmed by the hand that brought them into being, they find themselves cast in a desperate flight from the centre of their explosive world. Instinct with fear, they tumble head-long through the planes of the picture – areas that could be extended infinitely, with ever more shreds of matter – in a movement that they themselves have never understood or controlled. It is what Jean Grenier, in a perceptive foreword to the catalogue of Michaux's 1967 show at Le Point Cardinal, calls a *'Lebensgaloppade'* – a life gallop – a point that he develops: 'These black fellows who follow each other endlessly [...] make me think of what Bossuet says about death, the man in the grip of his perishable destiny begs the invisible powers to allow him to slow down his course. In vain. Move on, they shout to him, move on. No respite. The originality of Michaux is to have chosen this absence of respite and to have transformed a fatality into a challenge. He would not content himself with saying like Zarathustra: Again! He would like to say, he would like to shout: Never stop! Always further!'[15] Within these pictures (whose general theme Michaux is still exploring today) one feels the exultation of the charioteer, whipping his horses ever faster. But those creatures are not, of course, mere emanations from the outside: they are himself. 'Je voudrais bien savoir', he once wrote with clear-sighted self-mockery, 'pourquoi je suis toujours le cheval que je tiens par la bride' (I would like to know why I am still the horse that I am holding by the bridle).[16] Here the horse that is himself is being ridden in a spirit of unrestrained creation, with no heed for its four legs or its sense of danger. And from it emerges a fragmented vision of what, to the naked eye, is invisible: the cellular chaos that underlies all appearance.

*

By comparison, the mescaline drawings do not appear to have opened up such rich sources of invention. They are fascinating, certainly, just as the four books that Michaux published on his drug experiences continue to fascinate by the clarity brought to sensations that reach out far beyond words. Both attempts to capture the unrecapturable are, clearly, in vain; they cannot be more than descriptions or semblances of other states. Despite this, they do break new ground. Both the books and the paintings that attempt to record these hallucinogenic experiences commemorate an act of tremendous and sustained discipline; the lucid man tries to maintain a situation in which he both is and is able to comment on the drugged man. In the writings on his various, very soberly prepared experiments with drugs, Michaux describes extreme points of terror and ecstasy. There is no comparable explicitness in the paintings, naturally enough. One is confronted by forms apparently related to minute seismographs – seismographs of every flicker of the spirit, characterized at times by a hurry of thin, quivering lines across a predominantly white page, at others by a concentration, by an interweaving of such lines into an endless knot – a dark brooding mass that seems to have pushed roots down into the paper. Occasionally, dimly recognizable forms / heads that recall both humans and animals make their way out of some of these strange skeins. But they explain nothing, or at least nothing more than their author's view of mankind as a host of chance apparitions in a world of pain and confusion. And if they continue to bob up into our vision, it is because we are doomed to take a particular interest in them. Michaux makes '*hypocrites lecteurs*' of us all.

But more important, perhaps, is the obverse of this. The hand of the artist is hardly to be seen. Impersonality and passivity are the most evident characteristics: they provide the cleared channels through which the mescaline experience can run. In his attempt to describe the very flow of sensation, Michaux has relinquished the artist's traditional role as 'maker' and tried to let everything materialize as though unaware of his own participation. In this context, the concept of personality is meaningless; the artist has become purely a medium for conveying experience. It is an effort to fuse the outer and inner worlds, an attempt at totality, at stopping time with a statement of completeness. In *Passages*, he explains that: 'Instead of a vision to the exclusion of others, I would have liked to draw the moments that, end to end, make life, to show the inner phrase, the phrase without words, a cord that endlessly unrolls, sinuous, and, in the intimate, accompanies everything that presents itself from outside as well as inside. I wanted to draw the consciousness of existing and the flow of time.'[17] In other words, it represents the continuation of his search for the 'essential', for whatever it is that underlies the fleeting surface of things.

It is this search that has provided the greatest constant of all Michaux's work, both written and painted. His entire contribution to art can be seen as a concentrated and radical stripping away of appearances to find an essential new truth; a desire to formulate a vision of life irreducible to anything else because it obeys its own laws at every point. Michaux's definition of what is essential (which he has described, laconically enough, as the 'secret that he has since his early childhood suspected of existing somewhere and of which those around him are obviously not aware'[18]) remains highly personal but it is crucial as the main generator of his work. It is also one with the basic preoccupation of a great deal of contemporary creativity. The problem is not only how to express anything at all with the increasingly insufficient and devalued means at one's disposal, but how to arrive at a 'statement' (though the word sounds too definitive; 'suggestion' would almost be more accurate) about life that will survive its own faithless, ruthlessly and often indiscriminately iconoclastic age. Like one of his unfortunate blobs, Michaux has let himself be driven by every stray, often highly unconventional impulse – 'J'écris', he once noted, 'afin que tout ce qui était vrai ne soit plus vrai' (I write so that everything that was true is no longer true) – evolving an anti-logic that is always ready to undergo a further transformation rather than harden into a system. His art is in a constant bid to outwit itself, to avoid its own pitfalls and keep its own set of values, however curious, under constant scrutiny. The performance has been prodigious. 'Admirable Michaux', Maurice Blanchot writes, 'he is the writer who, closest to himself, has united with the foreign voice, and the suspicion comes to him that he has been trapped and that what is expressed here with the jolts of humour are no longer his voice, but a voice that imitates his. In order to surprise and recapture it, he employs the resources of a redoubled humour, a calculated innocence, cunning detours, retreats, abandonments, and, at the moment when he perishes, the sudden, sharp point of an image that pierces the veil of noise.'[19]

The desire for experiment, that cunning innocence, and the will to record have focused almost entirely on painting over the last few years. As far as the writing is concerned, one feels that the main body of work has well and truly been done, that recent publications like *Poteaux d'angle* and *Façons d'endormi Façons d'éveillé*, interesting as they might be, have no vital bearing on the existing texts. The latest paintings, however, continue in a tradition of research and enrich what has come before them by demonstrating the tremendous viability of the same themes.

The present scope of Michaux's painting is as wide as it has ever been: he appears to be continuing to work in all the very varied genres that he has so far invented (with the partial exception of the mescaline paintings; partial because the formal concepts that were suggested to him during his experiments continue to influence his work even though he has renounced all forms of drugs – purveyors in the end of a '*misérable miracle*'). Over and above being a writer and a painter, Michaux can be seen in fact as several painters in one. Each genre that he has developed, and not only in the two highly distinct media of watercolour and India ink, is its own separate province. There are, for example, the acrylic paintings to which Michaux gave such a degree of immediacy when he used them to translate his response to the May 1968 'events' in France. Their first impact is of brutal black-and-white puzzles, but then the peculiar, slight consistency of the paint makes one think of smears left behind by some body in transit – as though, in making a rapid departure, some organism had let some of itself rub off on the paper. True to a general, apparent absence of form, the whole is in a state of flux: as one baleful head-shape surfaces on the chaos, another collapses, while in the same set of thick black lines and smudges a third begins to appear.

Concentration has also been brought to bear on the gouache ideograms, which in their way could be approached as the very essence, the ultimate reduction of Michaux's art. They are the most rarefied and self-sufficient of all his experiments in form, a purely other and untranslatable language (with much in common, of course, with the Chinese calligraphy of which Michaux is so fond). These late gouaches have moved further and further into another universe. Twists and turns of a weightless fibre on a pale, horizonless blue ground, they are the very illustration of ethereality. They impart a sensation of freedom, like notes of music set afloat in eternity. Or, at other times, they are given as three swift squiggles on a pale grey banner, itself a mild concentration of the white of the surrounding air. In their utter simplicity, they stand like symbols for a vision that has no end.

1   The only one to precede it was at the Stedelijk Museum, Amsterdam, in 1964.
2   René Bertelé has recorded that: 'Les premières manifestations plastiques d'Henri Michaux que je connaisse sont datées de 1925 et de 1927. De 1925, une "tâche", peinte a l'huile, qui appartient à Jean Paulhan.' 'Notes pour un itinéraire de l'œuvre plastique d'Henri Michaux', published in the *Cahier de l'Herne* on Michaux.

3 Interview with Henri Michaux published in *Le Moruic*, 31 March 1971.

4 *Saoûls* begins: 'Magrabote, mornemille et casaquin / fortu mon père, forsi ma mère ...'.

5 Henri Michaux, *La Vie dans les plis* (Paris: Gallimard, 1949).

6 'Ce qu'Henri Michaux perçoit donc en lui lorsqu'il s'interroge et prend conscience de lui-même, c'est sa faiblesse ontologique. Pour se faire exister il se découvre sans force. Cette expérience n'a rien d'exceptionnel. De façon évidente ou dissimulée, elle se trouve au coeur de tous les *Cogito*, à commencer par celui de Descartes. "Je pense, done je suis", cela veut dire: "Je pense que je ne suis pas par moi-même, je pense que si j'existe, ça ne dépend que de moi." Donc je suis faible! Ma faiblesse, c'est d'être une créature évidemment contingente, à qui l'existence n'est donnée qu'au compte-gouttes. [...] De quoi respirer, oui! de quoi exister, oui encore, mais tout juste et sans garantie! de quoi être fort, heureux, égal aux conditions requises par l'existence? non, certainement, non! [...] On dirait l'histoire d'un être infortuné qui, dès sa naissance – pourquoi? est-ce qu'il crie trop? – se trouverait privé de la plupart des dons indispensables aux enfants des hommes. Privé et conscient de cette privation.' Georges Poulet, 'Henri Michaux et le supplice des faibles', in Raymond Bellour (ed.), *Cahier de L'Herne no. 8: Henri Michaux* (Paris: Editions de l'Herne, 1966).

7 Henri Michaux, *La Vie dans les plis* (Paris: Gallimard, 1949), p. 151.

8 'Du reste, nous ignorons si l'univers appartient au genre réel ou au genre fantastique', Jorge Luis Borges, 'Sur Henri Michaux', in Raymond Bellour (ed.), *Cahier de L'Herne no. 8: Henri Michaux* (Paris: Editions de l'Herne, 1966).

9 These and similar examples can be found throughout Michaux's early texts, especially in the anthology of them published as *L'Espace du Dedans* (Paris: Gallimard, 1944).

10 'Pon naquit d'un oeuf, puis il naquit d'une morue et en naissant la fit éclater, puis il naquit d'un soulier; par bipartition, le soulier plus petit à gauche, et lui à droite, puis il naquit d'une feuille de rhubarbe, en même temps qu'un renard; le renard et lui se regardèrent un instant puis filèrent chacun de leur côté. Ensuite il naquit d'un cafard, d'un oeil de langouste, d'une carafe; d'une otarie et il lui sortit par les moustaches, d'un têtard et il lui sortit du derrière, d'une jument et il lui sortit par les naseaux, puis il versait des larmes en cherchant les mamelles, car il ne venalt au monde que pour têter. Puis il naquit d'un trombone et le trombone le nourrit pendant treize mois, puis il fut sevré et confié au sable qui s'étendait partout car c'était le désert. Et seul le fils du trombone peut se nourrir dans le désert, seul avec le chameau, puis il naquit d'une femme et il fut grandement étonné.' Henri Michaux, *Plume* (Paris: Gallimard, 1938), p. 123.

11 'On change de gare de triage quand on se met à peindre. La fabrique à mots, mots-pensées, mots-images, mots émotions, disparaît, se noie vertigineusement et si simplement. [...] Plus d'envie, d'appétit parleur. La partie de la tête qui s'y trouvait la plus interessée se refroidit.' Henri Michaux, *Passages* (Paris: Gallimard, 1963).

12 'Les couleurs qui filent comme des poissons sur la nappe d'eau où je les mets, voilà ce que j'aime dans l'aquarelle. Le petit tas colorant qui se désamoncelle en infimes particules, ces passages, et non l'arrêt final, le tableau. [...] Eau de l'aquarelle, aussi immense qu'un lac, eau, démon-omnivore, râfleur d'îlots, faiseur de mirages, briseur de digues, débordeur de mondes.' Henri Michaux, 'En pensant au phénomène de la peinture', in *Passages* (Paris: Gallimard, 1963).

13 'Etions-nous nés pour la gangue / Etions-nous nés, doigts cassés, / Pour donner toute une vie à un mauvais problème?' Quoted in René Bertelé, *Henri Michaux* (Paris: Éditions Pierre Seghers, 1965), p. 71.

14 'Aux tâches maintenant. [...] Eh bien, je les déteste. J'aime l'eau, mais elles non. [...] Done je me bats avec elles, je les fouette, je voudrais être tout de suite débarrassé de leur bêtise éffondrée, et les galvaniser, les rendre éperdues, exaspérées, les allier monstrueusement malgré elles à tout ce qui bouge, à l'innombrable foule d'êtres, de

non-êtres, de fureurs d'être [...]. Vite. Il faut faire vite, avec ces grandes molles, capables de se vautrer partout. C'est tout de suite, avant qu'elles n'étendent leur domaine d'abjections et de vomissements. Insupportables tâches.' Published in the catalogue of an exhibition of Michaux's India ink paintings held in 1959 at the Galerie Daniel Cordier.

15 'Ces bonshommes noirs qui se succèdent sans fin [...] me font penser à ce que dit Bossuet à propos de la mort, l'homme en proie à son destin périssable supplie les puissances invisibles de lui permettre de ralentir sa course. En vain. Avance, lui crient-elles, avance. Pas de répit. L'originalité de Michaux est d'avoir choisi cette absence de répit et d'avoir transformi une fatalité en défi. Il ne se contenterait pas de dire comme Zarathoustra: Encore une fois! Il voudrait dire, il voudrait crier: Jamais d'arrêt! Toujours plus loin!' Jean Grenier, 'Un abîme ordonné', in *Henri Michaux: Choix d'oeuvres des Annees 1946–1966* (Paris: Le Point Cardinal, 1967)

16 Henri Michaux, *La Vie dans les plis* (Paris: Gallimard, 1949), p. 235.

17 'Au lieu d'une vision à l'exclusion des autres, j'eusse voulu dessiner les moments qui bout à bout font la vie, donner à voir la phrase intérieure, la phrase sans mots, corde qui indéfiniment se déroule, sinueuse, et, dans l'intime, accompagne tout ce qui se présente du dehors comme dedans. Je voulais dessiner la conscience d'exister et l'écoulement du temps.' Henri Michaux, *Passages* (Paris: Gallimard, 1963).

18 'secret qu'il a depuis sa première enfance soupçonné d'exister quelque part et dont visiblement ceux de son entourage ne sont pas au courant'. From Henri Michaux, 'Quelques renseignements sur cinquante-neuf années d'existence', republished in Raymond Bellour (ed.), *Cahier de L'Herne no. 8: Henri Michaux* (Paris: Editions de l'Herne, 1966).

19 'Admirable Michaux, il est l'ecrivain qui, au plus près de lui-même, s'est uni à la voix étrangère, et il lui vient le soupçon qu'il a été pris au piège et que ce qui s'exprime ici avec les soubresauts de l'humour, ce n'est plus sa voix, mais une voix qui imite la sienne. Pour la surprendre et la ressaisir, il a les ressources d'un humour redoublé, une innocence calculée, des détours de ruse, des reculs, des abandons et, au moment où il périt, la pointe soudaine, acérée, d'une image qui perce le voile de la rumeur.' Maurice Blanchot, from a section of *Le Livre à venir*, republished as 'L'infini et l'infini', in Raymond Bellour (ed.), *Cahier de L'Herne no. 8: Henri Michaux* (Paris: Editions de l'Herne, 1966).

Originally published in *Art International*, Lugano, January 1972

13

JEAN DUBUFFET'S WAR WITH CULTURE

Written for *Réalités* magazine in 1967, a year after my arrival in Paris, this perky essay recalls the extent to which Jean Dubuffet was shaking up the hidebound Paris art world. I immediately saw the point of Dubuffet's inventive iconoclasm, and he remained a touchstone for me as a young art critic starting out in Paris. Later, I was lucky enough to interview him and to write about his work at greater length, which he encouraged me to do because he was particularly keen to build up his reputation outside France. A decade or so later, his paintings and above all his extensive 'Hourloupe' series of sculptures seemed to me to be growing repetitive, even formulaic, and I began to avoid reviewing his ever more frequent exhibitions in galleries and museums around the world. Pantheons, like prisms, respond to every small shift, and just as my admiration for Picasso never quite recovered from having seen endless displays of his ceramics, so Dubuffet's inventive and courageous early work seemed to be smothered by acres of his later, repetitive red-, white-, and blue-striped sculpture. This did certainly not debar him from my pantheon, but like a noble in attendance on Louis XIV who has lost favour, he was obliged to take more of a back seat.

Two new periods have recently entered the history of modern art: before Dubuffet and after Dubuffet. 'He will be to the second half of the twentieth century', the pundits now say, 'what Picasso was to the first half.' At the height of his fame, Jean Dubuffet has become both a minor gold mine and a major star in the French cultural firmament. It was not always so.

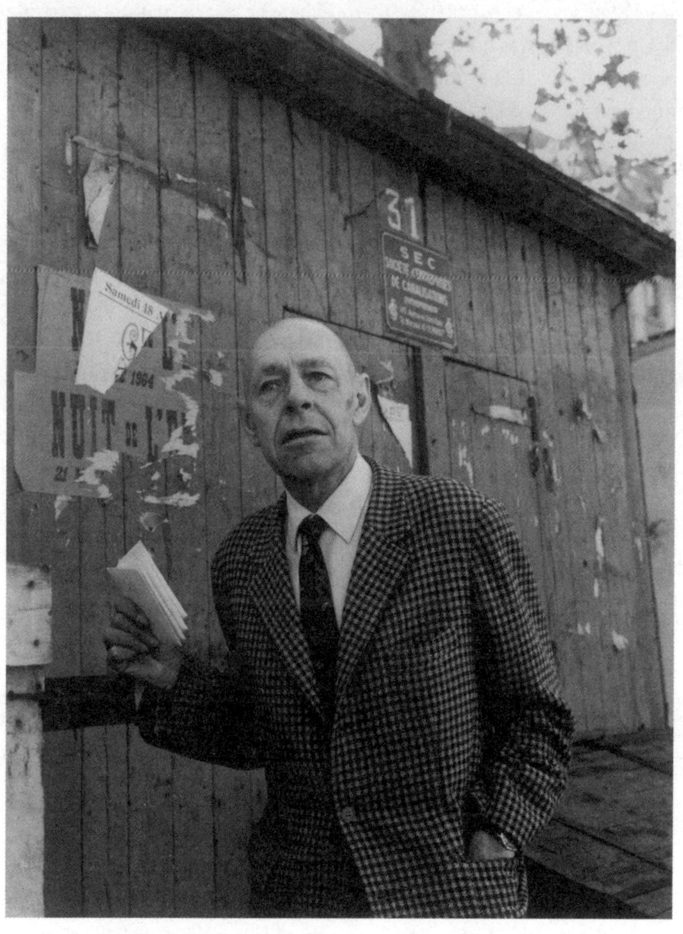

Jean Dubuffet, Paris, 1964, photographed by Ida Kar

Just twenty-five years ago, Dubuffet was a wine merchant – though admittedly not the most run-of-the-mill kind of that métier in Paris. At the age of seventeen, he left Le Havre, where he was born in 1901, to study art in Paris. He was quickly disillusioned. What his professors acclaimed as art – the revered art of the museums – left him painfully indifferent, and he drifted into a desultory study of music, languages, and literature. By the time he came to the end of his military service, one thing at least had become clear: that art, such as it was, was not for him. He had to find another career.

Footloose and ashamed of his inactivity, Dubuffet began to covet the at-home-in-the-world air of ordinary people like the local butcher and the postman. So, with deadly logic, he decided to join them. Wine had been his father's trade and, after a trial run in the family business, Dubuffet *fils* set up a wine shop in Paris. Poverty and an occasional urge to return to painting dogged him for several years. At one point, he embarked on a scheme for making masks and marionettes, but it proved so financially disastrous that he was soon driven back to wine. Then, to Dubuffet's disbelief, business picked up. By 1942, he was able to entrust the shop to a friend and go back to painting with a whole heart – and with a burning belief that the ordinary, the ugly, and the unheard-of were what art needed.

His aim was to create an art that would immediately go home to the man in the street, an art that was fresh and freed of the 'boredom' of the museum masters. He wanted to paint things that people would enjoy in the way they enjoyed fun fairs and strip cartoons. Anything was better than 'culture'. Not surprisingly, Dubuffet's choice agony at that time was to watch the good people of Paris yawning their way down endless galleries of 'improving' art on wet Sunday afternoons. That was one situation that his paintings could change.

The first Dubuffets were funny, childlike figures that shocked by their crude simplicity. All that had been sacred in art since the Renaissance was violently profaned. The noble human face became a comic blob; a woman's breast, a slipshod circle with a dot. Dubuffet seemed to be looking out on the world from a kind of nightmarish nursery: his adult sense of absurdity was being relayed in children's terms. But the initial simplicity of his approach deepened into thicker, more fascinating flesh.

A series of curiously alluring heads grew under Dubuffet's brush. Their crudeness was of a different order, for they appeared to have risen through the canvas by virtue of a brilliant, organic quirk. *Mr Chocolate*, *The Demoiselle of Stone*, *Cloudy Head*, and *Dead-Leaf Head*, quizzical and amorphous creatures of the kind one sometimes makes out on a rock face or in a drift of smoke, were the heroes of his new mythology. Magical *bonshommes* (fellows) of no fixed address or time, they were at the furthest remove from the psychological interest or the idealized beauty of classical portraiture. Mr Everybody had made his triumphant entry into art.

In them, too, lay the basis of Dubuffet's manifesto. They were a spearhead in his attack on what he considered the moribund values of the Western tradition in art. As a first step, the masters were to be thrown out of the museum windows because their presence crushed the viability of a truly contemporary art. Once their autocracy had been shaken off, thought Dubuffet, then a popular art could finally evolve, and it would be exhibited 'in the city, in the most living parts of the city'.

For a moment, it seemed possible that Paris, like La Paz, might see its uninhabited walls – its gaunt hoardings and the dreary corridors of its subway – brightened by a rash of vivid scrawls and funny faces. Dubuffet enlarged the scope of his idea by recommending that any kind of material could go into the making of such pictures. He laughed at the traditional artist's delicate brushes and tiny tubes of paint and found that new horizons were opened up by watching a house painter or a mason at work.

Eventually, everything from coal dust to oyster shells was worked into his own canvases. The artist's hand began to efface itself behind weird techniques and materials: he carved statues out of anthracite, made collages of butterflies' wings, landscapes of strips of bark and leaves. There were pictures larded with bread, and others where anything that came to hand, like a kitchen utensil, had been used to press the paint into new textures. The aim, said Dubuffet, was to create works as unexpected and fascinating 'as talking dogs'.

Dubuffet's other trump card was *art brut* or 'raw art'. The odd Surrealist apart, no one had ever taken the recorded fantasies of madmen, illiterates, and peasants very much to heart. Dubuffet hailed them as the new lifeblood of invention and after the end of the Second World War, began a huge collection of them. The common link between all raw art objects

– whose authors are sometimes unknown and referred to by titles such as the Prisoner of Basel or the Numismatist – was their (for Dubuffet) happy lack of artistic culture. Because of that, Dubuffet reasoned, they had been able to explore areas of experience forever closed to the traditionally trained artist. Since their being shown on a grand scale to the public, it has been suggested that their impact on the future of art could be as explosive as that of African and Oceanic sculpture fifty years ago.

For a long time, Dubuffet must have found a certain counterpart in these works to his own, not least since, at the outset, he himself was openly treated as a madman. His course, in style as well as within the channels of public recognition, has much altered since. Throughout the 1960s, he has worked mainly on a series of deft jigsaw-like paintings in which a world of close-knit figures and shapes is there for the searching. Like a succession of Siamese twins, one figure often springs from another; or an arm or a disembodied pair of lips disengages itself from the brightly coloured jumble. The language in these pictures has become far more difficult to follow: images that used to look like public property have been turned into private signs. Where, one wonders, are all the *bonshommes*?

On one score, the glorious Dubuffet must be said to have failed. His art has not reached the 'living places' of the city – it has gone instead into the 'sinister museums'. It is even doubtful that it has gone home to the ordinary man. When questioned, a museum attendant at Dubuffet's latest show stated that he hadn't much time for these particular works and that he had far preferred the previous exhibition – of religious art. It was noble but perhaps naive of Dubuffet to hold out such a hope. In art, the rule seems to be that only the very sophisticated are moved by the very simple.

Originally published in *Réalités*, Paris, 1967

14

FROM BRETON TO BECKETT: THE WRITERS IN GIACOMETTI'S CIRCLE

To Thérèse Tigretti Berthoud, one of the few remaining members of Alberto Giacometti's family, who generously lent a large part of her collection to the Giacometti exhibition that I curated in Hamburg.

The life and work of Giacometti constitute one of the pillars of my existence, as I have acknowledged here and later in 'Bacon / Giacometti: Parallel Visions of a Terrible Truth' on pp. 243–65. Of all the modern artists to whom I have been drawn, he is the one that seems to me to invite the most constant reflection and commentary. I have been writing about him for some fifty years, and yet I still feel that so much remains to be said. To an extent, this is because everything that relates to him, from his sculpture, painting, and drawing to his austere, obsessive existence in Paris, stimulates an extraordinary desire to describe, analyse, and attempt to trap the sensations they engender in words. But his images of man have proved not only inexhaustible in the face of every interpretation, but also evasive. Like a truth that cannot be pinned down in any other medium, his images demand total attention while all the while giving that focus the slip effortlessly. Giacometti not only made sculpture for the dead, as Jean Genet noted eloquently, he also made it for the yet unborn, so that it now belongs to that very rare body of art that, having transcended its epoch, is timeless.

It comes as no surprise, then, that Giacometti has attracted the highest level of critical and lyrical appraisal of any twentieth-century artist, from the

Surrealists through Sartre and Genet to later poets like Jacques Dupin (see my interview with him about his friendship with Giacometti on pp. 152–63). This fact has long fascinated me and, while the Hamburg exhibition came slowly together, I began to explore his unusually numerous and close relationships with writers for the lecture that I gave at the opening of the show.

When I originally chose to talk about Alberto Giacometti and the writers who were so important to him – both as fellow creators and as friends – the subject seemed quite straightforward, with a linear development leading from the pope of Surrealism, André Breton, to the pope of existentialism, Jean-Paul Sartre, then branching out to quite equally fascinating individualists like Jean Genet and Samuel Beckett. But the further I got into it, the more the story of Giacometti and his writer friends turned out to be full of complexities, containing endless, intriguing byways and a cast if not of thousands then at least of scores of poets and philosophers, playwrights and *hommes de lettres*, publishers and editors, art critics and journalists.

So although it appeared compact and manageable at first, the subject is in fact not only large and multifaceted but also so central to Giacometti's life and work that I now realize entire books could be written on the subject. Having recently looked through much of the vast literature on Giacometti, I am astonished at how little this richly diverse vein has been mined by the many other distinguished commentators to have devoted themselves to the study of the infinitely expanding Giacomettian universe. As a result, I found that as soon as I focused on a specific aspect of the theme – which in its broadest sense could be called 'Giacometti and Literature' – my attention was claimed by a dozen other considerations. Take Giacometti's very formative relationship with the domineering Breton, for instance, which cannot be properly understood until it is compared to the more equal friendships Giacometti developed with the other Surrealist writers, such as the amiable, dandyish Paul Éluard or the brilliant, tortured poet René Crevel, whom Breton excommunicated from the Surrealist church because of his homosexuality (and who later committed suicide). This in turn brings to mind Giacometti's almost lifelong bond with Michel Leiris, a writer who remained prudently on the fringes of both Surrealism and existentialism and who, possibly as a result of his repressed homosexuality, also attempted suicide, or his alliance with such

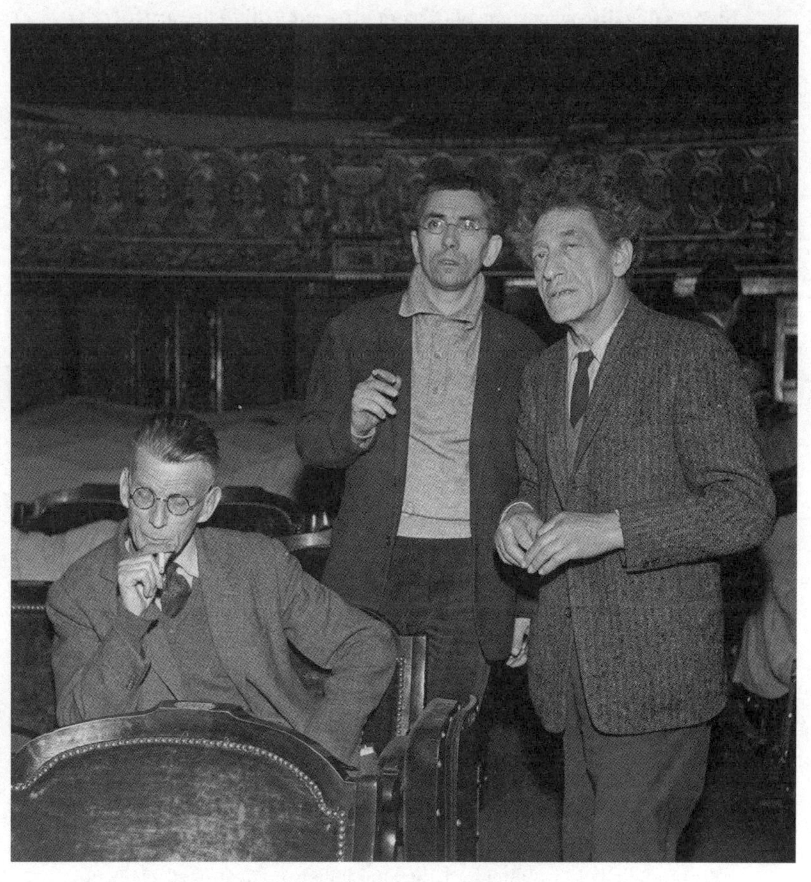

Samuel Beckett, Jean-Marie Serreau, and **Alberto Giacometti**
at a rehearsal of *Waiting for Godot*, Théâtre de l'Odéon, Paris, 1961,
photographed by Boris Lipnitzki

a complete outsider as Genet, whose taste for low life and petty theft had frequently landed him in jail rather than in any literary movement. And then, as one discovers some of Giacometti's many other literary friends, from Tristan Tzara to Georges Bataille, one is taken even further off one's original course into wondering how Giacometti found the time, stamina, and sheer depth of fellow-feeling to forge lasting, meaningful relationships with such a variety of outstandingly gifted – and often demanding and difficult – writers.

I feel sure that at least some of my fellow lecturers in this symposium would agree with me when I say that as one prepares a new paper on Giacometti one feels overwhelmed by the odds. So much has been written, by such distinguished hands – and yet so much remains to be said. Giacometti, one realizes more and more keenly as one attempts to approach him from whatever angle, serenely eludes any fixed definition. That, of course, is a sign of his greatness, of his universality. He is a sculptor who engraves, a painter who designs decorative objects, a draughtsman who writes (in French and in Italian), a recluse with a huge range of friends, both famous and obscure, a profound thinker whose nights are whiled away in louche bars and brothels, a great talker who loved rambling discussions on café terraces but whose whole life was a solitary struggle in the confines of a shabby, comfortless, chaotic studio.

Giacometti's studio has a very special importance for me, and I knew as I prepared this talk that I would be drawn back to it because I see it as the source, the *fons et origo*, of everything connected with Giacometti. For me, it has always been a touchstone by which one can test one's ideas about him and get them into proper perspective. I also, I must say, simply love the photos of the studio, because everything in this magic hovel speaks of solitary devotion to work: not only of a new head in clay being maniacally modelled, then obliterated, then modelled and destroyed again, but decades of work, whole carpets of crumpled, discarded drawings mixed up on the floor with books and newspapers and plaster bits and pieces – a hand fragment here, a whole nose there – and ranks of finished sculptures of every size, standing like a gaunt new race, a private army of aliens about to invade the world, while behind them on the pitted, peeling walls, there rises a sprawling fresco of prehistoric-looking sketches, staring skeletal heads and votive limbs with occasionally a poignant, scrawled reminder or a telephone number, footnotes to bring us back to the so-called 'real' world beyond the studio's grimy windows.

Over the years, Giacometti moulded this exiguous space to himself and his working needs like a shell. It became exactly what he needed, and with each hour he worked there it clove ever closer to him – which is of course why, even when the reclusive artist had become internationally famous and rich, he never moved, however crumbling and insalubrious the studio had grown. In fact, this shell – with its infinite memories of occasional triumphs but above all of repetitive, ultimately inevitable failures – clung to him so tightly that Giacometti had the greatest difficulty in prising himself out of it. But once he had at last thrown down the palette knife, removed the clay sticking to his hair and summarily brushed his clothes, Giacometti did eventually emerge from his cave around midnight and turn his steps towards the bright neon lights of Montparnasse, where a completely different life beckoned.

Once Giacometti had installed himself at his favourite table at the Coupole or the Select, with his newspapers and books and cigarettes positioned very precisely around him, he would look for someone he could talk to. The art of conversation – Giacometti listened as intently and intelligently as he talked – was so important to him that he once said he would give anything in the world for a good conversation; and, pushing the concept to the extreme as he liked to do, Giacometti also claimed that he would accept having both arms and legs amputated as long as he could be propped up as a mere trunk of a man on a mantelpiece and allowed to talk with everyone in the room to his heart's desire. Once Giacometti engaged in talk, a torrent of words, no doubt dammed up by the frustrations of the day's fruitless work, was let loose. The dishevelled, solitary sculptor who despaired of ever reproducing a nose or an eye as he actually saw it turned into a spontaneously brilliant conversationalist, ranging easily, inventively, and wittily over every topic that cropped up. Everyone of note who met him (and that included the best minds of his generation, including Sartre, Genet, and Beckett, as we shall see) agreed that as a talker Alberto was in a class of his own. And although we have no recordings of Giacometti in these epic discussions (Simone de Beauvoir once said how bitterly she regretted not having been able to tape Sartre and Giacometti talking together), we do have an extraordinary range of published interviews with Giacometti that reveal his restless verbal intelligence, his love of paradox, and his gift for analysing the contradictions of his own aesthetic attitudes.

This prodigious ability was underpinned by a barely less impressive – though never fully developed – gift for writing. Giacometti wrote in a variety of forms: poems, essays, and art criticism as well as abundant letters and whole carnets of studio notes. His collected writings and interviews add up to a volume of some six hundred pages, which by their diversity and lucidity rank with Delacroix's *Journal* and Van Gogh's *Letters* as an outstanding source of insight into an artist's imaginative world. One cannot grasp the full importance that writing and writers had for Giacometti until one senses his own literary ability and ambition. His earliest full-length piece, *Hier, Sables Mouvants* (Yesterday, quicksands) – published in 1933 – gives an excellent sense of the way Giacometti's literary imagination moves, so I will quote the last paragraph from it here:

> '*For months during the same period I could not get to sleep in the evening without first imagining that I had crossed a dense forest at dusk and come to a grey castle which stood in the most hidden and forgotten of spots. There I killed two men before they could put up any defence; one of them, about seventeen years old, always had a pale, frightened look, the other wore a suit of armour with something on its left side that shone like gold. I raped two women once I had ripped off their clothes – one who was thirty-two years old and dressed in black with a face like alabaster, then her daughter who wore loosely floating white veils. The whole forest echoed with their cries and their groans. I killed them too, but very slowly (night had fallen by then) and often beside a stagnant green pond in front of the castle. There were slight variations each time. Then I burnt down the castle and fell contentedly asleep.*'

Quite clearly Giacometti's biographical fragment was influenced both in choice of theme and technique by the dream-inspired, 'automatic' writings of his Surrealist friends. While he remained obediently within the fold, Giacometti struck up numerous alliances with writers in the Surrealist movement, as we have seen. He not only read their work, but from the mid-1930s on made prints specifically for their new publications, illustrating books by so many of the leading writers of his time – from Crevel to Bataille, Éluard to Tzara, Breton to Genet – that the list constitutes a kind of *Who's Who* of the Parisian literary world both pre- and postwar. The first of these writers to make a lasting impact on Giacometti as an artist and as a man was no doubt Breton, both by his position as uncontested leader of the Surrealists and by sheer force of personality. Although not that much older than Giacometti, Breton assumed momentarily the stature of a father figure for him when Giacometti's own father died in 1933. Breton, who addressed the young sculptor as 'mon enfant et mon ami' (my child and my friend) in the letters between them, invited Giacometti to be best man at his wedding to Jacqueline Lamba in 1934. He also welcomed the new Swiss recruit to his ranks as the Surrealist sculptor par excellence, and in answer to his own rhetorical question 'What is Surrealism?', he replied: 'It is Alberto Giacometti in his struggle with the angel of the Invisible who agreed to meet him in the blossoming apple trees.'

At the beginning, Giacometti rejoiced in his affiliation with Surrealism. Having arrived in Paris in 1922, he had not forgotten how obscure and estranged he had felt first as a student, then as a struggling young sculptor, in the great capital. Barely ten years later, under Breton's wing, he could claim to be at the very heart of le Tout-Paris des arts et des lettres and close to such movers and shakers as Salvador Dalí and Balthus, Luis Buñuel, and Antonin Artaud, to say nothing of cutting-edge tastemakers like Jean Cocteau, designers of the quality of Jean-Michel Frank, or discerning collectors like Charles and Marie-Laure de Noailles. But gradually his belief in the very tenets of Surrealism – above all in its insistence on imagination and the unconscious as the key sources of creativity – waned. Although his Surrealist sculpture had been outstandingly inventive and evocative, Giacometti felt he had got to a stage where he was creating objects rather than true sculpture and he wanted to return to the representation of reality as the touchstone of his art. He had also started to chafe under Breton's authoritarian control. Essentially an individualist and a loner, the young sculptor eventually threw down the gauntlet in a Surrealist meeting in February 1935 by loudly claiming that all his much-admired Surrealist work had been nothing but 'masturbation'. And as

Breton moved to excommunicate him for such outspoken disobedience, Giacometti beat him to it by announcing: 'Don't bother. I'm off.'

This act of rebellion cost Giacometti dearly. He lost many of his Surrealist writer friends, although a few dissidents, like Crevel, who died shortly thereafter, and Leiris, stuck by him. He then underwent a period of frantic experimentation and severe self-doubt that lasted basically from his expulsion right through his wartime exile in Switzerland. Even though in Geneva Giacometti managed to maintain his interest in contemporary writing through his close association with the leading art publisher there, Albert Skira, and his review *Labyrinthe*, it was not until he returned to a liberated Paris that his artistic fortunes and his friendships with the leading writers of the day revived. Although dilapidated and grimy, with despondent, poorly dressed people queuing endlessly outside the food shops, the Paris that Giacometti encountered was about to enter a period of intense intellectual ferment, as if the very fact of survival had engendered a burst of creativity. At first, he feared his favourite haunts might have disappeared, but the bars and bistrots and even the brothels, like the legendary Sphinx, were all very much open for business. Giacometti lost no time in resuming his nocturnal wanderings in Montparnasse and Saint-Germain-des-Prés, where he found many of his former and several new literary friends. One was Maurice Merleau-Ponty, the phenomenological philosopher, whose theories about the primacy of perception in art interested Giacometti to the extent that he adopted – or rather adapted – them as his own, incorporating certain basic phenomenological approaches in his own discourse about the problems that he faced in his attempts as an artist to convey reality. Others included the power couple that had established absolute sway over Saint-Germain and intellectual fashion in the whole of France and beyond: Jean-Paul Sartre and Simone de Beauvoir.

Giacometti's sympathy went first and more lastingly to de Beauvoir, the 'Beaver', as she was known for her tireless capacity for intellectual application and hard work. There appears to have been a spontaneous affection between the two, which resulted in Giacometti's making several notable portraits of de Beauvoir both in drawing and in sculpture. For her part, although she never wrote extensively about Giacometti's work, de Beauvoir did leave a very memorable pen portrait of the artist, recording her early impressions of him in a letter written (in her charmingly foreign English) to her American lover, the writer Nelson Algren. Dated November 1947, the letter also refers to the key exhibition that Giacometti was about to have at the Pierre Matisse Gallery in New York:

> *'I don't think I happened to speak about a very good friend of us who is a sculptor.... I admire him as an artist immensely. First because he does the best modern sculpture I know; then because he works with so much purity and patience and strength. He is called Giacometti, and will have a big exhibition of his works in New York next month. Twenty years ago he was very successful and made much money with kind of surrealistic sculpture. Rich snobs paid expensive prices, as for Picasso. But then he felt he was going nowhere, and wasting something of himself, and he turned his back on snobs; he began to work all alone, nearly not selling anything but just what was wanted to live. So he lives quite poorly; he is very dirty in his clothes. I must say he seems to like dirt: to have a bath is a problem for him. Yesterday I saw his house, and it is dreadful. In a nice little forgotten garden, he has an atelier where he works.... There are holes in the roof so the rain falls on the floor, and there are pots and pans to receive it, but there are holes in them too! He works 15 hours a day, chiefly at night, and when you see him he has always plaster on his clothes, his hands and his rich dirty hair; he works in cold with hands freezing, he does not care.'*

Giacometti's interaction with Sartre was perhaps less personal, although for a long period the two men enjoyed meeting regularly in the cafés to discuss everything under the sun (as mentioned earlier, de Beauvoir laments in her journal that these epic conversations, fuelled by cigarettes, ersatz coffee, cognac, and, in Sartre's case, amphetamines, were never recorded for posterity). However, it did prove very useful professionally. Although neither saw it as such at the time, their relationship might be regarded in retrospect as based quite spontaneously on self-interest. For Sartre, Giacometti came to represent the existential artist par excellence, and the philosopher lost no time in attaching the sculptor to the existential cause within a web of subtly suggestive concepts. I am not suggesting for a moment that this was a conscious decision on Sartre's part, any more than Giacometti's enthusiasm for having Sartre write the preface to the New York show in 1948 that put him on the international map was a strategic career move. But the two men gravitated towards each other instinctively because they knew it would serve both their purposes well.

To a notable extent, the collaboration worked. With his essay 'The Search for the Absolute', Sartre made some of the most lastingly memorable observations about Giacometti at a time when the best writers associated with and wrote about the best artists (a tradition that in France dated back at least to Charles Baudelaire). With Sartre, Giacometti's achievement was suddenly and durably put into dramatic perspective, as though it had come into public focus for the first time. Sartre's text – which Giacometti had read and carefully annotated – is shot through with *aperçus* so brilliantly phrased they can be taken out of context and still offer arresting insights. 'Thoughts of stone haunt Giacometti. Once he had a terror of emptiness; for months he came and went with an abyss at his side; space had come to know through him its desolate sterility', is one, for instance, and another: 'Giacometti knows that there is nothing redundant in a living man, because everything there is functional; he knows that space is a cancer on being and eats everything; to sculpt, for him, is to take the fat off space; he compresses space, so as to drain off its exteriority.'

For his part, Giacometti benefited demonstrably from having his work analysed within the parameters of the most provocative philosophy of the time and thence subtly incorporated into it. The obscurity in which he had laboured since his expulsion from the Surrealist movement thus ended in one fell swoop – to be replaced by a steadily growing reputation both abroad and in Paris. Sartre's preface marked a watershed in Giacometti's career. Perhaps because he later felt that his work had been appropriated into a system to which he had never subscribed, Giacometti nevertheless grew resentful of Sartre. Unlike Sartre, Giacometti believed, he – as a sculptor, painter, and draughtsman – had nothing to prove or promote. Rather than to convince a public, he had the more modest but more demanding task to convince himself that he could catch the fleeting reality of an instant's gaze and give it permanence. The union with France's leading intellectual had been extremely useful; it had even been fun, since no one more than Giacometti enjoyed supple philosophical wranglings with such a first-class mind. But gradually the connection wore thin, as it had done with Breton, and when the end came, it came definitively, even though it was ostensibly over a relatively small error of fact about an accident that Giacometti had once had as relayed by Sartre in his autobiography, *Words*. Thus, with a great show of indignation, Giacometti tried to end any association he might be perceived as having with a system of belief that he felt had been arbitrarily imposed on him and his work – which, he felt, owed far more to the ancient art of Egypt than to any modern philosophical system such as existentialism.

*

'Beauty has no other origin than the wound (unique, different in each person, hidden or visible) that we carry within us, that we preserve and to which we withdraw whenever we wish to leave the world for a temporary but profound solitude.... I think Giacometti's art seeks to uncover that secret wound in each being, in each thing, so that the wound illuminates them.'

Jean Genet's declaration at the beginning of his celebrated essay 'Alberto Giacometti's Studio' sets the tone for the most personal and in many respects still the most illuminating exploration of Giacometti's world. That wound – 'a kind of secret, painful heart', as Genet describes it elsewhere – is essentially what remains of mankind once the artist has stripped away all disguise. The essay, which remained Giacometti's favourite piece of writing on his work, moves fluidly from subtle aesthetic and philosophical inquiry to down-to-earth factual description and snatches of conversation between the two men, who became close friends during the mid-1950s. They would have been aware of each other's work well before they actually met in 1954, probably through Sartre, who had written memorably about both of them. Giacometti's curiosity would certainly have been aroused right away by a man as famous for his alarming criminal record as for his highly acclaimed plays and novels (the latter principally glorifying the former). He would also have been intrigued by Genet's reputation for lawlessness, treachery, and homosexual low living. But what really won the sculptor over was the sight of Genet's perfectly bald, domed head – first glimpsed in a crowded café – which he ardently wanted to capture in a portrait. Having accepted Giacometti's pressing invitation, Genet began to make tracks regularly to the artist's studio, to sit for what turned into a whole series of portraits of himself: three paintings and six drawings.

During one of these sessions, with Genet seated on what he described as a particularly uncomfortable kitchen chair, Giacometti scrutinized the writer intently, then rhapsodized: 'How beautiful you are! How beautiful you are!', adding 'Like everyone else, huh? Neither more nor less.' In one of the scattered notes he wrote constantly, Giacometti described Genet's head as 'stuck obstinately and violently forward with, at the corner of his mouth, an expression of pain mixed with disenchanted sadness as if in regret that life was nothing but a chasm.' But Giacometti also constantly underlined how impossible it seemed to him to convey the full reality of the man fixedly staring back at him from the chair: 'I'll never manage to put into a portrait all the power a head contains. Just the fact of living requires so much will power and energy.' When Genet was released from his duties as a motionless and mute sitter, he took the opportunity to run his hands over a finished figure in bronze while closing his eyes. This was his reward for so much silent concentration. 'I cannot describe', Genet later wrote, 'how happy my fingers were'; and elsewhere he praises Giacometti as 'a sculptor for the blind'.

The bond that formed between the two men, with their shared interest in the underworld and life lived outside social conventions, extended into long, free-for-all conversations once they had left the studio to drift from one Montparnasse café to another. Their relationship developed not only out of a deep mutual admiration, but also because they made few demands on each other. Giacometti would have immediately appreciated the fact that Genet did not seek his artistic support, unlike both Breton and Sartre, who had incorporated his work and his personality into their respective intellectual systems. With Genet, there was no hint of appropriation: Giacometti was neither Surrealist nor existentialist but more freely and more concentratedly himself, as if the acquaintance of another tortured but unshackled creator simply reinforced his own natural individualism. The exchange between them was based primarily on the ease and interest with which they could talk on any topic. While Genet might delight Giacometti with stories of life on the 'inside', Giacometti could have surprised his writer friend by the expert grasp he had of international politics and such unexpected subjects as historical military campaigns (including those of Napoleon, which Giacometti studied avidly). But it was also an exchange of gifts: if Genet wrote an essay on the sculptor, Giacometti drew a figure for the cover of his play *The Balcony*. As the friendship evolved, Genet put his scattered reflections and impressions into order, publishing the completed essay first in the catalogue to Giacometti's show at the Galerie Maeght in Paris in 1957, accompanied by three original lithographs by the artist, and then as a small book, illustrated by Ernst Scheidegger's eloquent photographs of the studio. Towards the end of his essay, Genet takes leave of Giacometti with a description that seems to capture him feverishly at work for ever:

> *'His fingers rise and fall like a gardener's pruning or grafting*
> *a climbing rose. His fingers play up and down the statue, and*
> *the whole studio vibrates and comes to life. I get the strange*
> *impression that, with him there, without even touching them,*
> *the older, already completed statues change and are transformed*
> *because he is working on one of their sisters. [...] everything is*
> *precarious and about to collapse, everything is about to dissolve,*
> *everything is floating: and yet it all appears to be captured in*
> *an absolute reality. When I leave the studio, when I am outside*
> *on the street, then nothing that surrounds me is true. Shall I*
> *say it? In that studio a man is dying slowly, being consumed*
> *and metamorphosing into goddesses beneath our very eyes.'*

By their very vision of the world, Beckett and Giacometti seemed predestined to meet. While Giacometti's skeletal figures came across as the visual embodiment of Beckett's plangent, pared-down prose, some of Beckett's utterances read like a manifesto for Giacometti's despairing attitudes towards his art. 'To be an artist is to fail, as no other dares fail', Beckett stated in 'Three Dialogues with Georges Duthuit'. And later in the same text, the Irish poet formulated the irreconcilable contradictions of his situation, which could have run like a caption under Giacometti's craggy, survivor-like figures: 'The expression that there is nothing to express, nothing with which to express, nothing from which to express, no power to express, no desire to express, together with the obligation to express.'

Giacometti and Beckett – who first met at the Café de Flore in autumn 1937 – tended to run into each other rather than meet by arrangement. Their friendship was based on mutual sympathy and respect, but even though they frequently let their hair down when they drank together it always retained a certain formality. Since they were both night owls and great walkers, and since both lived within easy reach of the boulevard du Montparnasse, they were bound to come across each other on a relatively regular basis. Certainly, poet and painter were a familiar sight and quickly passed into Montparnasse legend. According to the Greek painter Constantin Byzantios, who arrived in Paris just after the war, it was Giacometti who appeared to make the running in the relationship: 'One evening, or one night rather,' he relates, 'Giacometti came to sit next to Samuel Beckett in the Coupole. And he whom one normally listened to, around whom people gathered – he made an unprecedented effort to enter into his neighbour's thoughts, to surround him with an ever-tighter net of questions, as if driven by unbounded curiosity – which Beckett, however, seemed not to notice.'

In addition to their liking for late-night drinking and walking until dawn, the two men shared a fondness for prostitutes, mainly because they were drawn to the ease of having sex (or failing to have sex) without the emotional involvement of a relationship. Both men patronized the local brothels, notably the Sphinx, and both deplored the closing-down of this widely reputed and luxuriously appointed establishment, which Giacometti mourned as 'a marvel surpassing all others'.

When asked once whether he had ever sat to Giacometti, Beckett apparently looked surprised and said, 'No'. Beckett may have felt reticent about being portrayed, just as he avoided being photographed. Nevertheless, with his tall, spare, forward-leaning frame, Beckett himself came as close to a Giacometti 'Walking Man' as anyone could, while Giacometti might have been the model for one of Beckett's tramplike figures, faced by the absurdity of his predicament and possibly even trapped up to the neck by the rubble of his sculptor's cave. If many of Giacometti's works might easily – perhaps all too easily – illustrate Beckett's novels and plays, then Beckett's work abounds in phrases that give dramatic relief to Giacometti's stark imagery. One famous phrase from *Waiting for Godot* could stand as an emblem for Giacometti's funerary race: 'They give birth astride a grave, the light gleams an instant, then it's night once more.' And throughout the novels that Beckett wrote in the mid-1950s – *Molloy, Malone Dies,* and *The Unnameable* – there are countless parallels to Giacometti's universe. The greyish air that circulates through Giacometti's closely hatched drawings and seeps like ash into his sullenly coloured interiors finds constant echoes in Beckett's darkly humorous musings. Here, for instance, Beckett might almost be defining that distinctive, almost liquid element that Giacometti's figures are bathed in:

> 'Air, the air, is there anything to be squeezed out of that old
> chestnut? Close to me it is grey, dimly transparent, and beyond
> that charmed circle deepens and spreads its fine impenetrable
> veils. Is it I who cast the faint light that enables me to see
> what goes on under my nose? There is nothing to be gained, for
> the moment, by supposing so. There is no night so deep, so I have
> heard tell, that it may not be pierced in the end, with the help
> of no other light than that of the blackened sky, or of the earth
> itself. Nothing nocturnal here. This grey, first murky, then frankly
> opaque, is luminous none the less. But may not this screen which
> my eyes probe in vain, and see as denser air, in reality be the
> enclosure wall, as compact as lead?'

Curiously, the encounters between the two men have gone virtually unrecorded. Beckett described them in as early as 1939 in a letter to an old friend as being made up mostly of 'pleasant silences' (which is what Beckett tended to prefer, even with intimate friends). 'Things were insolvable' for Giacometti, Beckett stated at one point, 'but that kept him going.' As for Giacometti's attitude towards Beckett, there is even less on record. According to the Italian writer Giorgio Soavi, Giacometti once made the following comment about their friendship: 'Beckett and I saw each other now and then. He didn't like to be around people, in bars with women late into the night. He didn't like it. He must have been shy. But when we met accidentally, he and I used to stay together until six or seven in the morning.'

Even so, Beckett famously turned to Giacometti (and not to any other of his artist friends) to design the set for the new production of *Waiting for Godot* at the Théâtre de l'Odéon in Paris in 1961. By this time, the two men had known each other for a quarter of a century, and from relative obscurity both had become famous, having each fashioned a distinct, disturbing picture of what it was to be a human being in the postwar world.

The original production of *Godot* in the tiny Théâtre de Babylone in 1953 had met with a mainly hostile reception. However diffident in his attitude to success, Beckett was pleased to have a new production of the work put on in 1961 in the far bigger, more auspicious spaces of the Odéon. This time, and for the first time in his life, Beckett directed the play; as before, the script called simply for 'A country road. A tree' as its backdrop. In the event, almost anyone could have run up a skeletal tree, symbolic of death and rebirth. Being as exacting a director as he was a writer, however, Beckett had a very specific tree in mind, so he wrote to Giacometti saying that, if he could see his way to designing the set, 'we would all be very pleased'.

In the ramblings that the two men had taken together across Paris, trees had in fact played a prominent role. One anecdote, whether apocryphal or not, that comes to mind is the exchange that they had had, sunk no doubt in existential gloom, during one such amble when Beckett burst out: 'Je ne peux plus regarder les arbres' (I can't look at the trees any longer) to which Giacometti gently responded: 'C'est que tu les aimes trop, Sam' (That's because you love them so much, Sam).

*

However much passion, determination and patience he put into his work, Giacometti always remained unusually lucid about its place – and the place of all human creativity – in the larger scheme of things. In what appears to have been the very last note that he made before he died, Giacometti reflected on all forms of art and came to the serene conclusion that they had their 'place and nothing more'. The fragment, found after his death in the studio, is entitled simply 'Tout cela n'est pas grand'chose' (All that is not so very much):

> *'all that is not so very much,*
> *all the painting, sculpture, drawing,*
> *writing or rather literature.*
> *All that has its place and nothing more.*
> *Trying is everything.*
> *how marvellous!'*

Originally delivered as a lecture at the Bucerius Kunstforum, Hamburg, January 2013

15

REMEMBERING GIACOMETTI: AN INTERVIEW WITH JACQUES DUPIN

Having just reread this interview with Jacques Dupin about Giacometti, which I did in Paris a couple of years before Dupin's death in 2012, I regret that I did not spend more time talking to him about all the artists he knew, as well as the writers in his life and his own work as a poet. Since I admired both Dupin and his poetry, I think I felt particularly inhibited by the idea that I would be taking up his precious writing time and perhaps irritating him by posing insistent questions about things that he might not care to talk about. And this was a real concern, since Dupin was never a loquacious man, but rather taciturn and hard to get talking freely.

Yet I knew that he was an unusually valuable source for many aspects of twentieth-century art and literature that interested me. And I had had numerous opportunities to try to pin him down for a formal interview, since I first met him as early as 1966, when Francis Bacon had his initial show at the Galerie Maeght; and I went on seeing him regularly over the intervening years – above all when Bacon invited us both to meet for dinner on his frequent stays in Paris. But the fact that Bacon also admired Dupin made me all the more circumspect, since Bacon did not like friends of his getting together when he was no longer present. So we rarely met outside these dinners and the occasional vernissage, and I think the first time I did talk in depth with Dupin was, significantly enough, after Bacon's death in 1992 when I was doing preliminary research for my biography, *Francis Bacon: Anatomy of an Enigma*, which came out some four years later.

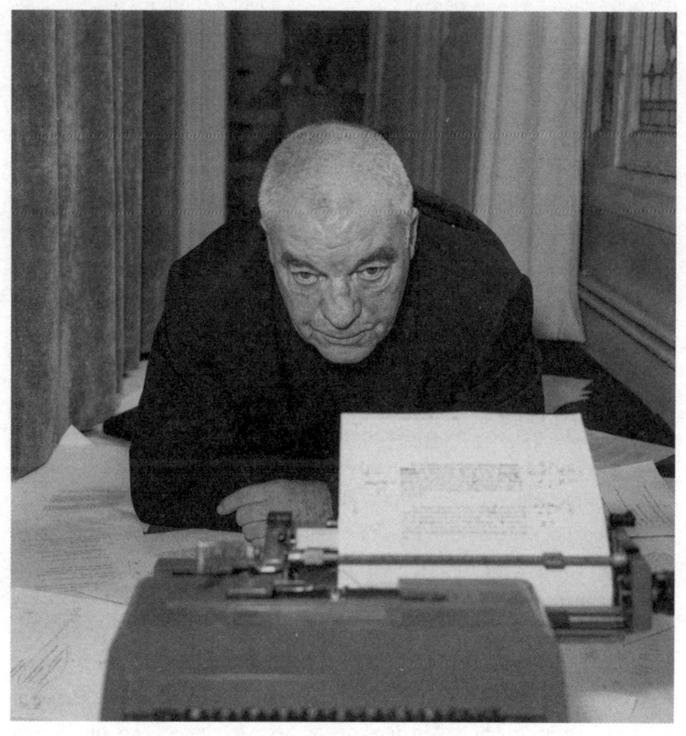

Jacques Dupin, at home in Paris, 2003, photographed by Lian Hong

Here I had a very specific and plausible reason for sitting down with Dupin and prompting him to speak. Faced with writing the first complete account of Bacon's life and work, I was all too conscious of how little information was available about him. Somehow, while making his opinions well known through various interviews (notably with the British art critic David Sylvester), Bacon had contrived to keep whole periods and aspects of his life quite secret. I knew perhaps as much as anyone about his overall existence since I had spent hundreds of hours talking to him essentially about himself, his early life, his career, his great loves and his despair; and Bacon had been unusually forthcoming, almost as if he had decided that I would be best placed to use the reminiscences that he was relaying (if I was wary of interviewing Dupin, I certainly was not of Bacon, since our friendship was in fact based on a kind of extension of the very first interview I did with him for a student magazine in 1963). Nevertheless, two problems remained. One was that Bacon was my sole source, and that he told me mainly what he wanted me to know in a form and style of his own choosing; and, secondly, that he talked only about certain aspects of his life and would not be drawn on the many others that any competent biographer would need to know about.

So I depended on all those who had known Bacon well to fill in some of the numerous gaps in my knowledge and understanding. However, much to my disappointment, I had already found that several of Bacon's closest friends either did not wish to talk about him (for reasons best known to themselves) or were quite happy to communicate but simply did not know how. And I will never forget, after a journey involving several trains that took up most of a whole day, talking to one of his oldest friends who, to my earnest queries about this and that, merely repeated: 'Oh, Francis did love a drink, didn't he?'

Dupin, on the other hand, came up trumps. He was not an old friend of Bacon's and he did not have a deep or extensive familiarity with his life and personality. But, with a poet's instinct, he reviewed his entire experience of Bacon and provided a summary of it in a handful of graphic stories and descriptions, all of which I managed to incorporate usefully into my budding biography. What I particularly appreciated was Dupin's retelling of a long drinking bout with Bacon, which culminated in Bacon's meeting an old flame, a huge wrestler, into whose giant embrace the artist fell enthusiastically and repeatedly, emerging only to continue the discourse on Velázquez that he had begun with Dupin earlier in the day when they had both been relatively sober.

As a result, when I came many years later to curate an exhibition of Giacometti's work at the Eykyn Maclean gallery in New York, I did not hesitate to contact Dupin with a view to including a full interview with him about Giacometti – whom he had known longer and better than Bacon – in the catalogue to the show. With the invaluable support of a key member of the Giacometti family, Thérèse Tigretti Berthoud, we managed to assemble an impressive, eloquent body of work, to which I wrote the catalogue introduction. But what was really lacking was the authentic voice of someone who had known Giacometti well and could bring that precious past back to life.

Dupin, as I hope you will agree when you read the following interview, did in no way disappoint, but the manner in which the event unfolded went way beyond any normal expectation. On the appointed day of our interview, I came over on an early train from London to Paris to meet Dupin at his apartment on rue de Bretagne, not far from République. The idea was that we should do the interview in the late morning, then perhaps have lunch together to tie up any loose ends and see whether further, recorded instalments would be called for. Nervous as I was, I arrived early and whiled away a long moment in the Square du Temple, musing on its earlier Templar history but above all fiddling and checking the two voice recorders I had brought to ensure that, if one machine failed, the other would not. At the hour agreed, I clambered up to the top of Dupin's staircase, thinking of the fine view that he must enjoy over the Square and beyond. I rang the bell and waited. Nothing happened. After a decent interval, I rang the bell again. Again nothing happened. Meanwhile I saw my whole trip wasted and the Giacometti catalogue I had promised my friends, Chris Eykyn and Nick Maclean, sadly truncated.

Then, just as I started my return path down the stairs, there was a scrabbling noise at the door. I turned round and, to my horror, I saw Jacques Dupin in pyjamas covered from head to foot in blood.

'Jacques, I'm so sorry to have disturbed you', I muttered, aghast.

'Come in', the blood-stained apparition said clearly.

'You must get back into bed, and I will call for an ambulance', I said, further alarmed by the pools of blood that stained the entrance and the tiled floor of the kitchen into which Dupin ushered me.

'There's no need for an ambulance', Dupin insisted. Meanwhile, I noticed, the blood coming from his head was still dripping noticeably down his cheeks.

'Well, then I'll call your doctor, Jacques', I said. 'Just give me his number.'

'No, we have agreed to do an interview', Dupin pursued implacably.

'But Jacques,' I said imploringly, 'we can't do an interview with you in this state. It doesn't matter. I'll come over from London some other time.'

'You've come all this way to do the interview', Dupin said grimly. 'We'll do the interview.'

We sat down at the kitchen table. Gingerly, I took out my two voice recorders, anxiously confirming that nothing had changed since I checked them a few minutes earlier.

'Jacques, we really could do this another time', I said weakly, watching the blood gather at the top of Dupin's brow before it snaked down his face.

'We'll do the interview', Dupin repeated. 'I slipped on this blasted, slippery kitchen floor and hit my head. It's not nearly as bad as it looks. I think I've got a cut on the scalp and of course that bleeds profusely.'

The voice recorders are now whirring in the silence. My questions take on a new urgency, as if I am addressing a man about to die before me. I fantasize that he might indeed suddenly pass away, and I will be left with the bloodied corpse and a very ambiguous situation to explain to the police. Dupin, on the other hand, seems not only totally focused, but almost jubilant. He answers every question directly and fully, building up a picture of Giacometti as he really was that no one who had not been there, frequently, and with a reporter's eye, could now reproduce for posterity. The rivulets of blood slow, but not completely, so that occasional drops splatter on the floor, on the table, and, most disquietingly, right onto the voice recorders as if they too want their presence to be acknowledged as we talk.

From time to time, Dupin lights up a cigarette, fully at ease now, pausing before continuing his story. He remains cogent and concentrated throughout. I already know that the interview has been a success, even if I feel slightly ashamed it had to take place when Dupin was at such an apparent disadvantage. He, however, seems to revel in this contradiction, and it occurs to me that he might never have talked so freely and unhesitatingly if he had not just come through his recent ordeal.

I pack up my things and Dupin accompanies me very slowly and carefully to the door of his apartment.

As I begin the descent, I turn round to wave one last goodbye.
Dupin's face, more bloodied than ever, cracks open in a farewell smile.
'Maintenant, au moins,' he calls out as I am halfway down the staircase,
'tu connais la couleur de mon sang!'[1]

*

Michael Peppiatt: Jacques, when did you actually first meet Giacometti?

Jacques Dupin: In 1953. I was working at *Cahiers d'Art*, Christian Zervos's art magazine, and they used to send me to various artists' studios to write an article and take some photos. And one day they asked me to go and see Alberto Giacometti and bring back enough text and photos to fill ten pages of the magazine. So that's how I first went to rue Hippolyte-Maindron, which is an ordinary little street in Alésia, just behind Montparnasse. There were six or seven studios at number 46. You just walked in because the main door was open, and Alberto's was the first on the left. I went in the evening, because Alberto led a noctambulant existence – he slept in the morning, went out for a coffee around two o'clock, worked until about seven in the evening, usually with a model – his brother, Diego, his wife, Annette, and later his girlfriend, Caroline. After that he went back to the café for more coffee and a ham sandwich. Then he worked until about midnight when he went out to Montparnasse to have dinner, with friends or with people – girls – he knew in the area. After that, he'd usually go back to the studio and go on working until dawn. I was very nervous when I went to meet him because I'd heard so much about him, but he was very amiable and courteous with me as he was with most people. He loved to talk, which made things much easier, so we talked about a whole range of topics. And I started going to see him every week, in the early evening, once he'd finished working from his model, and we'd go out to have a drink together. He liked the text I'd written that came out in 1954, and that's how our friendship began.

Then I left *Cahiers d'Art* and started working at the Galerie Maeght, where I looked after some of the gallery artists and Giacometti in particular – organizing his exhibitions and catalogues. And later he asked me to write a book about him, which I did – it was the first monograph on his work and it came out in 1960. So I went to see him often throughout that period because I wanted to get him to talk about his work. And Alberto also made some engravings for two books of poems of mine.

But I wanted to tell you a bit more about Alberto's studio. The studio was tiny, full of finished works or sculptures still under way, some of them wrapped in wet rags, and lots of canvases stacked against the walls, with the floor thick with plaster and clay. And there'd always be the easel with the canvas he was working on – he often worked on the same picture for ages, scraping it down, then starting it all over again. The only way of getting a canvas out of him was to carry it off for an exhibition. Otherwise he could have kept on working on the same canvas all his life. And when he wasn't modelling or painting, he was drawing, often on any old bit of paper or magazine. And if he didn't have anything to hand, he'd draw on the walls. It was as though he couldn't stop drawing, and of course for him drawing was the source of everything he did. He even drew in the dust, or when we went out to the café, he'd go on drawing constantly with his finger on the tabletop while we were talking. What struck me most about the studio was that there wasn't anything in it that didn't lead directly back to work – even the dust helped him. And that's why the studio suited him, because he was completely obsessed with his work. Everything else – such as looking for another studio – was secondary.

MP: How did Alberto himself strike you at the time?

JD: He made a deep impression on me. He always wore the same old clothes, with a shirt that he certainly didn't change every day, and a midnight-blue tie. He always wore a tie, at whatever moment of the day. And then with that great shock of hair and that angular, deeply furrowed face of a Swiss – or really Italian – mountaineer, you couldn't mistake him. He looked more like a tramp than an artist. He hobbled a bit when he walked because he'd had an accident. And he had this cavernous, gravelly voice and a thick, Italian accent when he spoke French. So he had a very distinct presence, but as soon as he began talking he became very welcoming and amiable.

MP: Once you'd discussed gallery business with him, what other things did you discuss?

JD: Alberto liked to talk about everything. Conversation was hugely important for him – sometimes I'd even hear him talking by himself when I arrived at the studio. He was particularly interested in politics. And also, curiously enough – this is a thing people don't know – he had a passion for military campaigns. He loved to re-enact Napoleon's battles, trying out all kinds of different strategies. And then of course he read constantly – all the literary reviews, like *Les Temps modernes* and *Nouvelle Revue Française*, for instance – so he knew everything that was going on in the literary world, and he and I used to talk about poetry and things we'd read. And, as you know, many of his closest friends were writers – Michel Leiris, who wrote the very first article about his work, Sartre and Simone de Beauvoir, Jean Genet. He liked writers more than other artists.

MP: Lots of people dropped in. Was everyone welcome?

JD: Alberto liked company because he loved conversation. He'd go on working and smoking all the time while he was talking to people, so it wasn't as though he was being interrupted – unless he was working from a model, and then he'd close the door and focus entirely on the model. On the whole, he was always pleased to see people, although every now and then someone would irritate him. He always used to say that whatever he was doing was hopeless, that everything he did was bad, dreadful, useless. And of course people used to say, 'Oh no, it's marvellous, that head is amazing.' And I remember Douglas Cooper came to the studio and Alberto went on about how bad everything was, and Cooper said, 'Yes, it is pretty bad', at which point Giacometti became absolutely furious and showed him the door! And Cooper never came back.

MP: If he didn't like his own work, did he like anybody else's?

JD: Alberto didn't like any contemporary artists. The one exception to that was Picasso – but not all Picasso, of course – and the regard was mutual. I know that, because I saw quite a lot of Picasso around that time, and Picasso always used to ask me: 'How's Alberto? What's he doing?' But you never really knew where you were with Picasso because he was always up to some game, pretending to like things he didn't like. Alberto was much more straightforward. He usually said what he thought, and he never tried to further his career. If anything, quite the opposite. He was very pessimistic, but he enjoyed company and he had a wide circle of friends.

MP: Did he talk to you about personal problems?

JD: Well, his personal life was complicated because he had a wife, Annette, but he also had other women friends, like Caroline, who used to come and sit for him in the evening, and afterwards they would go out to have dinner together in Montparnasse. Caroline had been a prostitute and she still had lots of links with the underworld. She used to get into trouble, and at one point she got a jail sentence. I think Alberto was attracted to that sort of life. He may have romanticized it, but he liked the fact there was less bourgeois hypocrisy between people like that. Obviously, their relationship made for difficulties with Annette. Alberto was in any case impossible to live with – sleeping by day, working by night, living in that kind of discomfort. But even after she had moved out, Annette used to come in every day to pose for him, to give things a bit of a clean and go through the accounts. There were always money problems. Although he gave drawings away very freely, Alberto was very tight with money. When I was there, Annette often used to come in specially and say hello. Then she'd say: 'I need money to pay for this and that.' And since I was sitting right there, Alberto couldn't really refuse, so he gave her a bit of money.

MP: Without much enthusiasm.

JD: No enthusiasm at all. But he was very generous with his work. I remember leaving the studio one evening and seeing a fantastic picture sticking out of the rubbish. So I went back to Alberto and I said: 'If you're throwing this out, I'd like it.' So he looked at it for a moment, then he said: 'Perhaps it's not that bad. Take it. But I don't want to see it again.' I've got it here somewhere, but I've never got round to hanging it.

MP: Did you come across Diego much when you went to see Alberto?

JD: Yes, of course. Diego was absolutely essential to Alberto. Not just because he depended on him for the casts and the patinas and the whole technical side of things. He asked Diego's opinion about everything – he'd call him in and say: 'Do you think I should make the arm a bit higher or not?' Things like that. And Diego was always on hand to help. Even though he often seemed to be grumpy and withdrawn, Diego absolutely adored Alberto and would have done anything for him. They were best friends; Diego was like Alberto's double. And in that sense Alberto could have done without marriage. The whole thing with Annette started during the war, in Geneva, and somehow it led to marriage. But, of course, the absolutely dominant woman in Alberto's life always remained his mother, Annetta. Annetta was the anchor for the whole Giacometti clan.

MP: Did you meet the mother?

JD: Yes, I went to Stampa twice with Alberto. And then I went a third time for his funeral. Alberto spoke Italian or at least the local Italian dialect of that part of Switzerland with his mother. He had an almost religious devotion to her. When he got back to Stampa, his mother used to get him to strip, then she soaped him from head to foot and washed him. And she used to insist that he eat proper, regular meals. She also used to sit for him. When he was in Stampa, Annetta was his main model.

MP: And you yourself sat for him. In fact, we have one of the two paintings Giacometti did of you in this show. What was it like to have your portrait done?

JD: Well, Alberto was quite demanding. He expected his models to stay very still and to look at him very directly in the eyes the whole time. If you moved the tiniest bit, he would get very upset and start groaning and shouting. 'Ah there you go! You've moved again!'. Of course, you can't keep that up for long. So we took little breaks every twenty, twenty-five minutes. But the whole séance went on for a good three hours. So it was quite tiring. But afterwards we'd go to the café and have a drink together – because of course he never had anything in the studio to make coffee or even give someone a glass of water. When he was there, he just worked, talked, and chain-smoked. He didn't drink much, he wasn't a real drinker, which as you know is a whole way of life. But he smoked continuously, stubbing one cigarette out, usually in the damp clay foot of a figure he was working on, then lighting another.

MP: Was he ever pleased with something he'd done – with your portrait, for instance?

JD: No. He always thought he'd failed. At the same time, he often felt he'd made a little bit of progress – that there was some light at the end of the tunnel. With my portrait, he scraped the paint off time and again and then very quickly repainted an image that, to me, looked almost identical to what had been there before. But he never thought it was finished. He wanted to come back and work on it again when he left that last time, when he was very ill, for Switzerland. But, of course, he never came back.

MP: Unfortunately, I never met him – not even when he and Francis Bacon got together in London. Were you with them?

JD: Yes, I spent a couple of evenings with the two of them. It was fascinating to see them together. Francis said he liked Giacometti's drawings above all – he was more reserved about the sculpture and painting. I don't really know what Alberto thought about Francis's work, but he was certainly impressed by its force, its power. Both of them talked a great deal when they were together – but I'm not sure they were actually listening to each other.

MP: I've often thought Giacometti's whole style influenced Bacon. You know, the chaos in the studio, the single naked light bulb hanging down, the fact that they both clung to their tiny, cluttered, uncomfortable studios even when fame came and the money poured in. Yet they were also so different in so many ways.

JD: They had a lot of points in common, it's true. Even their taste for low life and gangsters. I was just thinking of some of the times I went with Alberto to the late-night pick-up bars around Montparnasse – Chez Adrien and places like that. One evening, after we'd had dinner, we went on for drinks at Chez Adrien. I'd been carrying a folder of drawings by Alberto around all evening, about thirty of them, and suddenly I realized I'd left everything at the restaurant. And Caroline, who luckily knew the people at the restaurant, went back there and managed to retrieve them. Then another time, late at night, we were sitting in Chez Adrien, and suddenly these men came in and started shooting at the mirror over the bar. There was some kind of gang war going on. So Alberto, Caroline, and I got under the table until it was all over. When we got up, there was a lot of glass all over the place and most people had disappeared. We were a bit shaken up, so we went to another bar for a drink, and while we were sitting there the same lot of gangsters came in, but they had calmed down by then, and they simply stood there and had a drink too!

MP: And Alberto really liked all that.

JD: Yes, Alberto loved that. He thought that was really something.

1   'Now at least you know the colour of my blood!'

Originally published as the preface to the exhibition catalogue *Alberto Giacometti: An Intimate Portrait* (New York: Eykyn Maclean, 2010)

16

A BROKEN DREAM
OF BALTHUS

One of the reasons I wrote frequently about Balthus was that I met him (as I met Bacon and Dubuffet) when I was very young and impressionable, and the whole aura of romanticized enigma that enveloped him intrigued me and became part of my fascination for his work. I was too naive to realize that Balthus had knowingly mythologized himself while en poste at the Villa Medici by assuming a dubious title, 'Count Klossowski de Rola', although I did inwardly question his claim while I was interviewing him that he also descended from Lord Byron. At one point in our talk, he hinted that his real father might have been Rainer Maria Rilke, but since the poet had indeed been his mother's lover, I was inclined to give him the benefit of the doubt on that one. In any case, I rather enjoyed the make-believe atmosphere he spun out of the heavy summer air as we visited the Villa's gardens, with Balthus languidly indicating the view that Velázquez had sketched on his second visit to Rome in 1650.

Balthus mythologized his work, like his origins, by drawing on the great Renaissance tradition both in composition and in technique, deepening the noble glamour this conveyed, as if he were the direct heir to Piero della Francesca. But such legends were already wearing thin, in my mind at least, by the time of his big retrospective exhibitions of 1983–4.

My disillusionment, intimated below, has continued ever since, to the extent that, at Balthus's large exhibition at the Metropolitan Museum of Art in New York in 2013, where I once saw allusive mystery, I found shallow artifice and a dated period charm. Mythologizing served Balthus well while he was alive, but posthumously it has proved to be a cloak for a vision that,

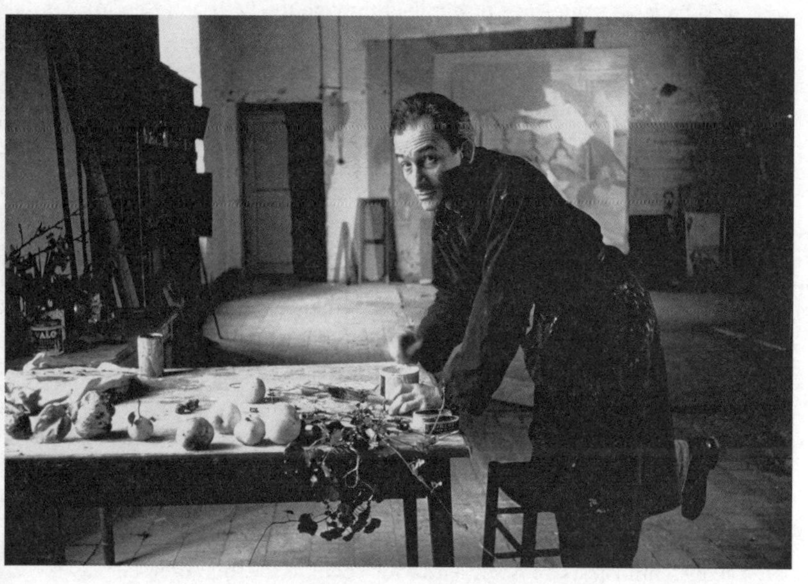

Balthus at work in his studio in the Château de Chassy,
France, 1956, photographed by Loomis Dean

while still painted with great mastery and flair, was never transformative or profound. Like Dubuffet, Balthus remains in my pantheon but, particularly in view of both his social and art-historical pretensions, he has slipped down the ranks.

The big salutes to Balthus have been fired. Vast crowds for whom Balthus was barely a name have now milled through the Paris and New York retrospectives. These exhibitions have been treated to a spate of critical opinion and intimate, biographical disclosure; and as a result, they have no doubt fixed the elusive artist, for the moment at least, in the pantheon of modern masters. Big shows, weighty catalogues, mass recognition: surely all admirers of Balthus are glad that his painting, for long the delectation of an enlightened few, has now become the object of such widespread publicity and attention?

Then why, I am forced to ask myself, has my deep, long-standing enjoyment of Balthus work not been heightened, but dulled, by the retrospective? It is true that I lived much of last summer in expectation of seeing the great Balthuses brought together. In preparation for the essay that I was writing to coincide with the Paris opening,[1] I read every obtainable text on the painter (including the voluminous and poignant correspondence between his mother and Rilke, and also an unpublished thesis tracked down in London). I talked by telephone to the artist himself, to the organizers of the exhibition, and to old friends of his, enthusiasts from way back with whom, as the show drew increasingly near, I developed a kind of 'Balthus fever'. Perhaps such expectation could only lead to a let-down. But there were good reasons for the disappointment that ensued. The best way of analysing them might be to compare the essay that I completed before the Paris retrospective with a 'Postscript' written (and published below) as the paintings were being crated for New York.

*

At seventy-five, Balthus is about to receive the highest accolade the contemporary art world can bestow: a retrospective at the Centre Pompidou, followed by another at the Metropolitan Museum in New York. At a time when interest has been so sharply refocused on figuration, these exhibitions will provide a long-awaited opportunity to reconsider the work of an artist one might describe, journalistically but accurately, as the least known of the great living painters. For comprehensive shows of Balthus's painting have been extremely rare, and written information about him has up until now been astonishingly meagre.[2]

Neither accident nor neglect but the artist himself is at the origin of this situation. From the outset, Balthus has been a solitary, a swimmer against the tide, appreciated by a small, though influential, number of people. As his reputation has grown and his painting become the object of a widening cult, he has been correspondingly reluctant to discuss any aspect of it. All interviews have been expertly discouraged. 'I don't see what one can say about my paintings', he replied to several questions I once put to him during a visit to the Villa Medici. 'After all, if they're any good, they should say whatever it is for themselves.'[3] A closely guarded secrecy also surrounds even the basic facts of his biography, which are simply not mentioned in most texts about him. One well-known critic, when preparing the introduction to a large Balthus exhibition, received a cable from the artist asking him to begin: 'Balthus is a painter of whom nothing is known. And now let us look at the pictures.'[4]

The mystery, or mystification, shrouding Balthus's life has whetted curiosity rather than allay it, of course. And the real biographical facts, little known as they are, are both interesting in themselves and vital to a fuller understanding of the work. However fragmentary, some outline of the artist's early life can be pieced together. Balthasar Klossowski was born in 1908, the second son of Erich Klossowski, a German of Polish descent, and his predominantly Russian wife, Baladine. Both parents were artists, and the father also wrote on art (notably a monograph on Honoré Daumier). Balthus – like the Renaissance masters, he was to use his first name as an artist – was taken from Paris as an infant and brought up in Switzerland. Highly cultivated and cosmopolitan, the Klossowskis attracted a variety of writers and artists into their family circle. Rilke was a passionate admirer of Baladine and a frequent guest. The great, reclusive poet became a kind of mentor to Balthus, encouraging his precocious talent and writing a text for forty drawings by the young artist of his cat – the whole being published as a small book, entitled *Mitsou*, in 1921. Since other famous visitors to the Klossowski household included

André Gide and Pierre Bonnard, one may conclude that when Balthus returned to Paris, aged sixteen, he was unusually well versed in the ways of the world, or at least the ways of artists.

He also gave early proof of the independence that was to characterize his entire development as a painter. Rather than undergo any formal training, the young Balthus copied the works of Nicolas Poussin at the Louvre and, a little later, the noble frescoes of Piero della Francesca at Arezzo (where he added Italian to his several languages and further rounded out an already markedly international cultural education). What he could not learn from his own experiments, he appears to have picked up from discussions with more mature artists, notably André Derain, whose return to classical values in the stylistic ferment preceding the First World War remained a major encouragement for younger painters of similar convictions. Certain early influences on Balthus – not only Théodore Géricault and Caravaggio, but also John Tenniel's illustrations for *Alice*, the drawings in Heinrich Hoffmann's *Struwelpeter*, and the *Images d'Épinal* of 1830 – have been noted; but he was also no doubt keenly aware of the Italian and German 'realist' painters of the period. Of the artistic friendships that Balthus made as he settled into Paris life, the most important and lasting was with Giacometti, who was to take as independent a course as himself. Literature had been a prime force in his imagination since childhood, and he was instinctively drawn towards writers. Jules Supervielle, Antonin Artaud, and, later, Albert Camus recognized the young artist's gifts sufficiently to commission theatre sets from him. These experiences helped to shape Balthus's concept of pictorial space: the figures in many of his early paintings are presented as if on stage.

Once these formative years have been sketched in, biographical detail becomes less relevant. The works take over, particularly as from 1933, the year in which the artist gave conclusive proof of a personal vision. Seen half a century later, Balthus's illustrations for *Wuthering Heights* have lost none of their angular malevolence and awkward passion: figures like puppets with outsized heads mime Emily Brontë's tale of headlong self-destruction in a mise-en-scène of grotesque eloquence. Painted in the same year, *La Toilette de Cathy* (where, once again, the artist depicts himself as Heathcliff) perpetuates the climate of suppressed violence and impending doom; but it has the monumentality of a complex, fully resolved pictorial statement. Narrative painting – works that tell a generally recognizable story – fell into such bad repute towards the end of the nineteenth century that it has been virtually shunned by artists in the twentieth. Balthus is the great exception. Not since Georges Seurat's *A Sunday Afternoon on the Island of La Grande Jatte*, perhaps, had there been so concentrated a narrative picture as Balthus's second (and vastly superior) version of *La Rue*, also begun in 1933. Through its nine figures precisely placed against a flat, theatre-like decor, *La Rue* recounts a whole universe going about its business and its pleasures – with the central somnambulist figure as the key witness, his deep, fixed gaze as if absorbing and transcending the intensely everyday humanity around him. One may analyse the curious combination of dreamlike unreality – of automatons come to life – and a perfectly balanced, classically conceived composition. Yet there remains the central mystery: of how this patently unreal scene transmits such a concentrated sum of real life. More tellingly, no doubt, the paradox may be inverted and *La Rue* seen as a powerful evocation of how unreal 'real' life frequently appears.

The late 1930s and 1940s brought several memorable portraits (such as the vast, pouchy-eyed *Derain*, portrayed with a dazed-looking model in unequivocally rumpled clothes, and the extraordinary *Vicomtesse de Noailles*, whose tubular limbs gleam like burnished bronze); a sumptuously painted *Still Life*, as violent, with its smashed decanter and stabbed bread, as anything Balthus has ever painted; and a number of hauntingly beautiful figure paintings. The latter are almost exclusively of adolescent girls, daydreaming in provocative attitudes or intently reading (like Hamlet, in the book of themselves). The atmosphere is heavy with suspended sexuality, imagined or remembered in settings that the artist lovingly builds up in rich tonal patterns of warm and cold colour – such as the cool green velvet and blazing red-and-yellow fire in *Les Beaux Jours*, a contrast echoed in the young girl's ivory skin and the boy's ruddy-hued back.

Between 1952 and 1954, Balthus painted what has remained his most perfect work: *Le Passage du Commerce Saint-André*. It is also arguably the most 'classical' painting of the century. As one's eye moves between the well-rounded figures and along the precisely delineated facades, it is led back several centuries to the early Italian Renaissance – to what one might call the still centre of the history of Western art. The compositional balance and sense of proportion, the ratio of parts to the whole, are deeply rooted in the tradition of the Old Masters. A forgotten harmony, long absent from painting, appears to have been re-established, and one wonders whether Balthus organized his composition with the Golden Section in mind. At all events, the golden key on the far wall is surely not only topographical but symbolic. And the number eight on the storefront might be seen (without being too fanciful) as representing both the number of figures and the first integer of the *divina proportione.*

The central figure in *La Rue* came towards us. Here, the principal personage marches away, straight-backed, at the peak of self-possession. The golden baguette in his hand is like an emblem, a sceptre, of his power. Balthus's power to maintain enigma and suggest deeper meaning in the most ordinary of scenes – like the *Passage* – lies at the heart of the fascination that his paintings generate. In the absence of myth, he has succeeded in giving ordinariness itself a mythical dimension.

Painted during the same period, *La Chambre* seethes with unnamed violence and eroticism. The curtain is about to go up, or be brought down, on a rosily naked adolescent girl thrown back in complete abandon on a chaise longue. She might be dead, exhausted by a rapist's assault, or simply in a deep dream of desire. The angular, dwarfish figure at work at the window acts like a figure of retribution, a spiteful Fury. The only witness here, as often in Balthus, is the cat, sagaciously squatting on a large book. While dramatic and beautifully painted in subtly accorded, sombre tones, *La Chambre* also contains a comic undercurrent – creating the impression that the protagonists might in fact be children simply play-acting in an empty house.

That 'childhood is the heroic age of man' is a basic article of faith for Balthus, and he once claimed that he himself had 'never felt any transition from childhood. Everything seems to have followed on in the same way.' Certainly, a childhood or adolescent vision of the world dominates his painting up until the mid-1950s. Its awkwardness and torments, and above all its self-absorbed freedom from the outside world, form the underlying theme of many of his pictures, giving them a peculiar psychological tension: the vision of adolescence still reverberates with the adversities of adolescence itself.

In 1954, Balthus left Paris for an ancient, isolated mansion in the Morvan, where he lived until 1961. This radical change of scene not unnaturally brought a change of subject. Landscape – which had hitherto interested Balthus above all as a setting for his figures – became a dominant concern. Unlike *La Montagne* of 1935–7, the new views of nature were virtually unpopulated: man is reduced to a speck, one small element among many others in an exquisitely constructed composition. In these landscapes, the last asperities of personal quirkiness are smoothed away. In their place come beautiful harmonies, built up layer by layer and thought out to the last grain of dry, crumbly paint, as in the deeply satisfying *Grand Paysage à l'arbre* of 1960. The artist himself, once so tangible in his work, has disappeared, become anonymous. He has, in James Joyce's phrase, been 'refined out of existence'. This also holds for the figure paintings of the post-Paris period. The artist as a distinct personality is no longer present. *Golden Afternoon* (1957), for instance, is a marvel of colour combination, as daring as it is delicate. But the subject – the narrative implications and psychological tensions – has gone, and we are left here with consummately skilful patterning.

Balthus moved from the Morvan to take up his post as director of the French Academy in Rome in 1961. For some fifteen years, he assumed the duties of that prestigious office, and also supervised the restoration of the Villa Medici's frescoes. His production during that time slowed down markedly, with the occasional new painting often taking several years to complete. The technical mystery of these works is undeniable, and most of them radiate a deep aesthetic charm. But aestheticism began to exclude all else. The veiled threat and sardonic humour that had captivated Artaud and Camus might never have existed in this universe of suavity and seduction. The concerns here are with formal values only: how the female limb and the table leg balance each other out in *La Chambre turque* (1963–6), for instance, or the occasional, deliberate, refreshingly bitter dissonance of colour.

This accomplished aestheticism was not a phase, however. It continued after Balthus's retirement from the Villa Medici. And the insistence on purely pictorial qualities has led increasingly to a lack of meaningful content. *Le Château au miroir* (1977–80), for example, is a divertissement of remarkable technical virtuosity, but while it charms the eye it provides nothing for the mind. Some recent paintings also seem to have undergone a deliberately archaizing process so that their dragged, grainy pigment imitates ancient frescoes miraculously preserved in all their original freshness. With this antiquarian note, and the growing insubstantiality of the recent paintings, a certain mannerism has crept in. In *Le Peintre et son modèle* of 1980–1, acquired by the Centre Pompidou, the two attenuated figures float in an atmosphere of ethereal delicacy. There is no longer any 'what', only a 'how'. One need simply compare the work with one of the Centre's other major Balthus pictures, *La Toilette de Cathy*, painted nearly a half-century before, to measure the loss of vigour and conviction.

The loss would seem far less marked, of course, if Balthus had not achieved such intensity while still a young painter. It has been said that the main difficulty in assessing his work is that it can be compared only to that of his masters: that long line of supremely classical artists from Piero via Poussin to Seurat (though, of course, Caravaggio and Courbet have also played an essential part in his development). In this sense, it will be fascinating to see how the new generation of figurative painters relate to an art so profoundly rooted in the grand tradition – and to paintings, moreover, that take years of patient and precise labour. What is certain is that Balthus appears quite unique in our century, for no other painter has succeeded in communicating a complete vision while remaining so tenaciously within the time-hallowed conventions of fine art. Because of, rather than despite, these 'constraints' – these well-tried, infinitely adapted 'rules of the game' – Balthus has fathered a whole universe, which has its heroes and many heroines, its unmistakably Balthusian atmosphere, and, above all, its mystery – which words attempt to single out but cannot explain. In the end, the greatest tribute a writer can pay to Balthus's best pictures is that, having undergone every kind of analysis, they re-emerge with their essential secret untouched and as potent, as magical, as before.

POSTSCRIPT

The last line of this essay leads straight on to the underlying problem. In the Centre Pompidou retrospective, the 'essential secret' of Balthus's art certainly did not appear 'as potent, as magical' as before. My initial dismay no doubt came from the confrontation, suddenly and en masse, with the physical reality of paintings that I had written about from memory and reproductions. Many of the works, it seemed, had taken on a peculiarly seductive patina in my mind. I had appropriated them in thinking and writing about them; and they occupied a precariously high place in my mental landscape. So when I was faced with their distinct otherness, on wall after exhibition wall, I could not shut out *my* Balthuses … nor, indeed, the insidious echo of Eliot's: 'That is not it at all, / That is not what I meant at all.'

This is a regular *risque du métier*. Things rarely have the impact one expects, especially when expectations are excessive. But what was the fundamental reason for my disappointment: that Balthus had turned out to be a less fine artist than I imagined, or that the retrospective did not do him justice? Or both?… It's obvious that retrospectives are most likely to disappoint the people who know an artist's work best, because they already have a kind of ideal exhibition in mind when they arrive. Thus, they are particularly quick to find fault with the choice, the hanging, and the lighting; they are also most sensitive to the 'rightness' of the place where the event is being staged.

Almost all the great Balthuses had been assembled at the Centre Pompidou. So, whatever the circumstances, the raw beauty was there. It was in the sharp song set up between a blazing red and an unripe blue, in the ancient harmonies of exact proportion exemplified in *Le Passage du Commerce Saint-André*, in the unexpected notes of quirky humour and sardonic observation, in the perfect silences of deeply structured landscapes. It reappeared in the astonishing monumentality of *Nu devant la cheminée*, where the traditional language of volume is revived with an eloquence unsurpassed, I believe, in our century. Was I hampered from appreciating its grace to the full merely because it was glimpsed between two hats and three chattering heads; was the charm shattered by the swirl of groups and the inescapable, inexcusable trumpetings of their guides?

In part, certainly. My experience of Balthus until then had always had an agreeably private side to it. I had been lucky enough, as a young critic of twenty-five, to have spent the day with the artist at the Villa Medici, during his tenure as director of the French Academy there.

Several friends of mine owned works by him, others had known him well, in Paris or Rome; and over the years a sense of complicity, of belonging to a kind of *Balthuskreis*, had developed. And this is perhaps central to a deep appreciation of the paintings. Balthus's is above all a private art, made about a few people, and for a few people, by a man of manifestly aristocratic inclinations. It is addressed, in the first instance, to a certain elite that Balthus knew and admired in his youth, in the Paris of the 1930s. In this sense, and also in its hidden affiliations with the great classical tradition, it is a hermetic art. No one has been more conscious of the fact than the artist himself; it was for this good reason that he discouraged all publicizing, through large shows or books or interviews, of himself, his work, and its sources until very recently.

How right the artist's instinct had been became dismally evident in the Centre Pompidou retrospective. The private art destined for private rooms hung here not on real walls, of course, but on temporary partitions; not in a normal, closed space, but beneath the Centre's thick festoons of exposed pipe, and under unnecessarily harsh lighting. Few buildings could have been so directly inimical as this contemporary culture machine (whatever its undeniable merits) to the spirit of Balthus. The rare perfume of a delicately cultivated, secret universe rose into the wide, functional, glass-and-girder-encased spaces – and was lost.

But walking round the exhibition and following the curve of the artist's fifty-year development, I realized I was troubled by something far more important. The real impetus of the show, and thus of the oeuvre, lay in the first half, lasting until 1955, let us say, when both *Le Rêve* and *Nu devant la cheminée* were painted. From then on, as I had suggested in my essay, the work grew increasingly insubstantial – with occasional exceptions, such as the *Japonaise au miroir noir* (1967–76), where sheer beauty prevails; and reached a high point in ethereality in the elegantly empty *Le Peintre et son modèle*, on which the exhibition ended. At this point, it became clear that Balthus's work simply does not lend itself to large-scale retrospectives, however worthwhile they may be in art-historical (as opposed to aesthetic) terms. Since Balthus is the great modern painter of enigma and subtlety of sensation, his work requires a correspondingly spare, subtle presentation. The great Balthuses are not legion, but they are worlds unto themselves. A dozen of the finest of them, hung with some outstanding drawings in a few well-proportioned rooms, would constitute the most apt – and the only real – tribute to his unique, and uncannily elusive, achievements.

1 Published in a French translation in *Connaissance des Arts*, Paris, November 1983.
2 The situation has of course changed entirely since the retrospective took place. Meagreness is no more. On the contrary, the Centre Pompidou catalogue is a formidable tome of some four hundred pages and nearly as many illustrations. To a conscientious roundup of the main texts on Balthus – by Artaud, Camus, Jouve, Pierre Klossowski, and John Russell – it adds some more recent aperçus. In all, it constitutes the foundation stone of what will no doubt gradually become a monument of Balthus scholarship.
3 See *Réalités* (English edition), Paris, October 1967.
4 See John Russell, catalogue to the Tate Gallery exhibition (London: Tate Gallery, 1968).

Originally published in *Art International*, Lugano, April–June 1984

17

THE SHAMEFUL LIFE OF SALVADOR DALÍ

What to make of Salvador Dalí, then as now? As brilliantly talented for public relations and creating his own legend as he was at inventing disturbing pictures, he has slipped into a category all his own, a kind of genius-buffoon whose clowning is as much admired by a wide, appreciative public as his meticulously rendered imagery. And he deserves his reputation on both counts: some of his works still astonish by their blend of weirdness and technical mastery, and no other artist has been as outrageously witty both in person and in writings such as *The Diary of a Madman*. Still, it remains doubtful whether the painting would have developed beyond his brand of shock Surrealism into a more complete oeuvre had he not had his eye so firmly fixed on fame and money, becoming increasingly the 'avida dollars' of André Breton's brilliant anagram right up until the end. Dalí created his own persona so meticulously that we can probably do no better than to accept him as he presented himself: an alarming amalgam of visionary artist and self-serving showman.

Dalí might have perfected the art of showmanship, but he was certainly not alone among twentieth-century artists in hotly pursuing publicity and international fame. His compatriot Pablo Picasso skilfully fed the press to create a legend around his life and work, while building far more solid foundations than Dalí for lasting artistic success. Very aware both of Picasso and the Surrealists, Francis Bacon realized early on that the conjunction of savage imagery and a scandalous private life would not fail to draw the art world's attention. Even Alberto Giacometti, who seemed to show success the back of his plaster-caked hand, allowed every photographer of note to

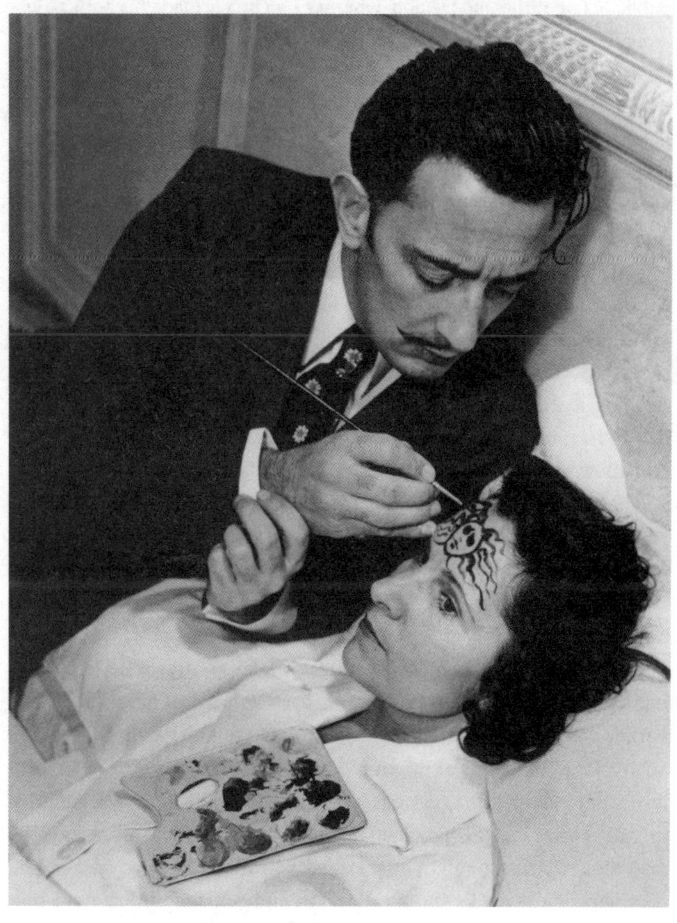

Salvador Dalí with his wife Gala, 1942, photographed by Philippe Halsman

capture the eloquent squalor of his tumbledown, sculpture-filled studio in widely distributed reportages. But none of them allowed myth-making and publicity to get the upper hand, whereas Dalí finally made his antics more arresting than his art.

By the time he became a household name, Salvador Dalí was already perceived above all as a performer – an outrageous self-publicist and riotously witty clown. In France, where he spent part of the year, he could always be relied on to liven up any event or public debate. But even in that role, which he abused shamelessly, he began to pall. I remember almost literally bumping into him in 1971 at the Francis Bacon retrospective at the Grand Palais in Paris. He was unmistakable, with his manic stare, pointy moustaches, and exotic clothes. 'They're very, very *"raisonnables"*,' Dalí repeated loudly to those around him, pointing his silver-topped cane at the most alarming of Bacon's images; and he was visibly annoyed when this bit of Surrealist upstaging failed to turn more than a few heads. Somehow, even his clowning had grown predictable.

The story of how Dalí went from the subversive brilliance of his youth to an increasingly hollow, money-making exhibitionism is told with exemplary clarity in Ian Gibson's big, new biography of the Catalan artist. It is ultimately a depressing tale, because it chronicles in great detail how Dalí progressively cheapened and squandered his enormous natural talent. Gibson has chosen to concentrate on Dalí's early career, because it is by far and away the most interesting part. 'Two thirds of this book', the author declares in an afterword, 'are devoted to one third of Dalí's life. Such a structure was not imposed artificially, but shaped itself irresistibly as my research progressed. Dalí's work, after he moved to America in 1940, grows increasingly hackneyed and repetitive' (p. 684). And the man himself, Gibson might have added, became increasingly grotesque.

Signs of the ruthless manipulation and self-aggrandizement that characterized the later Dalí were nevertheless discernible in the artist as a very young man. When he was barely sixteen, for instance, he announced confidently in his diary: 'I'll be a genius, and the world will admire me. Perhaps I'll be despised and misunderstood, but I'll be a genius, a great genius, I'm certain of it' (p. 109). Slim and strikingly handsome, he let his jet-black hair grow down to his shoulders and began dressing in stylishly

Bohemian clothes for maximum effect. Although paralysingly shy, the adolescent Dalí was already fully launched on his conquest of the world.

Gibson begins his biography with a full description of Dalí's forebears and the area north of Barcelona, around Figueres and Cadaqués, to which the artist, forever conscious of being Catalan rather than Spanish, was to remain so deeply attached. Dalí's childhood comes across as relatively normal (above all if one discounts the artist's later, myth-making version of it), except that he had had an older brother, also called Salvador, who died some nine months before he himself was born. His parents, who were comfortably off and relatively cultivated, made all the more fuss of him, giving in to his every whim. But even at a very early age, according to Gibson, Dalí suffered intense feelings of shame, making it 'extremely difficult for him to maintain normal relations with the people around him' (p. 62).

Other signs that Dalí was not just any boy growing up in provincial, middle-class Catalonia were not long in coming. Extreme timidity coincided with an array of obsessions, such as buttocks (fascination with, both male and female) and locusts (pathological fear of), that were to stay with him throughout his life. As he grew into adolescence, Dalí also became fixated on his unusually complex sexuality. First, there was the realization that he was poorly equipped for intercourse. However disturbing the discovery, Dalí himself related it with typical verve: 'For a long time I experienced the misery of believing I was impotent', he observes in his 'Unspeakable Confessions'. 'Naked, and comparing myself to my school friends, I discovered that my penis was small, pitiful, and soft. I can recall a pornographic novel whose Don Juan machine-gunned female genitals with ferocious glee, saying that he enjoyed hearing women creak like watermelons. I convinced myself that I would never be able to make a woman creak like a watermelon' (pp. 111–12). This discovery was normal enough, except that, for Dalí, masturbation was to be the main, indeed almost the only, sexual activity throughout his life.

These facts would hardly be relevant if they were not vital to an understanding of Dalí's subsequent behaviour and his art. An overriding sense of sexual inadequacy was surely one of the factors that drove Dalí to create with such single-minded intensity, and most of the self-styled Great Masturbator's best paintings bristle with erotic allusions. Gibson rightly emphasizes Dalí's tortured sexuality, and in an intriguing passage he examines what appears to have been a protracted but unconsummated love affair with the poet Federico García Lorca, whom Dalí was later to describe as the greatest friend of his youth. Dalí's other close companion during this period was, of course, Luis Buñuel, and Gibson's account of the interaction of this fabulously talented Spanish trio, who had come together as students in Madrid, makes for one of the most exhilarating passages in the book. In retrospect, it seems almost uncanny that the three most artistically gifted young men in the country should have met and had time to share their dreams, thus influencing each other for life. Gibson gives a tantalizing glimpse of Lorca, whose biography he has already written, and records with gusto how Buñuel and Dalí came to make their subversive first film together, *Un Chien andalou*, which was shown in Paris in 1929.

Around this time, there occurred two events that were to shape the rest of Dalí's life. One was his conversion – the word is not too strong – to Surrealism, which took place (if Dalí's own, unreliable memoirs are to be believed) when the artist met the movement's leader, André Breton, on his second trip to Paris: 'I felt at the time that I had been granted a second birth', Dalí stated many years later. 'The Surrealist group was for me a sort of nourishing placenta and I believed in Surrealism as if it constituted the Tables of the Law' (p. 255). As he describes the artist's new involvement, Gibson also conjures up the effervescence surrounding the movement, with its constant battles, internal and external, and its fierce resolve to turn all preconceived notions about culture and life on their head. For a while, Surrealism's ideology kept at bay the monstrous egomania and self-serving cynicism that later claimed the artist entirely. The other cause that he began to serve did not: on the contrary, it began from the outset to egg them on.

Gala appears to have dominated Dalí, both fascinating and terrifying him, from the moment they met in 1929. She was then married to the poet Paul Éluard, but the couple accepted and even encouraged each other's infidelities, to the point where Gala felt that her husband was actually pushing her at his friend Dalí. Not long thereafter, she left Éluard to live with the painter. For Dalí, the highly sexed, Russian-born Gala – nicknamed the 'Sibyl of the Steppes' – brought some form of physical release and the promise of intelligent companionship. For Gala, the artist seems to have been a career and a fortune waiting to be made, as well as a husband who would tolerate all the lovers she craved. In the end, they seem to have been a monstrous match for each other, and much of the latter part of this biography traces their mutual degradation.

On the way, there are moments of respite. Dalí's visit to Sigmund Freud, for instance, is one of those vignettes that seems suddenly to speak volumes about the twentieth century. And with his incredible energy, Dalí carries even the growing weight of his empty clowning and repetitious image-making before him. As the money poured in, from paintings, endless prints, and all kinds of Dalí-inspired merchandizing, the artist surrounded himself with a court of beautiful young people and managed to meet virtually everyone who took his fancy, from the Pope and Franco to Clark Gable and Bob Hope. Once Gala died, Dalí went into rapid decline, and his own end is as gruesome as this master of unpleasant fantasies might himself have devised. One wonders whether the painter was in fact as ashamed of himself as his biographer claims. It hardly matters. The book provides not so much a cautionary tale but a trustworthy, even-handed account of a life that continues to haunt our imagination.

Originally published as a review of Ian Gibson's *The Shameful Life of Salvador Dalí* (New York: W. W. Norton, 1997), in the *New York Times Book Review*, New York, 22 December 1998

18

LOOKING BACK
AT NICOLAS DE STAËL

My first contact with Nicolas de Staël's painting came at *Réalités* in 1966 when I was given a sheaf of reproductions and told to work up the requisite number of words around them. I had got used to commenting on Pisanello or Patinir one week, then Calder or Dubuffet the next. But Staël was different: the tension coming off these great, fractured compositions hit me like a scream.[1] I saw him as a man torn apart by painting's ever more insistent claims on him to go deeper and deeper into the ambiguous, treacherous ground that he had opened up between figuration and abstraction. I identified with him and his destiny, since like many young people I felt deeply divided by my own self-doubt; and although I was far from suicidal, I regularly rehearsed in my imagination Staël's dizzying leap to his death at Antibes.

This identification led me to write on several other occasions about Staël's work and also to get to know his widow, Françoise, and his children during stays in Ménerbes, the fortified hill village where the artist had bought a retreat. Since I thought his work deserved greater recognition, I tried to curate an exhibition of it in London, a city he loved, but the project eventually failed through lack of support. Years later, when David Nash, another great Staël enthusiast, invited me to write the preface to the Staël show that he was organizing in his New York gallery, I leapt at the opportunity, and I was immensely pleased, when I stood again in front of Staël's astonishing images, to find that my interest in him and his unique achievement was as strong as ever.

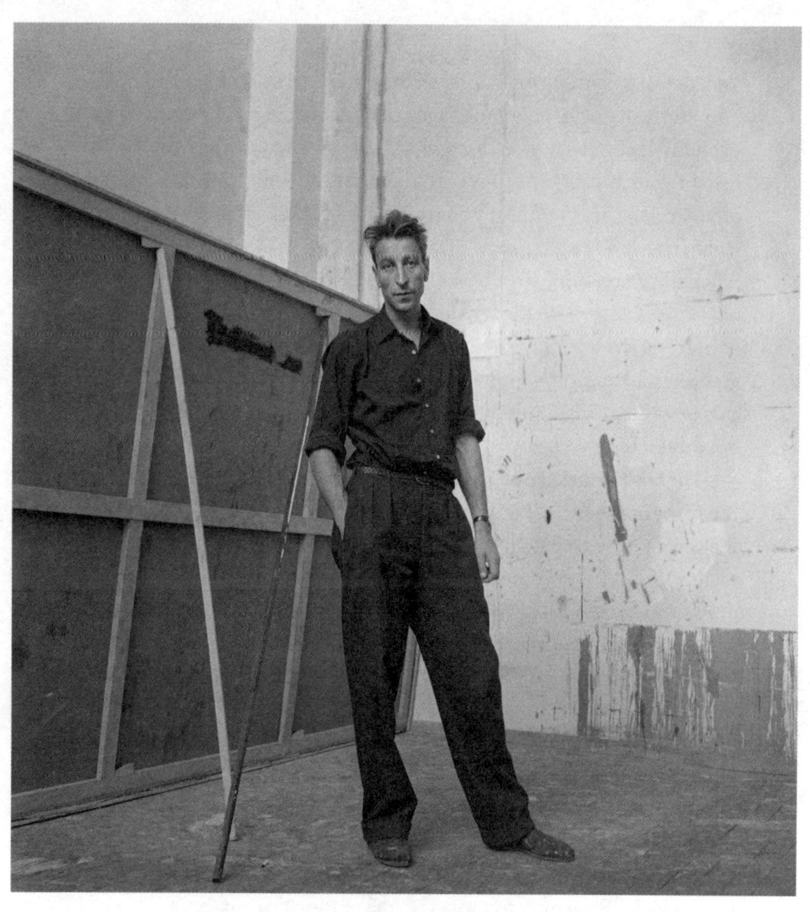

Nicolas de Staël, in his studio on rue Gauguet, Paris, 1954,
photographed by Denise Colomb

'Black A, white E, red I, green U, blue O: vowels,
One day I shall reveal your secret birth'
Arthur Rimbaud, *Voyelles* (1883)

You look at a painting by Nicolas de Staël with the eyes of a child because you are learning a new language. Take any section of a canvas and examine it closely. It is as though, with brush and palette knife, he had lifted the skin off paint to reveal an unknown world of colour, a mass of vivid clash and sumptuous harmony. A streak of white gives way like cloud over sun to a glimpse of incandescent yellow. Two slabs of fractured black imprison a lozenge of sullen blue. These warring elements rest on a knife's edge, with the tension between them so acute it is as audible as a stifled scream. The paint bristles with menace: an insidious metallic green surface, seeping round the edges of every chromatic truce. But for this instant, plucked out of chaos and re-enacted on canvas, the fragile balance holds.

The whole notion of balance is key to understanding Staël's achievement: the artist himself was the sum of extreme emotional contradictions that constantly threatened to tear him apart. He veered abruptly from exultation in his own artistic powers to the depths of self-doubt and despair just as in his own life he moved from abject poverty to heady success and from domestic security to anguished solitude. Those close to him have described how he would break into a dance of frenzied joy in the studio at one moment, then sink into a silent, black depression. Staël was driven by his inner conflicts to become a painter: only through painting could he hope to keep his Furies, however precariously, at bay. 'All through my life I have needed to think painting,' the artist said in 1953, 'to look at paintings and to make paintings to help me to live, to free me from all the impressions, all the sensations and all the anxieties from which I have only found a way out through painting.'

Painting was the arena in which Staël could let his conflicting impulses loose. Once they were contained in the infinitely pliant medium of paint, where his fluency and cunning knew no bounds, the artist would allow the hostile forces to skirmish and battle until they were trapped into a miraculous stasis – light against dark, tone against tone – that gave him a moment's respite. But Staël's tensions were innate, forever demanding new solutions, pushing the artist constantly to reinvent the means by which he kept their discord in check and his own life together.

Staël by no means sprang ready-armed into this all-consuming fray. From the very beginning, he had known the hardness of life and the fortitude it took to survive. Born in St Petersburg in 1914 into an aristocratic family close to the Imperial Court, he saw the whole world of Tsarist Russia overturned as a small boy, then experienced a bitter exile in Poland and the loss of both parents by the time he was eight. Brought up (but never understood) by kindly foster-parents in Brussels, Staël only found his bearings again in late adolescence when he discovered his passion for painting. He studied, often in painfully reduced circumstances, the entire history of art, choosing his masters carefully, from Rembrandt and Velázquez to Courbet and Manet. He also travelled widely, with whatever money he could muster, frequenting the great museums and sketching the exotic sights that came his way. A Northerner from top to toe of his towering, taut frame, he was drawn most to the Mediterranean's sparkling colour, in Barcelona and Naples, in Sicily and Morocco.

The long apprenticeship to become an artist had begun, for Staël was no child prodigy. He spent most of the war and postwar years in Paris, struggling to find a voice of his own in the cacophony of prevailing styles. He copied at the Louvre and enrolled briefly at Fernand Léger's Académie libre, later destroying almost all of the stridently angular compositions that he made at the time. The friendships he formed with other painters, above all with Georges Braque, were to prove of lasting importance to the determined young outsider, who was ready to starve in pursuit of his artistic ambition. But in 1946 his life took another tragic turn when, not long after the birth of their first child, his wife died, partly of malnutrition. Shaken to the core, Staël threw himself even more intently into his work, producing a series of criss-crossed explosions of dark, angry brushstrokes with such unambiguous titles as *Black Composition*, *The Hard Life*, and *Resentment*.

Staël's talent and dedication as well as his unusual intelligence and charm nevertheless began to be acknowledged even in the notoriously closed circles of the Paris art world. The more adventurous dealers began to buy a few of his works, and Jeanne Bucher gave him a one-man show in her prestigious gallery on the boulevard du Montparnasse. He remarried, started a new family, and found a large studio – close to Braque's by the Parc Montsouris – which gave him the space and silence to work obsessively, as well as regular contact with the older painter, whom he venerated. Although living conditions were still spartan (with the family housed in a converted garage), and the artist's mood continued to swing between manic high spirits and brooding melancholy, there followed a period of relative calm during which Staël's palette began to lighten and the forms that he created grew less violently fractured. It was as if a new warmth had come into his life and the dark confusion of the war years had begun to lift, giving way to planes of softer, brighter colour.

By the end of the 1940s, Staël was acknowledged as a rising star of abstraction, well regarded in France and soon to have his first one-man shows in New York and London. But he had never thought of himself as 'abstract', since he claimed his pictures always had a subject (even if it was the grimy fissures in a dilapidated wall); and he was in any case the last person to accept categorization. Staël was Staël, and now that he had gained the experience and technique that he required, his adventure had just begun. It was not abstraction or figuration he was after, but life itself. He was in awe of the world, whether it took the form of a vast sky on a low horizon, dark dead leaves on the ground, or the clustered roof-tops of Paris. 'My passion is to trap a marvellous thing that passes by in a second', he said. 'I am an impaler of images.'

Staël was also a taker of risks whose temperament always impelled him to push back the boundaries and negotiate the unknown. And as he became increasingly confident in his visual gifts – an instinctive sense of composition, an unerring eye for *le ton juste*, the exact tone – the stakes grew higher. He would find a subject, mosaics of infinitely subtle shades or the sea under clouds at Honfleur, exhaust it in a series of oil studies that grew into huge canvases, then move on with mounting impatience. He travelled, again mostly southwards, in search of subjects that he would note on the spot, then work up once he returned to the monklike seclusion of his white-walled studio. What Staël wanted least was to belong to a school of like-minded souls with shared theories. It was not an aesthetic programme that he sought but its opposite: the freedom to explore whatever style or subject he fancied to the point of provoking 'accident' – the element of pure chance by which a random mark could make or break a picture. 'I believe in accident,' Staël wrote in one of his eloquent letters, 'and I can only progress from accident to accident.'

His life also appeared to progress – or at least lurch – from accident to accident. He provoked chance, like an adept at Russian roulette, forever defying the odds. Athletic and endowed with huge energy, the artist was already working day and night with a single-minded intensity that would have killed a lesser man far earlier. This rhythm, which allowed him to produce nearly nine hundred paintings in the last five years of his life, did not however stop him from enjoying the pleasures of life and long evenings with friends, fuelled by extravagant meals and epic quantities of wine. This was all part of the same seductively excessive temperament, but there was never any doubt about Staël's priorities. 'Have as many children as you like', he told his new wife. 'But never forget that for me painting comes first.'

By the early 1950s, Staël's focus settled unequivocally on the seen world. 'I don't paint before seeing', he remarked. 'I am not seeking anything but painting that is *visible* to everyone.' The conclusive experience came totally out of left field: a football match seen under floodlights at the Parc des Princes. Staël was so excited by the clash of form and colour on the pitch that he translated his impressions into a series of works in which the figures ('a ton of muscles', as he called them) were built out of thick wedges of red, white, and blue but were nevertheless fully recognizable as footballers. But of course they – and all the landscapes, still lifes, and nudes that followed – would not have made such an extraordinary visual impact had they not emerged from the matrix of abstraction like a new race with all its formal strangeness and rigour woven into their frames.

After several prolonged stays in Provence and a crucial new friendship – a brotherhood – with the poet René Char (long resident in the Vaucluse), Staël found the lure of the South overwhelming, not unlike Van Gogh, whom Staël resembled in more than one way. After his return from his second exhibition in New York in 1953, he made a decisive trip through Italy all the way down to Sicily, where he was entranced by the light, and particularly the evenings that he witnessed and noted in sketchbooks 'when the sky is yellow and the sea is red and the sands are violet'. From this point on, most of his work until his death centred round the Mediterranean rim. In autumn 1953, on the proceeds of recent successful shows, Staël bought a fortress-like, half-ruined old house in Ménerbes, a hill village in Provence, and for a while installed his growing family there. But he had already begun a new liaison, with a woman who became the subject of his great series of 'Nudes'. The relationship cut the artist off from his family but did not evolve, although Staël himself had already made the ultimate commitment – for him – of putting his new lover at the heart of his painting.

None of his close friends seems to have noticed then, in March 1955, that Staël was suicidal, any more than anyone now can fully explain his last desperate act. Nevertheless it seems impossible not to view the artist's entire work through the prism of his dramatic death. The decision appears to have been premeditated, since Staël wrote three letters of veiled farewell before he threw himself off the terrace above his studio. Still in the studio at his death was the unfinished *Concert*, the huge composition that he had been working on, in thinned, translucent pigment, which was inspired by a recital of Schoenberg and Webern that had deeply moved him. Also left behind was his *Seagulls*, grey birds in a lightless pale sky, eerily reminiscent in their forlorn flight of the crows in Van Gogh's last painting. The inhuman tension and solitude in which Staël had lived so long, strung between extremes of emotion and exhausted by the demands of his work, had ended by taking the ultimate toll.

If the mystery of Staël's death remains, so more importantly does the mystery of his painting, which absorbed and transcended the bitter contradictions of mid-twentieth-century art. The artist fulfilled his destiny by confronting the language of paint and reinventing it, syllable by elusive syllable, to express both the wonder of the world and his own turmoil. Several generations later, the uniqueness of Staël's vision outlives him, entrancing us by its poignant daring and eloquence.

1 Nicolas de Staël is frequently referred to in English as 'de Staël'. The correct usage is simply 'Staël', which is how he would have introduced himself and how his surname is used in France – in the same way that 'de Sade' should be referred to correctly, in English as in French, as 'Sade' or 'de Beauvoir' as 'Beauvoir'.

Originally published in the catalogue for the exhibition *Nicolas de Staël*, Mitchell-Innes & Nash, New York, 2013

19

ZORAN MUSIC:
ART AFTER DACHAU

I met Zoran Music in the late 1970s because I had been asked to write the introduction to a show of his work, which I had seen on and off over the years but did not know well. Courteous and reserved, Music struck me right away by the fact that he did not, like so many artists whom I knew, rattle off set pieces about his painting but on the contrary seemed to find it very difficult, try as he would, to make any satisfactory comment about it at all. I was also aware that he had survived internment at the Dachau concentration camp, but that for years after the war he had continued to paint the evocative scenes of Dalmatia and Venice for which he was best known. Some years earlier, however, images of the death camp had burst as if uncontrollably into his work, replacing picturesque *vedute* of the Dogana and Karst landscapes with mounds of the dead and dying, their corpses stacked like logs in a pyre.

Very gradually over the next twenty years, Music, who had never talked at length about his Dachau experience, began to open up during a series of interviews I did with him. By this time, we had become close friends, frequently spending the evening together, either in Paris or Venice, or occasionally travelling across Europe for the opening of one of his exhibitions. Music continued to paint well into his nineties, focusing on a series of bowed, solitary figures that were clearly studies of his ageing self. Painting has been described as '*un métier de vieux*', and Music certainly added credence to the view. In my experience, the same might be said of writing: so many aspects of its execution that seemed obscure or complicated are suddenly not, and the way forward, '*la diritta via*', is clear.

Like a tragic figure at the end of a play, Zoran Music finds himself alone on a dark, silent stage. From time to time, he enacts a familiar gesture, leaning forward with his shoulders hunched, his arm outstretched to paint or his head buried in his hands. Pale as a ghost and faintly outlined, he remains visible for an instant, then blurs and fades into the background, a shadow among shadows.

Over the past few years, Music has concentrated all his powers on this one theme: an old man confronted by the closeness of death. Nothing could be further removed from the gaiety of the artist's early Dalmatian and Venetian scenes than these relentlessly searching, sombre effigies where every outline threatens to dissolve. The late self-portraits haunt the imagination with the insistence of after-images, as if one had looked too directly at a dark sun. They form the absolute and irreducible statement of a life that has witnessed nearly a whole century and left an unforgettable record of its beauty and its horror. Yet while they explore the extremes of human experience, Music's works remain astonishingly discreet, their forms barely delineated, their colours hardly staining the canvas: even when they describe in the most graphic detail the piles of corpses at Dachau, they remain understated. It is this delicate reserve in the face of joy as well as suffering, I believe, that gives Music's art its power to move and to convince.

Music began life in a world already so distant from our own that we have to make a conscious effort to reimagine it. The Austro-Hungarian empire still dominated central Europe when he was born, in 1909, in Gorizia, a small town on the border between Slovenia and Italy. Music grew up speaking Slovenian, Italian, and German, changing from one to the other according to circumstance; he went on to learn Serbian, Croatian, a little Czech, and later Spanish and French. When the First World War broke out (a moment he remembers vividly), Music was evacuated. With his mother and brother, he wandered from town to town behind the front, picking up a little schooling and seeing other outposts of the Dual Monarchy.

Those wanderings set a pattern. Music studied in Zagreb, Prague, and Vienna. Then he went for a year to Spain, copying Goya and El Greco at the Prado and marvelling at the rich, dark interiors of the cathedral in Toledo. The Civil War broke out shortly after the young artist arrived

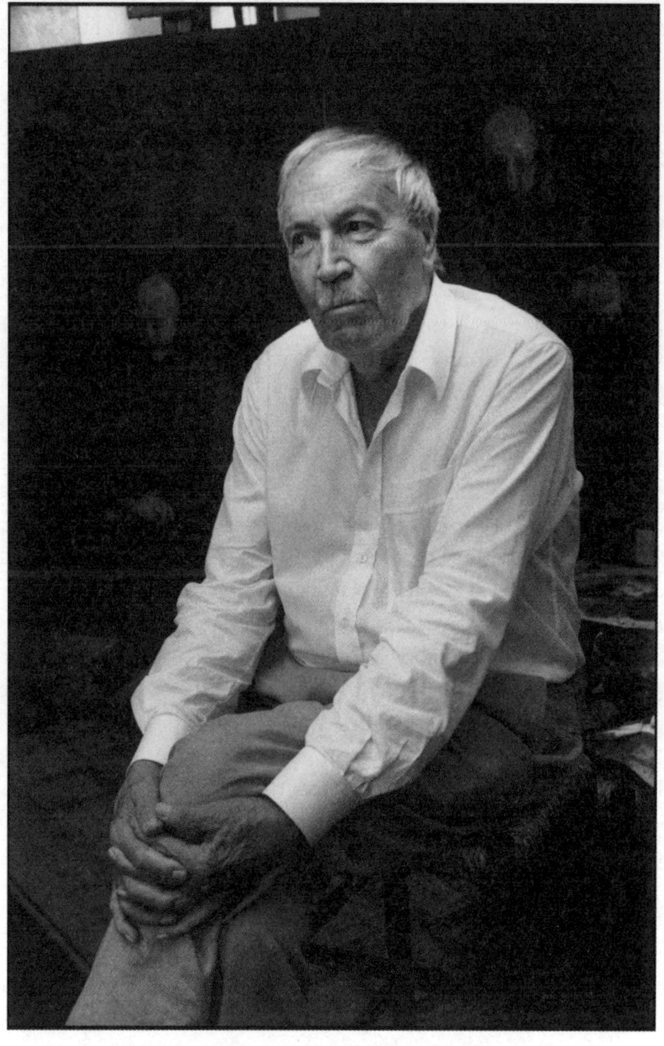

Zoran Music in his Venice studio, 1997, photographed by Martine Franck

in Barcelona; he made his way back home, then travelled further south along the Dalmatian coast to the island of Korcula, where he began painting landscapes of the Karst mountains. Music had admired the Karst since his childhood, and he had been constantly put in mind of the range's barren grandeur by the sierras that he had seen in Castile. These mountains became Music's first real subject, as the result – like all the artist's subsequent themes – of a deep, persistent attachment. Later, he called the Karst the 'matrix' of his art.

Venice had always beckoned both the traveller and the artist in Music. War had been declared yet again. By 1942, both Dalmatia and Slovenia were occupied; and Venice had become all the more alluring since artists and intellectuals from every corner of Italy had taken refuge there. In 1943, Music made his first visit to the city that was to entrance him for the rest of his life. During an exhibition of his work nearby in Trieste, he met Guido Cadorin, director of the prestigious Academy of Fine Arts in Venice, and his young daughter, the painter Ida Barbarigo, who was later to become his wife. Emboldened, Music returned to Venice, held an exhibition of recent paintings at the Piccola Galleria, and haunted the edges of the city to sketch its hallucinatory merging with sea and sky. His fascination with the lagoon and the boats that plied across the Adriatic did not fail to awaken suspicion, as did his friendship with certain members of the Resistance and other signs of his political allegiance. In 1943, Music was arrested by the Gestapo, imprisoned in Trieste, then deported to Dachau.

In the interviews with him that I have published elsewhere, Music gives the most movingly restrained account of his death-camp experience. Horrifying and degrading as his situation became, his desire to make images never lessened; and the moment a typhus epidemic swept the camp, allowing him to draw amongst the dying without fear of detection, the most poignant records of what he had seen were rapidly scratched out on bits of purloined paper and hidden until he was released. 'Without Dachau,' Music remarked memorably, 'I would have been a merely illustrative painter. After Dachau, I had to go to the heart of things.'

Once his health was sufficiently sound, Music went back to Venice. The city seemed like a mirage of beauty and freedom, and he began almost feverishly to record his joy in watercolour sketches of the Palazzo Ducale sparkling in the early morning light, and of the boats jostling on the canals or gliding past the Giudecca. From then on, Venice was to remain one of Music's best-loved themes: he was to return to it in more reflective, even sombre, moods, capturing the glimmering darkness inside St Mark's and the melancholy, ochre facades of its forgotten palaces. Most recently, he has painted the city as he has painted himself, with unsparing insight, as a survivor against the odds. Here Venice becomes a mere veil of buildings stretched against a malevolent sky.

But this adopted city, where the recent internee was soon established in a studio at the top of the Palazzo Pisani, did not drive out earlier memories. Music was already painting only those things that haunted his imagination and which he could see most clearly when he was day-dreaming or sitting with his eyes closed, allowing the images to form of their own accord, stripped of inessentials; he wanted mountains eroded into rock, and figures without masks, caught in full view of their fate. His fascination as a much younger painter with Dalmatian landscapes and the gypsies on horseback that he had known there flooded back, almost as if the nightmare of Dachau had lifted and allowed the recollection of happiness to return. Music painted these memories of his pre-war life with marvellous delicacy and verve, with the flattened perspective and thin, dry colour that he had admired in the frescoes of ancient churches in the Dalmatian hinterland. He also painted evocative little heads of his new wife, Ida, who appears with all the immediacy of a Fayum portrait, gazing across centuries with a clear message of immortality in her eyes.

The nightmare of Dachau never lifted. It had penetrated Music's life more deeply, influencing everything he undertook. If the light danced with such frenetic gaiety on the lagoon, was it not partly in contrast to the darkness of the concentration camp that loomed behind? The memories of Dachau were intensely present, but the painter had not found an adequate form to convey them. And when they first surfaced in his painting, they came so indirectly that they took even Music by surprise. He had been travelling by train through the countryside around Siena, looking closely at another range of mountains that attracted his attention by their strange shapes. They were stripped of all vegetation and looked almost white in the sunlight; down their sides, runnels had formed dark streaks, making them look like ribcages lying side by side. Music was deeply, inexplicably moved. And as he began to paint them, he realized that they reminded him inevitably of the corpses piled several metres high that were part of the everyday landscape of Dachau.

With its evocative subject matter and highly personal style, Music's work began slowly to attract recognition. By the mid-1950s, he felt sufficiently confident to move to Paris, where he joined the Galerie de France and took over a studio from the well-known photographer Brassaï. Thereafter, Paris became the other pole of Music's life, complementing the melancholy beauty of his beloved Venice by its importance as an intellectual and artistic capital. At first, the French cultural climate, still in its vigorous postwar ferment, had an unsettling effect on Music. He had always been prone to self-doubt, constantly questioning the validity of his art; and in Paris he found that most of the successful artists and the influential critics had been won over to the abstract cause. Little by little, Music's belief in his own vision began to fail and he started experimenting with abstract landscapes: beautiful, mysterious combinations of form and colour that nevertheless left him confused and dissatisfied. With his implicit attachment to the great figurative tradition of Western art, the painter began to feel that he had lost his way, and possibly even his identity. A painful crisis followed, during which Music was unable to work at all. Out of the agonizing, self-questioning, and frustration, the first cadavers and walking dead of *We Are Not The Last* emerged.

Once the series had begun, there seemed no end to the memories that clamoured for release. Version after version of the mounds of emaciated corpses, their arms and legs criss-crossed like dead roots, poured out of the survivor, like a recurring nightmare where each time a few salient details – the glittering eyes, the darkness of dead mouths – came back altered in the hallucinating monotony of horror. This was how it was. Like Goya, whose records of atrocity had taken on an altogether different intensity in his eyes, Music could say: '*Yo lo vi*' (I saw it). In Dachau he had seen the dead and the dying piled together 'like logs', often in such numbers that the camp authorities were at a loss to know where to stack them prior to incineration. He had heard the bodies in these piles moving still, limbs creaking like branches, as night fell, and in the morning seen them covered with light snow, never to move again. He had felt the eyes of the corpses following him as he moved among them, and he had been witness to every kind of macabre event in the unreal ceremony:

the official who, with lowered eyes, counted the gold teeth extracted from the dead by marking his notebook each time he heard the metallic sound of a tooth hitting the bucket; the dying prisoner sitting on the head of a dead prisoner as he ate his soup; the corpses not declared so that the living could share their rations.

'You saw so much that you became numb to the horror', Music remembers. 'They would line you all up, and if they sent you to the left, that was to the gas chamber, and if they sent to the right, you would go on living for a few more days. But you became so indifferent you no longer knew if you had been sent to the left or to the right, and you no longer cared. Little by little, you came to accept this universe of cruelty, with its strange, precise rules, as inevitable.' Nevertheless, the painter in Music had not been alienated. He had been deeply moved by what he called 'the tragic elegance' of the corpses, with their long emaciated limbs and fragile fingers, their gaping orifices, and the almost transparent fineness of their skin. It was this vision, above all the suffering and indignity, that came back to haunt him. It was of course specifically a painter's vision. Music was entranced by the unearthly beauty of the bodies, not unlike Claude Monet who had been impelled to set to work as his wife died to capture the bluish pallor of her face. Music even came to see his memory of the cadavers as a kind of treasure, to the extent that he had a nightmare in which he saw them slipping away from him and disappearing out of sight.

It is Music's tenderness that gives such poignancy to these memorials to Dachau's dead. There is no declamation, no hint of vindictiveness or outrage. 'It is something that happened', Music says in his calm, gentle voice. 'It would have been much better if it had not happened. But it did.' The facts are relayed without any attempt at narrative description: there are no commandants or watchtowers, no gas ovens or quicklime graves. There are simply nameless corpses, victims beyond time and place, portrayed with an astonishing painterly restraint. They barely mark the canvas's coarse, open weave with their extinguished presence, as if they had suffered and died with utmost gentleness. Yet they rise up to haunt us with the indictment that never ceases to be true: 'We Are Not The Last.'

Music returned to the Dachau theme several times before he felt that he had expressed it fully. Other subjects closer to hand were not lacking. He made some wonderful studies of roots, which harked back to his experiences in abstraction while incorporating his fascination with the attenuated limbs of Dachau's dead. From there he moved on to landscape, making memorable images in watercolour and oil of a barren, rock-strewn mountain that mirrored his love of nature stripped to its skeleton form. Here Music had found his way back to the earliest source of his art, and it allowed him to spend many contented days watching, thinking, and sketching in total solitude. Venice, lost in mist or glimpsed in the desolation of its rain-soaked facades, was also constantly suggestive. But Music seemed nevertheless to be in search of a subject that might attain the resonance and universality of his Dachau images.

The artist's brief essays in abstraction had made him a more resolutely figurative painter than ever. He had always believed in painting what was closest to him and what he could see most clearly behind closed eyelids: the residue of experience, coming into focus like the glimmerings of light for which he had waited in Toledo's dark cathedral. Being a creature of habit, like most artists, Music went to his studio without fail every day; and even if he was not in a working vein, he would spend his time there pottering around, looking at old pictures, fixing a pastel, or preparing a canvas. Nothing was closer to him as a subject than himself in his studio, and one day in the early 1980s, when Venice and the mountains had temporarily lost their hold, this is what Music began to sketch. The initial sketches developed into more finished drawings, which were taken up in watercolour and gouache, and finally in oil on canvas; and the artist in the studio became the theme of a long series of evocative images in which a lone figure looms out of and merges back into a cavernous space.

With its delicately layered colours – umber and ochre flecked with white, brownish cadmium, and scumbled sky blue – this series radiates the melancholy charm of Music's Venetian scenes. The artist, dressed in the kimono-like gown that he wears to paint, is occasionally represented with his wife, or seated beside an ominously dark rectangle of canvas. Mostly small in format, these studies touch by the simplicity with which they convey the painter's daily round; they allow the spectator behind the scenes, as it were, to witness the strange compulsion and ceremony of image-making. Yet after the 'lesson' of Dachau, such an *intimiste* approach could no longer satisfy Music's need to pare his subject down to an irreducible essence. Delightful though they are, the studio paintings can be seen in retrospect as a prelude to the much grander, more unsparing self-portraits that have occupied the artist almost exclusively ever since.

Nothing in Music's early work prepares us for the *terribilità* of his latest series of self-portraits as an old man. From the picturesque allure of the tiny gypsies on horseback and other Dalmatian motifs to these forbidding recluses, wrapped up in their despair, lies a life of unspoken introspection and suffering. This is Music's truth, the eventual meaning of his journey. At one point, it seemed as if the horror of Dachau had been absorbed and that he would be able to resume, with Mozartian lightness and skill, the joyful themes of his youth. But rather than lightening, the shadow of Dachau that forced him to look profoundly into the nature of human existence has lengthened with time. None of the honours of Music's subsequent life – a retrospective at the Grand Palais, accolades, and decorations – have diverted him from the most troubling questions. Why did I survive? How does one live after Dachau? What is this deferred darkness that awaits me?

The questions are addressed point-blank to the silhouette of an old man sitting naked as he ponders his fate, or edging closer into the shadows, as if to escape scrutiny. He has been shorn of everything, like King Lear, and surrounded by bare canvas. In this meditation, old age does not 'burn and rage at close of day'; it accepts the end with resigned melancholy and a touch of the resilient survivor's black humour. One would be hard put, I think, to find any hint of redemption in these spare, sombre self-portraits. But by tirelessly seeking an answer through the medium of his art, even as the light fails, Zoran Music has given us the most memorable occasion to believe in the spirit of man.

Originally published in *Art International*, Lugano, August–September 1981

20

DADO AND THE ATROCITY OF EVERYDAY LIFE

Miodrag Đurić, universally known as Dado, was, like Music, a close friend of mine, as well as an artist I admired for his extraordinary inventiveness and his readiness to take risks. As I pointed out in the Introduction, as a near-contemporary brought up in a different part of postwar Europe, I understood and shared his view of life as a series of extreme situations. In 2009, when he was already too unwell to travel, Dado asked me to curate a show of his sculptures for the Venice Biennale, where we were offered the courtyard of the elegant Palazzo Zorzi to display the large, complex, and often outlandish works. Dado followed the installation closely from afar, making major and minor changes to the overall look of the show right up until a delegation of Montenegrin government officials arrived by plane and, with traditional plum-brandy toasts and folkloric dances in native costume, declared the event open. What follows is the text I wrote to accompany the exhibition.

Dado is our deeper conscience. Each day, on all the media, we are assaulted by the cruelty and suffering that surges up from disputed border and dark street corner across the globe. The piles of blood-soaked casualties, the sobbing relatives, the villages in rubble, the dead or abandoned children. We know it so well, we wax indignant, then we move on with relief to the football results or the latest misdemeanour of a hapless star.

But Dado does not let us off the hook so easily. He has channelled into his grotesque (but not so exaggerated) imagery all the sufferings of the world. There is hardly a dismemberment or a deformity he has not seized upon, then transformed with infinite, plastic ingenuity into a hundred

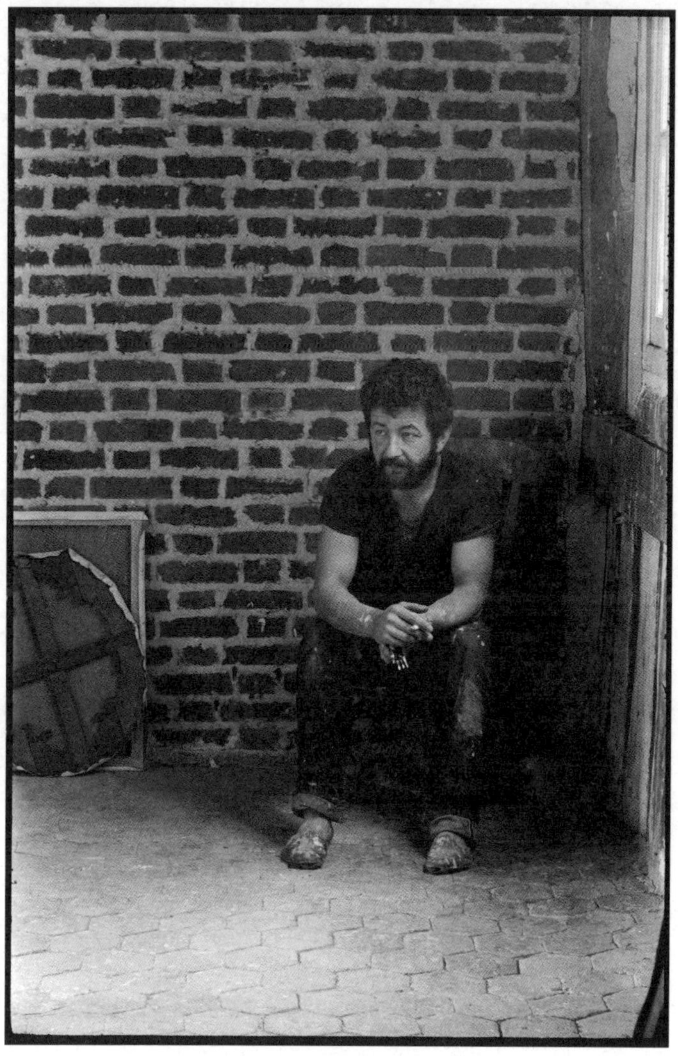

Dado in his studio at Moulin d'Hérouval, Normandy,
France, 1967, photographed by Denise Colomb

variations. If there is any joy in Dado's world, with its hard, sunny colours and merciless blue skies, it is the joy of an endless, pointless proliferation of grotesque misery. There is no end to this multiplication of death and indignity; under Dado's brush and pencil, horror reinvents itself, in ever more intricate refinement, ad infinitum.

At times, one even suspects a certain complacency, as if Dado had become overly at ease in the invention of atrocity. But that would be to misunderstand the artist fundamentally. If, in a memorable aphorism, Churchill concluded that 'the history of mankind is war', Dado would add 'and suffering, deformity, and humiliation'. This is not some game of mock horror that Dado has been indulging in and refining throughout his long career. It is the way he sees life and what he considers most real. What strikes certain spectators of his work as twisted and macabre is Dado's truth, the touchstone by which all else is judged. In his eyes, all pleasantness is a veil, all peace, a camouflage. Under the green grass, the corpse moulders, and in the delicate rose the worm has long been at work.

These are the realities that Dado cannot forget, and which we cannot evade, glutted though we are with daily reports of horror. When we see them transposed and reinvented under Dado's fluent hand, we are not simply reminded of the latest atrocities happening all around us. We are plunged into an awareness of our own mortality – of the precariousness of all life, and the responsibility we share in protecting it against all odds.

THE 'ZORZI ELEGIES'

Some time in the early 1970s in Paris, probably at an opening at the Galerie Jeanne Bucher on the rue de Seine, I got into conversation with an artist who introduced himself simply as 'Dado'. He was unusual in appearance – small and wiry, with dartingly bright, intelligent eyes, chuckling and laughing through a jungle of hair and beard. He was even more unusual in his talk, that jumped from art to scandalous gossip to arcane historical references; and his whole being seemed electrified by what was said in rapidly mumbled, thickly accented, colourful French. I was immediately drawn into his world, first by his vivid personality and unexpected charisma, then by the delicate, haunting strangeness and horror of the paintings he showed me. We saw a lot of each other in the years that followed, in all kinds of scrapes and circumstances, and I began to write about him – the odd review, interview, or catalogue preface. Soon I also had some impressive works of his staring down at me (and staring me down) as I worked, notably a huge collage of painted human fragments floating against an azure sky and a chaotic 'portrait' that he had drawn of me sunk amid a motley selection of other monsters. My 'Dadoization' had well and truly begun.

Then, in the early 1980s, after many sympathetic encounters and a few weird adventures, our ways parted. From being a regular art critic, I became totally wrapped up in editing and publishing the magazine *Art International*; and a decade later, when the publication ceased, I left Paris with my young family to return to London. For his part, Dado no longer hung around so much, full of tall stories and infectious laughter, in the galleries and cafés along the rue de Seine. He withdrew more and more to the old mill he had bought near Gisors in Normandy – to work, to bring up his large family, and to receive the visits of a growing, if somewhat specialist, court of dealers, collectors, and admirers.

Then, a couple of decades later, quite out of the blue (but thanks nevertheless to the loyal friendship of Dado and his wife, Hessie), I was invited to become the 'commissioner' – that strange mixture of art critic, event organizer, confidant, and bodyguard – for his present exhibition at the Venice Biennale.

So, nearly forty years after our first encounter, I returned to Dado and the strange world that he inhabits, both in 'reality' and in his art. What had happened essentially in the meantime? Above all, I realized as I talked to the artist and caught up on his activities, the relatively small tribe of Dadoesque beings trickling from his restlessly inventive hand had since expanded exponentially. Not only had they crowded pell-mell into galleries and museums, books and catalogues: they had overflowed onto entire walls, filling rooms in the artist's home as well as in complicit local pharmacies, deconsecrated chapels (including the amazing, nearby Chapelle St-Luc), forgotten farmhouses, and abandoned coastal block-houses, trailing their eloquent despair and degradation over every surface that allowed him within reach. Somehow the Dado phenomenon – the '*syndrôme Dado*', as the artist likes to refer to it – had gone unchecked, popping up and proliferating in the most unlikely places like spawn or cells – an offensive clearly led by a master strategist (which the artist most certainly is, needing every stealth and invention merely to survive the hectic confusion and demands of his own life).

In other words, in the interim, we have all become increasingly Dadoized. How was it possible? How did we allow ourselves to be invaded more and more deeply by these insidious creatures insolently parading their flayed bodies and lubricious intimacies under our very nose? Could it be that we were drawn in some half-conscious way to these beautifully delineated horrors that tumbled out of the artist's inexhaustible fascination with the macabre? Did we enjoy his ritual humiliations of humankind – as inventively repetitive as the sex acts in the Marquis de Sade – because they pushed back the notions of what was socially and artistically acceptable? Or was it more that they touched us by their vision of our own vulnerability and metaphysical disarray? And in that case were we not seduced by their implicit promise to take us deep into the dung heap of human history – thereby, perhaps, revealing a forbidden truth.

A TRUTH FORETOLD

'History is a nightmare from which I am trying to awake.'
James Joyce, *Ulysses* (1922)

From childhood on, we all know that existence is filled with dark secrets best left unexplored. Peer into the night and you will find the shapes and shadows of terror; shut your eyes, shut your mind, and the unnameable might go away, the fear might subside. Yet Miodrag Đurić, better known from childhood on as Dado, never shut his eyes. On the contrary, he peered further and further into the well of horror until it became his only reality – the truth behind even the most beguiling appearance and the bedrock of his convictions about life.

It is true that there was no lack of horrors for Dado to feed on as he grew up in an occupied, war-torn Montenegro further plagued by internal dissension, famine, and earthquakes. When questioned, as he inevitably is, about his obsession with anguish and pain, Dado will talk about the Italian partisan being led away beneath the window of his family's house in Cetinje to be shot, as well as the corpses he saw hanging for days on end from the gibbet in the main square. (The memories are still fresh and vivid: the soldiers dancing round the partisan's dead body; little Dado's oversized, hand-me-down shoes filling with snow as he crossed the square in fascinated horror; the hair on a decapitated head being carefully combed by the victim's widow.) Some of the horrors seen were soon channelled into drawing, most specifically when Dado's precocious graphic talents were called on by a local surgeon to record the harelip and tiny pointed milk teeth (motifs that still crop up insistently in Dado's imagery) of a boy on whom he was about to operate. It was hardly surprising then that the first picture to make a lasting impression on the young artist was Rembrandt's *Anatomy Lesson*, which hung ominously in reproduction in the study where Dado's grandfather, a physician, received his patients.

All this has a familiar ring, of course. The gifted, sensitive child, traumatized not only by early encounters with cruelty and privation, but also, far worse, by the loss of his mother when he was barely eleven, becomes fixated on the necessity of pain and suffering for the rest of his existence. But such neat explanations miss the point. Hordes of children suffered fates far worse (characteristically, Dado remembers his birth date primarily as the year in which Hitler came to power) than the young Montenegrin prodigy. And very, very few of those who survived went on to dedicate their lives to acting out in thousands of images a drama of imbecility and degradation in which there is no progress, no redemption, and no end in sight. 'I don't know where this obsession I have, this virus, comes from', Dado admits, barely disguising the gusto with which this notion fills him. 'It's as much a mystery to me as to anyone else. Let's just say that my life is a nightmare, and my work is another nightmare.'

THEATRE OF HORRORS

'When you stare into the abyss, the abyss also stares into you.'
Friedrich Nietzsche

Artists are very adept at covering their tracks. Once they have become who they are, they reinvent the paths they took to circumvent the obvious and avoid facile interpretations of their work. 'Never believe what an artist says', David Hockney once said (quoting Sickert, I think), 'only what he does.' One of Dado's great artist heroes, Francis Bacon, was past master at confounding preconceived ideas about himself or his painting. If he were taxed with the apparent horror of his paintings, he would merely reply that he thought people found them horrific because they tended to see life through veils, which his images to some extent removed, confronting them more directly with reality. Similarly, Dado (the 'tender torturer', as he calls himself) looks surprised, even somewhat hurt, when asked the reasons why the figures he creates undergo such delicately and endlessly inventive 'mutilation'. It's not mutilation, he is at pains to explain, as much as a deeper exploration of the complexity and beauty of the human body. Anything less, he continues, is superficial – mere 'dermatological creativity'.

Disingenuous though it sounds, this is how the artist views his own work; and while anxious to protect the secret springs of his creativity, Dado is not merely sidestepping the question or camouflaging his real intentions. Yet there are other, far simpler explanations that have a more direct ring of truth. From his earliest years, Dado showed a prodigious gift for drawing. As soon as he got to school, he began amusing everyone around with the caricatures he produced so effortlessly of his classmates and teachers. The drawings were so sharp and witty that they won him local fame, causing his mother to exclaim proudly that he would be the Walt Disney of his generation. Capitalizing on this, Dado got his friends to make the most ferocious grimaces they could muster as he caught them alive on paper, reliving the thrill of being terrified and terrifying in turn. At this point, of course, the horrors of war, as well as the local hospital that excited his precocious morbidity, were all grist to his graphic mill. The child was father to the man. Even before the trauma of his mother's death and the trauma of exile, the future artist had assimilated all the subjects that he was ever going to need.

An overview of the entire development of Dado's work (an impressively varied achievement now spanning nearly sixty years) reveals that while technique and composition vary constantly and radically – the pigment itself changing from dry and powdery to a diaphanous smoothness then to a rough, unmediated impasto – the themes themselves are almost constant. From the Montenegrin childhood to the present day, reality for Dado has remained rooted in pain, distress, and humiliation. In his unbroken paean to suffering, humour is never altogether distant, erupting through scenes of physical deformity and defeat in flashes of lubricious or satirical hilarity (it is not unknown to find Dado's family and friends – as well as his dealers – surfacing quite recognizably in the human wreckage that he depicts). The outlines of torture and degrees of deliquescence are reinvented with endless resourcefulness and delectation, just as the colours – especially the nursery pink and baby blue – cast a benign light on the worst atrocities, making them just bearable enough to sink deeper and more durably into the viewer's psyche.

Dado would, of course, argue that nothing in the varied aspects of his oeuvre – from engraving and drawing through fresco and easel painting to sculpture and mixed media – in any way equals the violence and horror of the natural world (and a fortiori the man-made world). A walk with him through the woods and fields of his adopted Normandy soon reveals, amid luxuriant foliage beneath a cloudless blue sky, Nature red in tooth and claw: the skeleton of a bird, a dog left to die, an unidentified but perfectly intact ribcage. Such discoveries fascinate and reassure Dado, who then happily returns to his studio to consult some fine ancient prints of animal skeletons in his haphazard studio library or a monumental *Atlas de dermatologie*, whose coloured photographs of the most alarming skin diseases afford him a pleasant interlude. 'A child with two heads', he announced to me once jubilantly, during the perusal of an old volume devoted to such phenomena, 'is in the end merely Nature's way of amusing itself.'

THE ARTIST IN EXILE

> '*One does not inhabit a country; one inhabits a language.*'
> E. M. Cioran

Every night, before he goes to sleep, Dado claimed recently, he sees the silhouettes of the mountains of Montenegro rise up before him. A good half-century after leaving Montenegro (after a spell in prison for minor political disobedience, and to avoid military service), the artist still dreams of the landscape of his childhood as of a paradise lost. From the blonde wheat fields and abundant orchards of the Véxin Normand, where he has spent most of his adult life, Dado revisits a vertiginous rocky landscape rising up ominously, with little for the unusually clean, unusually white sheep (a detail that he underlines) to crop since virtually nothing will grow there. He longs for it and talks about these scenes and the history underlying them eloquently, but he knows he will never go back, sincerely delighted though he is that Montenegro has recently once again become a thriving, independent republic. Long ago, like so many artists and writers during the twentieth century, Dado knew that the only path towards full self-realization lay in exile.

He was indeed so conscious of the fact that in the end he chose a double exile. Highly gregarious by nature, loving to talk and share every kind of experience, Dado was par excellence a metropolitan man when he arrived in France in 1956. A year or two thereafter, there was barely an interesting quartier, bar, or café in Paris that he did not know and did not frequent without falling in with some exotic friends and drinking companions. How he kept going on his slender means, where he slept or ate, remained a mystery even to those close to him. But rugged and resilient as a mountaineer, he reappeared seemingly unscathed from all the bouts of night-long carousing and conversation, eager to tackle a new series of engravings or complete a couple of large intricate canvases for an exhibition.

But the need to work (as well as the need to look after a rapidly growing family) gradually got the upper hand, and as mentioned earlier Dado could be found less and less frequently drifting with friends around Saint-Germain-des-Prés. His capacity for work had always been exceptional; and even when he was haunting the cafés or engaged in banter his hand rarely ceased drawing feverishly on any bit of paper napkin or tablecloth that came to hand. Once he had withdrawn to the unlikely agricultural solitude of the Véxin – in a second exile that isolated him once again from what was comfortably familiar – his powers of production knew no bounds. There, cut off in the oddly beautiful desolation of a mill consisting of several half-timbered, and half-ruined, buildings scattered around a large pond, Dado was able to project the seething mass of imagery within him on to every available surface. Having frescoed vast wall areas, he rested by painting one canvas after another; to draw breath after so many easel paintings, he settled down to sketch out in pencil and pen the supernumerary images that continued to bubble up in his brain.

There appeared to be an irrepressible spontaneity in all the various works that poured from his hand, but in fact Dado, who is a voracious and unpredictable reader – a scholar even, in his highly selective, idiosyncratic fashion – mulls over numerous themes and researches them thoroughly before beginning to incorporate them like a fresh disease into his stream of imagery. The range and diversity of these themes, which can be seen simply by referring to the titles of works listed in catalogues, closely mirror his interests and his reading. Running through one such list at random, one is struck by titles such as: *Histoire naturelle, Buffon*; *Le Livre de Job*; *Haendel Jephta*; *La Révolution française*; *Sterne des Inca*; *Meisodem* (a reference to his friend, the writer Henri Michaux's *Meidosems*); *Galerie des Ancêtres*; *Projet pour 'REPONS' de Pierre Boulez*; *Homage à Newton*; *Le Cardinal de Retz*; *La Passion selon Saint Mathieu*; *Vaisseau de Capitaine Cook*. Thus the natural sciences and religion, music and history, literature and physics are just some of the source material that Dado delves into to spin out new diaphanous evocations of the proliferating weirdness and death-bound bounty of life.

In response to the double exile that he had constructed for himself, I think Dado created two homelands where he was intensely himself and fully at his ease. One quite obviously was his art: a country entirely of his making and where he was the sole, acknowledged king. The other grew simultaneously out of the strange medley of learning, lore, and fantasy that Dado gleaned from old tomes, bizarre encounters, and discussions with experts and enthusiasts in the various fields that fascinate him. This knowledge illuminates Dado's daily discourse and has become so much part of his personality that discussions of the most practical or banal order – train times, a hospital appointment, cashing a cheque – are ineluctably interwoven with choice quotes from Kierkegaard or a national Montenegrin poet, a little-known historical fact about the ravages of the Black Death or Gilles de Rais's preferred modus operandi after raping peasant youths, a reference to an early Renaissance painting or to George Frideric Handel (for whose operas Dado has in fact designed some impressive stage sets). Then, of course, there is nearby Gisors, believed to be the cradle of the Priory of Sion and the site where the Templar Knights buried their treasure, which gives Dado a special local opportunity to indulge his passion as universal historian and myth-maker – the skilled weaver of bad dreams for a generation seeking comfort over truth and which has forgotten how to look directly at the realities of life and death.

DIALOGUES WITH THE DEAD

> *'Every death is an end of the world.'*
>
> Aleksandar Leso Ivanovic (Montenegrin poet, friend of Dado's father)

Having too much talent, too great a facility, has always been a problem for Dado. His virtuoso line conjures up a medley of monsters in minutes, complicating then resolving and refining forms with the ease and conviction of a past master, just as his brush works in the right, slightly off-key pastel hue to set our nerves most on edge. Being strikingly lucid for someone in daily pursuit of delirium, the artist is quite aware of the danger of mere virtuosity, and he has always sought in his art to counter what he can do without real difficulty. This has led him over the course of a long career to try his hand at virtually every genre available, from frescoing large surfaces to book illustration. Nevertheless, for a long time, the very different world of sculpture was only an occasional activity; and it might never have occupied more than a secondary place in Dado's creativity had a disaster not catapulted it to the forefront of his imagination.

In 1989, a fire broke out in Dado's studio at Hérouval, destroying most of the contents, including a number of sculptures that Dado had been working on. Although deeply shaken by the incident, Dado did not allow it to devastate him, as many a lesser mortal might have done. The following day, he returned to his charred sculpture incorporating some of the blackened utensils and detritus that lay still smoking on the studio floor. Thus, as in some ancient legend, Dado's adventure with sculpture was truly born.

Keenly sensitive, as he of course would be, to the catastrophic origins of this new race of objects, Dado thenceforth clutched sculpture closely to his bosom, allowing his febrile imagination free rein on every combination of lowly rubbish with emotionally charged item, creating a new realm for merging the sacred with the profane. An entire new vocabulary thus opened up to Dado and he ransacked it with his habitual fervour, turning his walks through the countryside and into town into intensive forays for the unusual, poetically disinherited element that would offset or top off a particular work. In this new dimension, Dado showed himself to be no less fluently inventive than in everything else he had undertaken. The exact combination of doll's head, tree trunk, and half-melted saucepan or of a homunculus submerged in a bucket welded to an ancient washing machine was the result of constant, agitated restructurings on which Dado's paintbrush would intervene regularly, adding delicate touches with the solicitude of a hen tending to her brood until the whole assemblage of mismatched elements would be dispatched with a generous stripe of colour – like the sudden tricolore of their creator's official recognition.

That this is no exaggeration – no easy piece of artist's myth-making – was amply borne in on the present commissioner. Not only was the choice of work to be presented in the Palazzo Zorzi's evocative courtyard changed on a daily basis, with many of the sculptures eventually being created especially for the site; but the sculptures themselves changed from minute to minute as the artist savagely rearranged their parts – excluding some, grafting on others – while wielding a loaded paintbrush for yet one more coloured accolade. Not even the final photographs for the catalogue could dissuade the artist from the continuous transformation that he lavishes on his work; and only when they had been expertly packed and removed from their origins could they be said to be – at least temporarily – finished.

From the fire that destroyed his studio, Dado drew yet another creative element. His son Domingo had taken numerous photos of the damaged remains, and to his great delight the artist rediscovered them by chance years later. These he had blown up into immense banner-like images to be used as a backdrop to the sculptures in as carefully a choreographed production as any Handel opera. Into the photographs were also incorporated – as if the contents were not already sufficiently dramatic – some of the extravagant imagery that Dado retains after falling into a six-day coma during a recent, severe illness.

However alive they are with references to everything from saints to shoes, the 'Zorzi Elegies' are all dedicated to dead friends and artists that Dado holds dear. Highly charged with personal associations, Dado's most recent sculptures bristle with messages between the living and the dead. Never less than totally generous with the manic flow of his own thoughts, the artist has incorporated scores of lasting obsessions into these impressively varied assemblages. One is his half-humorous, half-sincere Montenegrin's revenge on the Serenissima, long the distant (and of course tyrannical) ruler of Dado's native land; and with customary thoroughness, Dado has read much of the existing records of Montenegro's long subjection by both the Venetians and the Turks.

Taken all together, the sculpture, the banners, and the paintings on wood that have invaded the harmonious, early Renaissance courtyard of Palazzo Zorzi form a single requiem. They reclaim art's primary function, not to entertain with superficial effects, but to concentrate our eyes and minds on the awareness of ourselves and our fleeting passage on Earth. Visitor, as you pass by, stop and feel the tremors. This is no ordinary exhibition. Veils have been lifted, and graves opened. Here the living and the dead commingle. Here you can sense for once accurately and directly your precarious bearings in existence. Here, in the 'Zorzi Elegies', is the fragile but persistent song of what we all become.

Originally published as the preface to the exhibition catalogue *Dado*, Pavilion of Montenegro, Palazzo Zorzi, Venice, 2009. A very personal portrait of Dado can be found in my memoir *The Existential Englishman: Among the Artists in Paris* (London: Bloomsbury, 2019).

PART V

21

IN MEMORIAM:
ANTONI TÀPIES

I was never as close to Antoni Tàpies as I was to many of the other artists discussed in this book, but we met on several occasions in Barcelona and Paris and occasionally spent the evening together. I very much appreciated his extraordinary conversation, which ranged learnedly over all kinds of esoteric subjects, from Eastern philosophy to quantum physics and early Catalan literature. Tàpies could also be slyly ironic and, when he relaxed, unexpectedly earthy and funny. The tribute below was written first as a talk for an exhibition of his work that I organized in Rio de Janeiro, then slightly revised as a catalogue text for a posthumous exhibition in Catanzaro, the capital of Calabria.

I first became aware of Tàpies's work in the late 1960s and early 1970s, when I was making my way as a young art critic and writer in Paris. Anybody in the Paris art world at that time was in fact bound to have to come to grips with Tàpies's painting because it was so uncompromising, with its provocative use of unusual techniques and materials. But at that time, a whole range of artists were using violent or destructive techniques and incorporating base materials and other detritus in their work. Why Tàpies stood out from this particular crowd – and continues to stand out even more clearly today – was that beneath this apparently random chaos of marks and materials there has always been a profound culture and an immense humanism that has informed the work, running beneath it, as it were, like a secret language, lending meaning to what at first sight appears to be chaos. And this has surely been the task of all significant artists, particularly in the twentieth century: to let in the chaos swirling all around us and attempt to refashion it in a way that gives it meaning.

My attraction to Tàpies's work was strengthened by the fact that not only other writers I respected but several artist friends of mine kept a close eye on what he was up to. I remember Francis Bacon, who was never tender towards his fellow artists, above all those who were successful, went back twice to see a show of Tàpies and was clearly impressed. And having reviewed Tàpies's shows regularly and having met him briefly at various vernissages, I took the opportunity, once I had my own magazine, *Art International,* of planning a special issue on his work and travelling to Barcelona to spend some time with him in order to prepare it.

It was a marvellous experience to spend most of the day with the artist in his studio, not only because being able to talk at length to Tàpies was very enlightening, but also because you can find out so much about an artist from the studio itself – from its space and light, from all the finished or half-finished works, the preparatory sketches, all the brushes and other tools scattered around the place and the variety of materials (not unlike the raw ingredients of a meal about to be cooked) lying on the tables and on the floor. And when we left the studio, it was to go to the artist's very impressive library on another floor of the house. And in this particular case, of course, the library was almost as revealing as the studio since Tàpies is not only a legendary reader, reading widely across all the disciplines, but also a scholar, researching deeply into particular areas as apparently, but only apparently, diverse as Oriental philosophy and modern physics.

Tàpies himself was particularly genial during that visit, partly, I think, because he felt he had reached a particular pinnacle in his already long and highly successful career. After much preparation and many delays, the Tàpies Foundation had opened to considerable acclaim, and the artist was very gratified that it was now possible for visitors from all over the world to come and discover the whole trajectory of his work. So this was a moment of recognition and triumph, and although Tàpies is never less than modest and discreet in his manner towards other people, it was clear that he was deeply gratified by the surge of acclaim that the foundation had attracted.

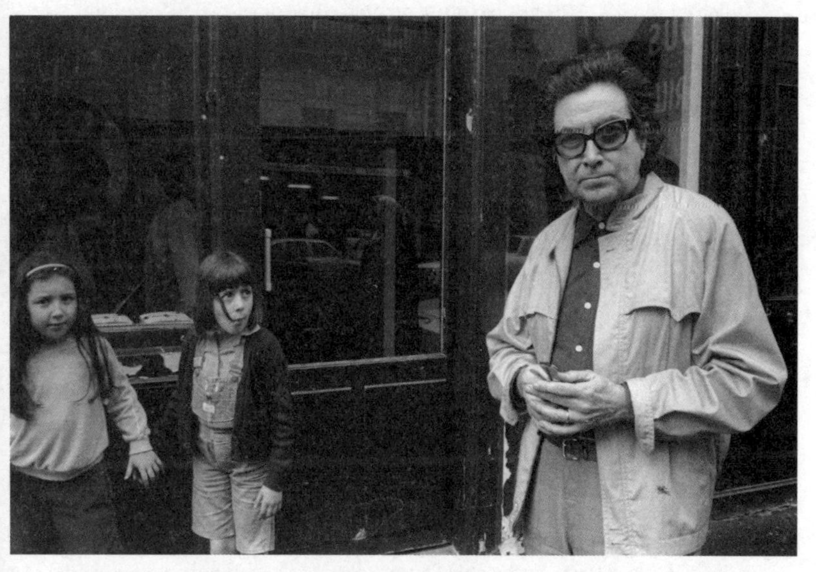

Antoni Tàpies in Paris, 1981, photographed by Sophie Bassouls

Of course, it had not always been so. Tàpies's early career had been arduous, fraught, and even occasionally dangerous. Although born into an educated and comfortably middle-class family (his father was a lawyer with close connections to Catalan public life), Tàpies had lived through the Civil War as an adolescent, which helped forge his lifelong commitment to the left. Before he turned twenty, a long, distressing struggle with lung disease put his plans for the future on hold while nevertheless providing him with the leisure to read widely, listen avidly to music, and draw to his heart's content. In that smouldering gaze, under a smart hat no doubt brought especially from Barcelona, one senses not only a young man's desire to impress, but a kind of unwavering self-belief and determination. For anybody setting out on the thorny path of art, those qualities are indispensable, and Tàpies has always shown an unusual talent for knowing how to put his many qualities to good use. Thus we find that before he arrived in Paris, despite ill health and his family's insistence that he study the law, Tàpies had already set up his own studio in Barcelona, made numerous contacts in the artistic and literary worlds (including what was to be a lifelong friendship with Joan Miró), and exhibited quite frequently for such a young painter.

And in some of the works that he was doing around that time, one can discern a number of preoccupations, as well as techniques, that were to stay with him and develop throughout his career. *Zoom*, for instance, which is one of the earliest works now on show at the Tàpies Foundation, attests to the artist's early interest in symbolism, a movement that flourished in Barcelona and influenced many of the city's most creative spirits, including the remarkable architect Antoni Gaudí. It also points to Tàpies's interest in the problem of the spiritual separated, like this floating, disembodied head, from the more material aspects of the human body. And in *Newsprint Cross*, one of Tàpies's earliest collages, we find the problem revisited: in symbolism, the cross represents the synthesis of the material (the horizontal bar) and the spiritual (the vertical). But what is already particularly characteristic of Tàpies is that he takes the allusive nature of the work a dimension further by creating a cross out of paper torn from the obituaries page of a local newspaper. You also get a hint of Tàpies's deeply ironic and sceptical turn of mind when you notice how much the other paper scraps around the cross look very much like toilet paper, an association that would have been seen as especially subversive in the repressive Franco regime of the time. But it would also be a mistake to limit the introduction of this humble paper – so much part of our daily human routine – to mere iconoclasm. For Tàpies, everything about life and the universe is dual. There is spirit and there is matter, and everything we see and know is a meeting of the two. Both the cross, with its spiritual and mystical connotations, and the lowly paper, with its base associations, are connected – not only because both come from the same source – wood – but because they both participate in the conjunction of spirit and matter. I think this sense of duality runs right through Tàpies's work: spirit and matter commingle, and to illuminate this principle the artist has gone deliberately out of his way to 'elevate' the basest materials – bits of string, rags, empty tins, old shoes, detritus of any kind – into the realm of art as a way of revealing that all elements are fundamentally interlinked and parts of one entity.

As soon as you begin to delve a little bit beneath the surface of Tàpies's work, you begin to realize what a huge, stimulating subject you have opening out in front of you. Tàpies can be read at numerous different levels, approached from a variety of angles. This is no doubt true of any important artist, at any period, but in our present age Tàpies seems to me to stand out by the breadth of learning that underlies and informs his work and the diversity of the influences that have gone into creating it.

For anyone who is familiar both with the artist and his art, the starting point would almost certainly have to be Tàpies's deep-rooted identity as a Catalan – not as a Spaniard, but specifically and unwaveringly from the moment he was able to think, as a Catalan. Catalan history and culture, the Catalan landscape, and the great Catalan city of Barcelona – where Tàpies was born in 1923 and brought up by parents who were both con-scious of their Catalan heritage. And to this list of Catalan attributes, one should certainly not forget to add the Catalan language, which Tàpies considers his unalienable birthright, all the more so since he and his fellow Catalans were forbidden to speak or to write in their mother tongue throughout Franco's long dictatorship. And one could go on and make a complete lecture on the importance of all things Catalan to Tàpies – what he himself calls his 'Catalan consciousness' – but I should like to touch on some of the other important sources of his art.

Since his earliest childhood – and above all during the years he was confined to a sanatorium in the mountains outside Barcelona as a very young man seriously ill with tuberculosis – Tàpies has been a prodigious learner, a devourer of books and images as well as an avid and knowledgeable listener of music. He has long made culture in its widest imaginable form, Eastern and Western, contemporary and historical, artistic and scientific, his own personal province. It began with the books in his cultivated father's library, with the images and records in the family home, and it has never ceased stretching out since. To give some idea of its extent, I will simply cite some of the artist's strongest intellectual passions: Asian literature and philosophy – into which he has gained an unusually deep insight, above all into the knowledge and practice of Zen Buddhism, the whole of European literature and philosophy as well, with a list of admired authors stretching from the arcane (such as the Catalan mystics) to the obvious (Nietzsche, the great Russians, Sartre and existentialism, etc.), modern scientific theory, psychoanalysis – especially Jung and his theories of the collective unconscious and its symbols, Surrealism (which partly defined Tàpies's early artistic development), music (particularly the great classical composers from Bach to Schoenberg, but also concrete music and contemporaries such as Stockhausen), art of course from every period, but with special admiration for Max Ernst, Paul Klee, and his fellow Catalan Miró, all of whom have influenced his art deeply, as well as photography, and so on ...

But to stop the list from becoming too overwhelming and Tàpies appearing as some kind of monstrous egghead, always buried in a book, I should say that he has also always been extremely aware of and highly fascinated by life lived on the streets – and, indeed, many of his paintings have been directly inspired by inscriptions, political slogans, and graffiti found scrawled on walls around Barcelona. Similarly, the great political and social upheavals through which Tàpies has lived – from the Spanish Civil War through the Second World War to the end of the Franco regime – have had quite as great an impact on the artist as any of the areas of more or less specialist or recondite knowledge that I have just enumerated. Tàpies has been politically aware since childhood, not least because his father and his father's friends were politically active, and he himself has been committed to the left since his student days. And he is so much a political animal that he will not accept that any human attribute or action is apolitical, believing that everything we do and think has some eventual political implication. And this belief permeates his art, which he sees as having not only a metaphysical import but a specifically political and social one.

Tàpies has reiterated this conviction repeatedly in texts that he has written and in numerous interviews. There is a passage in the artist's autobiography, written of course in Catalan and entitled *Memòria personal*, that is worth quoting because he brings together a memorable definition of artistic identity with a defence of the artist as a political activist. He is describing his hyperawareness of all kinds of hidden dimensions and forces in the universe and his receptivity to them: 'This mystical consciousness – almost indefinable – seems fundamental to an artist. It is like a "suffering" of reality, a state of hypersensitivity to everything that surrounds us, good and bad, light and darkness. It is like a voyage to the centre of the universe which furnishes the perspective necessary for placing all the things of life in their real dimensions.' And then he adds: 'If one believes that art can constitute a means of obtaining knowledge, then it is absurd to reproach the artist for becoming involved in morals and politics. The only authentic knowledge is born of universal love. When we love we suffer from all the forms of oppression of all dictatorships; and we desire to fight for liberty, for justice and for all that fosters human dignity.'

So that one can say that all Tàpies's paintings, from the artist's own viewpoint, are at one and the same time metaphysical and political, because there is no real division between them – just as he sees no division between mind and body, spirit and matter. But while there is a political undercurrent or political implications in many of Tàpies's works, there are also specifically political paintings. A militant Catalan anarchist, Salvador Puig Antich was one of the last political prisoners to have been executed under Franco. He was arrested after a car bombing in which a policeman was killed – apparently by another policeman. Despite obvious flaws in the case for the prosecution, Puig Antich was sentenced and, despite worldwide protestations, garrotted, at the age of twenty-four. In commemorating this brutal act, Tàpies has produced an almost achromatic painting, with the colour, like Puig Antich's life, draining away in a few last drips. This is underlined by the small colour chart added at the top of the canvas, which can be seen as a memory of colour – a reminder that somewhere outside the drabness of the present, with its harsh tyranny, colour and the normal freedoms and joys of life still exist.

It is interesting to note that, while colour plays a vital role in Tàpies's art, the range of colours he employs tends to be restricted. Black and white, greys, browns, and ochres tend to dominate his palette. Tàpies himself has said that he looks for 'colours that are close to a visionary, mystical world, the colours that are beneath superficial reality, the colours of illusions, dreams and visions, the colours of emptiness and space … For me, the colour of emptiness is an aid towards meditation.' This subdued palette – particularly when compared to those used by artists who depend on the language of colour, like Mark Rothko, say, or Sean Scully – this subdued palette springs no doubt from the artist's natural asceticism and reserve, but also because Tàpies feels that he does not need bright or violently contrasted colour to make his point, like someone who does not have to raise his voice in order to be heard. The colours are very much of the town, the urban landscape with its peeling facades and gritty, graffiti-covered walls that have so deeply penetrated the artist's consciousness. (It is perhaps worth recalling here that, by strange, some might say predestined, coincidence, Tàpies means 'walls' in Catalan.)

And although Tàpies is quite capable of startling us with a sudden, unfamiliar gash of crimson or intense blue, he derives quite as much expressive means from the actual texture – gritty, lumpy, scoured, gouged, scratched, dotted – of his paintings. Or from their very materiality, which is an aspect of Tàpies that comes back time and again – even in his titles. From early on, the artist says in his autobiography, he was 'obsessed with materiality, with the pastiness of phenomena which I interpreted using a thick substance, a mixture of oil paint and whiting like an inner raw material that reveals the "noumenal" reality which I did not see as an ideal or supernatural world apart, but rather as the single, total and genuine reality of which all things are composed'.

In the latter part of his career, Tàpies has gradually evolved a whole parallel universe of fully fledged, unconditionally three-dimensional sculpture, often elevating humble objects such as a forlorn bathtub or a chunky bag to an unexpectedly iconic status. Here, very graphically, it is as if he were bringing his political belief in the equality of all members of society to the realm of objects: nothing is too lowly, neither a foot, a bunch of straw, or a discarded bathtub, to be considered on a level with a Rodin or a Brancusi. However seemingly banal, they too can be set on a pedestal and admired by all and sundry. And of course, thanks to Tàpies's magic touch, they do become objects of importance, even veneration. Think of the muscles warmed, the cares soothed, the dreams released in this tub, or the changing contents of that bag, and you have the whole of life, in all its aspirations and fragility.

While we are on the subject of the very different and demanding medium of sculpture, which Tàpies has explored with such innovative and startling results, it would be good to mention the diversity of his artistic means. There is not a medium or area of artistic production, I think, that Tàpies has not made his own. Alongside painting and sculpture is his devoted activity as a printmaker. He has also produced numerous illustrated books, above all in conjunction with his close poet friends, and made theatre sets. He has, of course, participated in numerous films about his work and, above all, written and published widely, not only on his life and work, but books on culture and society in general. And in all these various areas, he has never been less than prolific. It is enough to make one despair!

More seriously, I used the expression Tàpies's 'magic touch' earlier for a very specific reason. For Tàpies, art and magic are essentially synonymous. Some of you may have seen the video on the artist and his work that accompanies the present exhibition. It begins with Tàpies walking round and round a blank canvas stretched out on the studio floor, dragging his feet, clicking his fingers. This was not done as some atmospheric gimmick for the camera: this is how Tàpies approaches a new work, often after days of indecision, circling the studio, sometimes even chanting to himself, not knowing what he is looking for, but waiting, waiting attentively for the moment where he feels various forces coalesce, giving him the sudden sense of a unity within the vast diversity of things and allowing him suddenly to bring forth the splash of paint or a sudden jet-black ideogram from which a fresh image will arise.

The main function of a work of art, in Tàpies's view, is to make the spectator see and think anew. We are so surrounded by visual messages and subtle propaganda of all sorts, he believes, that the artist's principal function is to clear the eye and the mind to allow a re-questioning and re-evaluation of reality. 'When you look,' Tàpies says in one of his texts, 'never think what painting (or anything else) "should be" or what most people would like it to be. A painting can be everything. It can be a burst of sunlight in a tempest. It can be a storm cloud. It can be a footprint on a road or – and why not – a foot that stamps on the ground meaning "enough!" It can be the air of dawn filled with hope or the acrid mustiness that rises from a prison. The blood stains of a wound or the song of a whole people under the blue or yellow sky. It can be what we are, today, now and always. I invite you to play, to look attentively.… I invite you to think.'

And on this all-important theme of looking, Tàpies goes on to say: 'How can we learn to look at things properly and not find in them only what we are told is there rather than what is there? Here is an innocent game I suggest that you play.… Look at the simplest object, take, for instance, an old chair. It does not appear to be of much importance – but think of the whole universe that is within it: the hands and the sweat of the man who sawed the wood that was once a robust tree, full of life, in the heart of a dense forest high in the mountains, the weariness it has soothed, the joys and sorrows it has doubtless supported.… All this, absolutely all, represents its life and has its own importance. Even the oldest chair has in it the initial force of the sap which once came up from the earth in the forest and again provides the heat when one day, having become kindling wood, the chair is burnt in someone's fireplace.'

Inevitably, I have only been able to touch on a certain number of the important aspects of Tàpies's art. I realize now, to my chagrin, that I have barely mentioned his extremely rich and inventive use of a huge range of materials and techniques. His whole oeuvre is in fact a kind of technical *tour de force*, and whatever Tàpies undertakes, its conceptual originality is synonymous with the actual way it is made and the materials – from marble dust to a chair leg – that go into it. Tàpies is an alchemist, a transmuter, taking the dross of daily life and turning it into the gold of a more penetrating vision. And this, in the final analysis, is how Tàpies sees his pictures – as windows onto another reality, cleared of certain illusions and opening into perspectives that are often vaguely sensed, in dreams or the odd epiphany, but rarely followed up and explored. This is what Tàpies does for us: he explores the unconscious, the deepest roots of the imagination, and gives it a form that encapsulates its disturbing strangeness. And I should like to leave you with a last quote from Tàpies himself: 'A picture is nothing', he states with finality. 'It is a door that leads to another door. Art, however excellent, will always simply be another manifestation of the *Maya*, of the deception that is everything. And the truth we seek will never be found in a picture; it will only appear behind the last door that the viewer succeeds in opening by his own efforts.... For art is like a game, and only by becoming very innocent – and perhaps this is true of all human activities – shall we grasp the profound meaning that it possesses.'

Originally delivered as a lecture at the exhibition *Tàpies*, Centro Cultural Banco do Brasil, São Paulo, October 2004

22

THE PARADOX
OF FRANCIS BACON

I have spent a great deal of my career writing about Bacon, from reviews to catalogues and whole books. This piece for the *Sunday Times* does not add much, but it has the advantage of brevity: I had to boil down everything I know about him into an essence that could be easily absorbed. I have had some practice at it in conversation because people always ask me what he was 'like', in a nutshell. Insofar as you can contain such a complex and contradictory phenomenon in a nutshell, this is as good a summary as I can provide.

'How marvellous he's taking you everywhere and telling you everything', John Deakin, Soho wit, and Francis Bacon's favourite photographer, said to me in 1963. I had come to London some weeks before in the hope of interviewing Bacon for a student magazine, and Deakin had introduced me to him with muttered misgivings at the bar of the French House. Deakin was visibly delighted that we had hit it off. 'Now make sure you get it all down, my dear', he admonished in high-camp tones. 'It could be very important one day!'

I did get it down, one way or the other. While weaving my way woozily back to a friend's sofa late at night or to my digs in Cambridge, I copied out all kinds of half-understood phrases – 'shorthand of despair', 'unlocking the valves of sensation', or 'homosexual love is both more tragic and more banal'. But I hardly needed to. Having been absorbed with vast quantities of champagne, I still had Bacon's definitions bubbling up in my mind, and I could reel them off, staggering around the room with exaggerated imitations of the Bacon voice and the Bacon gestures.

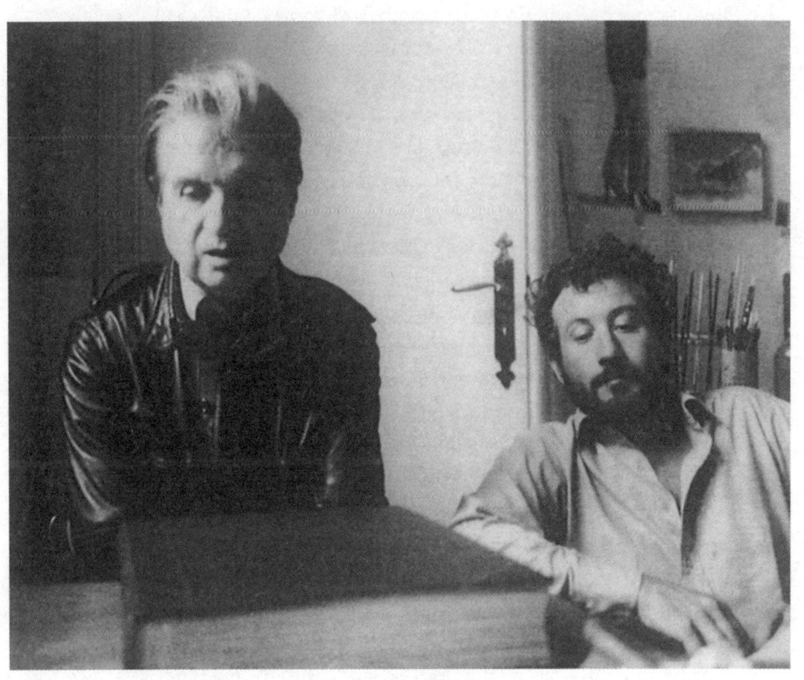

Francis Bacon and Michael Peppiatt in David Hockney's Paris studio, 1975, photographed by David Hockney

'Well that's all there is', I would repeat with a smile to alarmed friends. 'We are born and we die, and in the interval we attempt to give life a meaning through our drives.'

I did not realize it at the time but, more than grappling with Bacon's pronouncements on art, love, and death, I was attempting above all to get a measure of the man. It is rare to meet a genius at any point in one's life. But to meet one when you are twenty and know no one even remotely comparable – in brilliance, compassion, and devilry – marks you for ever. I have been lucky enough to meet a few remarkable people since, but I am still coming to terms with that initial resounding impact on my life that began in the bars and clubs of Soho, then continued to rise, in London, Tangiers, and Paris, for some thirty years until Bacon's death.

What was Bacon *really* like – behind the myth that grows almost daily around him? I have often tried to put it in a nutshell, only to realize that whatever formula I come up with is at best half true. 'Whenever he came into a room, any room,' one of my quick answers runs, 'you could feel the temperature go up. Suddenly there'd be a new vitality, with people outdoing themselves in talk and laughter and drink and generally carry-ing on.' Bacon put you, and anybody else who was drawn to him, on their mettle. When you were with him, you were subtly but inexorably obliged to think more penetratingly and express yourself more clearly. You became unusually self-aware, often painfully and disturbingly so. 'You've ruined my life by making me think about myself!' Bacon's lover, Peter Lacy, once shouted, suddenly rounding on him and no doubt meting out the violent punishment that Bacon craved. But in the end Lacy could not take that heightened self-awareness, and he drank himself deliberately to death – his end coinciding, as we now know so well, with the opening of Bacon's first retrospective at the Tate in 1962. Similarly, poor George Dyer, more vulnerable by far and the other great love of Bacon's life, killed himself with drink and drugs on the eve of Bacon's great triumph as the Grand Palais retrospective of his work opened in Paris in 1971.

What he was like *really* was a man strung perpetually between the extremes of his temperament. Bacon could, quite literally, be one thing and its opposite. Thus the painter of doom and gloom would regularly emerge from a drunken gambling spree with thugs in Soho to take tea with upright and uptight collectors, charming them into buying another of his terrifying (and already terrifyingly expensive) pictures. Or he would demolish another painter's reputation with a few waspish asides, then worry that his guests hadn't had enough caviar and Roederer Cristal and hurriedly order more. Or, again, he might abandon himself to the further reaches of a sadomasochistic orgy before hurrying to the bedside of a sick friend with the most delicate and thoughtful of gifts.

During our long, involved friendship I was very rarely the recipient of his nastiness. Once, emboldened by a mindless quantity of fine Bordeaux, I challenged his interminable put-down of David Hockney's work, and he rounded on me like an animal at bay, the hair bristling at the back of his neck. On another occasion, during a dinner with some young artists at the Coupole in Paris, I dared to differ from one of his repetitive diktats on Van Gogh and received the rough edge of his tongue for my pains. And more interestingly, and for me at least more incomprehensibly (since he had accepted my marriage without demur), Bacon grew white and breathless with fury when I told him, during a dinner at Bibendum in London not long before his death, that my first child was about to be born.

On the other hand, I was constantly the recipient of his attentiveness and generosity. It was not just a question of being invited to countless banquets at the best restaurants and grandest hotels – or, on a few memorable occasions, being backed (with sums I myself could not possibly have afforded) to try my luck at roulette, and when I won being commanded sternly to keep the winnings. Bacon's largesse permeated our relationship in much more subtle and telling ways. When a close friend of mine had a bad fall and broke her back, the first person to call, offering advice and funds, was Bacon. Having taken on an art magazine that I was trying to relaunch from Paris with little money and less business sense, I was considerably helped by Bacon's enthusiasm and his practical support, which included introducing me to potential backers for the project.

Bacon could also be a tower of strength when things went wrong in very personal areas of one's life. My father's death in the mid-1980s sparked various, mid-life crises and my whole existence in Paris fell apart. Bacon picked up instinctively on the difficulties that I was going through, and when we next met he took me on a trip through London that I will never forget. After dinner in the art-deco splendour of Claridge's, we went gambling and I – as happy in gaming as I had recently been unhappy in love – had a considerable win. We then swung round to Annabel's for more champagne and a midnight supper accompanied by a sublime claret. At this point, buoyed up by Bacon's wit and vitality, my spirits began to revive. But Bacon, who had staged all this to pull me through my despair (as he might have described it), did not stop there. 'There are all these girls – why don't you ask them to dance', he kept saying to me until I overcame my shyness and pranced dementedly about on the spangled floor until dawn. No therapy could have worked better. The following day I woke up giggling (for the first time in months) at the extravagances of the night.

However Satanic Bacon might look, trussed up in his Nazi-style black leather greatcoat, however venomous his drunken tirades waxed, this instinctive compassion never left him. It was one of his many paradoxes, just as he seemed at times the most feminine of men, intuitive and yielding, and at others the toughest, most daring, and dominantly masculine. Similarly, he would interrupt a mammoth drinking bout taking him from pub to club across London to consult his doctor, or top up on some bizarre health food (he took garlic pills addictively) after having consumed the richest dishes on every fancy menu in town. The man who thundered against God and the universe would allow himself to be taken meekly in hand by Valerie Beston, his diminutive minder and nanny-figure ('Valerie at the gallery', as Bacon called her), who told him which appointments he needed to keep – from art-world bigwigs to the electrician. The high roller who squandered fortunes on roulette went home on the Tube.

All these contradictions stretched Bacon's sensibility and kept him in a state of tension that was as palpable in the man as it is in his pictures, radiating waves of intensity. But the greatest paradox he kept to the last. Whoever could have imagined that Bacon, the virulent, lifelong atheist – painter of screaming popes and bestial couplings – would choose to be cared for by nuns when he became very ill? He had actually gone on record saying that he could conceive of nothing worse than dying amongst nuns. Yet on his last trip to Madrid, when he knew he was at death's door, he returned to the Servants of Mary, dying under a crucifix and being cremated to the sounds of Gregorian chants. Of all the enigmas that hover over Bacon's tumultuous life, this is surely the most hauntingly mysterious.

Originally published in the *Sunday Times*, London, 28 September 2008

23

THE LEGACY OF GENIUS: VAN GOGH AND BACON

When my wife, the art historian Jill Lloyd, was organizing her ground-breaking *Van Gogh and Expressionism* exhibition in 2007 for the Neue Galerie in New York, she invited me to contribute an essay to the catalogue. I knew that of all the painters Bacon admired, from Velázquez to Picasso, there was none he felt closer to, as an artist and as a man, than Vincent van Gogh, whose letters he constantly reread and referred to. Van Gogh, Bacon always held, was a 'realist', just as he himself was a realist, endeavouring to convey as intensely as possible the 'reality' of his deepest sensations about life. Attractive and convincing as this argument sounded as Bacon repeated and refined it over the course of numerous champagne-fuelled discussions, it hardly withstands sober scrutiny. Degrees of 'realism' are impossible to gauge for the simple reason that the very concepts of 'realism' – and, a fortiori, 'reality' – resist any durable definition. Bacon thought of himself as a 'realist' because he felt that his art derived directly from lived experience.

But Bacon's insistence on 'realism' was also a way of rejecting claims that he had been influenced by Surrealism or, in his mind worse still, by Expressionism. Indeed, he went to lengths to dissociate himself from all movements, partly because he believed that purely stylistic, comparative analysis would weaken the power of his imagery. Nevertheless, he would have seen Expressionist (and Neue Sachlichkeit) shows in Berlin, just as he followed aspects of Surrealism during his stays in Berlin and Paris in 1927–8. Rereading this essay about Bacon's near-identification with Van Gogh makes me want to explore other influences on his work – namely those that he rejected of Expressionism and, to some extent, Surrealism so peremptorily.

From our present perspective, it is easy to see how the influence of Vincent van Gogh's life and work has drifted like a pollen through the entire course of twentieth-century art, affecting it in ways that range from the obvious to the widely but barely perceptible. Van Gogh had a formative impact on the leading German and Austrian Expressionists, as this exhibition reveals in depth for the first time. But while the painters gathered in this show were demonstrably his most direct heirs, Van Gogh proved no less vital to Henri Matisse, André Derain, Maurice de Vlaminck, and the entire Fauve movement. Van Gogh's influence has in fact been so pervasive that he might be regarded, with Paul Cézanne, as one of the two great sources of inspiration for the course of twentieth-century art. In Nietzschean terms, the two painters could be seen as contrasting forces, with the Apollonian Cézanne focusing on underlying structure and classical balance, while the Dionysiac Dutchman insists on the primordiality of instinct and expressive directness.[1]

REALISM OVER EXPRESSIONISM

Countless artists have been touched by Van Gogh, whether by his art, by his life, or indeed by his letters, with their poignant account of his inner torments, his ambitions, and his devotion to his art. But surely none of them showed as complete an identification with Van Gogh, both as a painter and as a human being, as Francis Bacon, for whom, early on in his career, the Dutch artist took on a talismanic importance. Bacon identified above all with Van Gogh's overriding desire to recreate reality, however exaggerated or distorted the means used, since for both artists, nothing counted more, or was more difficult to achieve through art, than the recreation of life intensely lived. As we shall see, both artists were convinced – for all that both have been termed 'expressionist' – that they were first and foremost realist painters, involved in the most direct and telling representation possible of the world as they experienced it.

The high point of Bacon's involvement with Van Gogh came in the latter part of the 1950s, when Bacon painted an extensive series of variations on *The Painter on the Road to Tarascon*, which Van Gogh had executed in July 1888, during the richly productive summer of his stay in Arles. Originally in the collection of the Kaiser Friedrich Museum

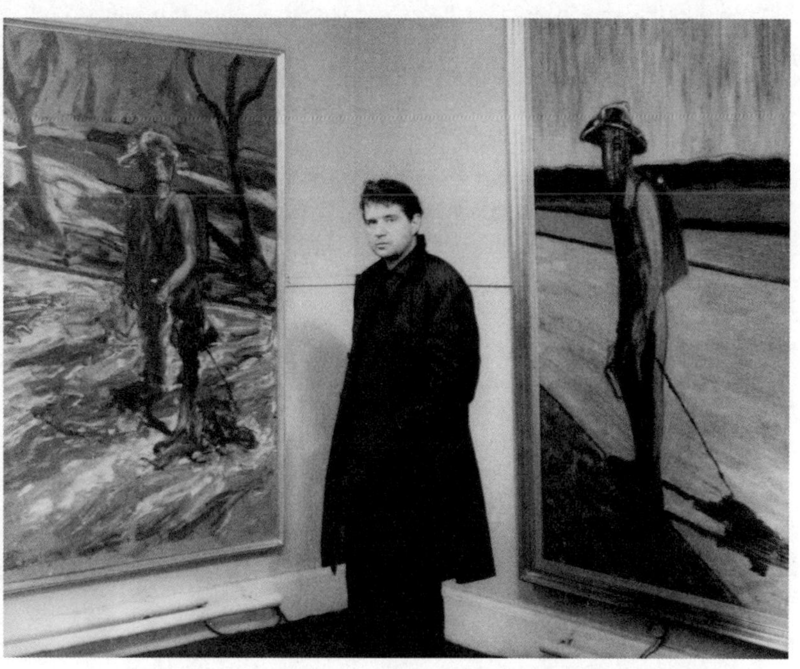

Francis Bacon in 1957, with two paintings from the series inspired by Vincent van Gogh's *The Painter on the Road to Tarascon*, photographer unknown

in Magdeburg, this poignant portrait of Van Gogh on his way to paint *sur le motif* was destroyed by a fire bomb in 1945, some eleven years before it became such an obsessive focal point for Bacon.[2] Only a colour reproduction of the work survived; and it was copies of this – ripped out of art books – that Bacon used as the starting point of what was to become an intense, anguished homage to Van Gogh.[3]

By this stage in his career, Bacon was quite accustomed to painting in series. As a very young artist, he had produced a number of Crucifixions and, more famously, from 1949 onward, an extensive series of variations on Velázquez's *Portrait of Pope Innocent X*. Bacon had also worked on other subjects in a serial fashion (partly because of his fascination with images in motion), creating seven versions of *Man in Blue*, for instance, and several studies of *The Sphinx*. In fact, like many painters – including Van Gogh himself – Bacon tended to work on specific themes obsessively until he felt he had exhausted their possibilities.

ROADS TO EXCESS

At first, there seems much more to oppose Van Gogh and Bacon than to associate them. Whereas Van Gogh came from a parson's family, of restricted means but with relatives in more prosperous, commercial activities such as art-dealing, Bacon was born into a family where new money (from his mother's steel-manufacturing family) had given a temporary boost to his father's faded aristocratic origins (his forebears were landowners of recognized military valour, with claims of kinship to the original Francis Bacon, of statesmanly and philosophical renown). Both artists tried and troubled their families to such an extent that they were kicked unceremoniously out of their childhood homes. But where Van Gogh was drawn to the service of God and the plight of miners in the Borinage, Bacon turned to the fleshpots of London, Berlin, and Paris – painting and prostituting himself with what we may now safely call gay abandon.

'The road to excess', William Blake suggested, 'leads to the palace of wisdom.' From the outset, both artists were almost outrageously excessive. Van Gogh's faith peaked early on into an intolerable religiosity (even his sister Willemien commented wryly about his being 'drunk on religion'); and his beliefs, whether about God or later on about art and society, were clearly of an intensity that frightened or alienated most people. There is a description of Van Gogh coming into a gathering in Montmartre, where among others Henri de Toulouse-Lautrec happened to be present, placing his pictures (unannounced and uninvited) all around the room, then waiting with all-too-obvious pent-up urgency for a reaction. From these and numerous other anecdotes, one can imagine how painfully awkward and embarrassing he must often have been, pure and ultimately sound though his motives were. Whether he is mounting the pulpit to expound on a chosen scripture or explaining his faith in a particular theme or form of painting, Van Gogh seems to scorch the ground in front of him by the fire of his conviction. Bacon had deep convictions too, but he also had a keen sense of life's vanity, not to say its futility. This encouraged him to push every situation to its limit, sometimes dangerously (after his death, his friend Lucian Freud summed him up as 'the wildest and wisest man I ever knew'). Whereas Van Gogh never relinquished his belief in an overarching metaphysical structure that gave all acts an ultimate significance, Bacon – also very much a man of his own time – bolstered his existence on Earth with the existential conviction (much repeated, like a tantra) that 'we come from nothing and we go to nothing, and in the short interlude between we give life a meaning through our drives'.

As their careers and their highly distinctive styles developed, the differences between the two artists grew ever more marked – at least, on the surface. Unkempt and visibly eccentric, Van Gogh trod a lonely path with little encouragement and no social or financial success. Impeccably dressed and at ease in every situation and milieu, Bacon meanwhile had a knack for making himself the centre of attention; and however pain-filled and repellent his early paintings seemed to the postwar world, he gradually built up a devoted following of collectors, museum directors, critics, and dealers until he became internationally famous. Where Van Gogh eked out a meagre existence, with his extravagances limited to visiting low-class brothels and drinking absinthe in workers' cafés, Bacon was a high roller, gambling for vertiginous stakes at exclusive casinos and treating his friends to champagne and caviar at the Ritz (although, as a very heavy drinker, Bacon would undoubtedly have echoed Van Gogh's poignant confession: 'If the storm within gets too loud, I take a glass too much to stun myself').

Both artists were preyed on by inner demons (Romantic and approximate as the notion remains). Sophisticated, wily, and a great accommodator of opposites, Bacon appears to have entered into some Faustian pact with his tormentors, at least to the extent that they fed his myth and did not come to claim him while he was alive. Even so, Bacon was highly aware of their presence in his life: he saw them as Furies, the Erinyes of Aeschylean tragedy, and he believed they punished him in other ways, through guilt and the death of those he loved most. Van Gogh was eventually overwhelmed by his demons, although the reasons for his suicide on that particular summer's day in 1890 have never been entirely understood. Yet had Van Gogh's personality not been so irremediably split, one cannot help but wonder, could his paintings have radiated that unique discordant intensity? Was his fractured spirit not the condition of his genius and the horribly high price he had to pay? William Butler Yeats observed that 'no mind can engender till divided into two'; to which one is tempted to add, in the case of both Van Gogh and Bacon, that the more deeply divided the mind is (short of incapacitating madness), the more creative it has to be merely to survive.

TRUTH TOLD BY A LIE

This catalogue of differences could be extended, but the links and similarities between the two artists are in fact more numerous and more striking. Both men were virtually self-taught, for instance, and long depended on scrounging tips from other artists before they evolved their own highly idiosyncratic techniques (or what French artists call familiarly '*la cuisine*'). Partly as a result of this, both painters manifest a certain awkwardness not only in their compositions but in their handling of paint, which was to give their imagery an unusually direct, unmediated force (although Bacon lost some of this rawness of transmission in the latter part of his career). Each artist, in his distinct way, became a consummate portraitist, focusing on an inner circle of friends and acquaintances and thereby creating the most memorable portrait gallery of his time (thanks to what Van Gogh aptly termed the 'radiance and vibration of our colourings').[4] Both also chose to paint on rough canvas, with Van Gogh experimenting with jute and Bacon preferring the unprimed side of the canvas because it had more 'tooth' and gave his paint a dragged effect. Like Van Gogh (and it may well have been a notion he adopted from Van Gogh), Bacon regarded many of his pictures as studies, rather than fully fledged compositions, and he entitled a great many of his paintings 'Study of' or 'Study for'; like Van Gogh again, as mentioned earlier, Bacon worked above all in series, and when he worked, he painted with great intensity and at breakneck speed – as of course did Van Gogh.

Most importantly, however exaggerated or distorted their imagery appeared (to their contemporaries, above all), the two artists insisted throughout their careers that they were realists. As outlined earlier, they were concerned above all with portraying as intensely as they could the reality they found before them and within them. And a quality the two painters undoubtedly share is the sheer force of their vision: when seen in a roomful of other artists, both Van Gogh and Bacon 'leap' off the wall, their very paint-marks conveying a greater urgency than those around them. For Bacon, who loathed being viewed as an 'expressionist' ('after all,' he would say archly, 'I have nothing to express'), the belief in the realism of his images went to the core of his artistic credo; he would spend hours attempting to define his own notion of realism, notably when talking to his great friend, the French writer Michel Leiris, to whom he once wrote a much deliberated letter in order to set out his own understanding of the concept.[5] In the interviews I had with him, for instance, Bacon returned repeatedly to the notion of realism: 'It's a very complex thing', he insisted. 'After all, it's not the so-called "realist" painters who manage to convey reality best. I mean, I saw an extraordinary picture by Monet the other day.... It was one of his views of the Thames, but you couldn't make anything out in the first instant because everything was covered in seagulls. It's the most extraordinarily inventive thing, and yet very real – a kind of fog of seagull wings over the Thames.' And again, in discussing Picasso, Bacon came back to the theme: 'The period that interests me the most is the late twenties and early thirties – you know, the beach scenes at Dinard where you see those very curious figures turning keys in the beach huts. And for me that is real realism, because it conveys a whole sensation of what it's like to be on the beach. They're endlessly evocative, quite beyond their being extraordinary formal inventions.'[6]

Significantly, talking about the way a great image takes hold of our imagination put Bacon in mind of Van Gogh, notably when he said to David Sylvester: '[The great image] has its own power, because it has reinvented its own realism. And Van Gogh is one of my great heroes because I think he was able to be almost literal and yet by the way he put on the paint he gives you a marvellous vision of the reality of things. I saw it very clearly when I was once in Provence and going through that part of the Crau where he did some of his landscapes, and one just saw in this absolutely barren country that by the way he put on the paint he was able to give it such an amazing living quality, given that reality the Crau has of just plain, bare land.'[7] In both Van Gogh and Bacon, there can be no doubt that the realism in question consisted of a subjective realism. As Van Gogh put it in a phrase that has become famous: 'True painters ... don't paint things as they *are* ... but as *they* feel them.' And Bacon echoed this repeatedly, coming up with parallel statements, such as, 'I am only trying to make images that come off my nervous system as accurately as possible.'[8]

In the same letter, Van Gogh continues with a phrase that Bacon frequently quoted: 'My great desire is to learn to make such inaccuracies, such variations, reworkings, alterations of the reality, that it might become, very well – lies if you will – but – truer than the literal truth.'[9] And Bacon puts this concept into his own terms when he discusses this remark of Van Gogh's in an interview: 'I believe that realism has to be reinvented. It has to be continuously reinvented. In one of his letters Van Gogh speaks of the need to make changes in reality, which become lies that are truer than the literal truth. This is the only possible way the painter can bring back the intensity of the reality he is trying to capture. I believe that reality in art is something profoundly artificial and that it has to be recreated.'[10] And later Bacon returned to his admiration for the unique intensity of Van Gogh's painting in the following little-known remark: 'Van Gogh got very near to the violence of life itself. It's true to say that when he painted a field he was able to give you the violence of grass. Think of the violence of the grass he painted. It's one of the most violent and abominable things, if you really want to think about life.'[11]

Van Gogh's *Letters* were prominent among the handful of books (with Aeschylus, Shakespeare, Proust, T. S. Eliot) that Bacon kept by his bedside and reread constantly. Alongside his admiration for Van Gogh's art, Bacon became fascinated by the spontaneous variety of ideas and depth of insight that characterize the Dutchman's letters. This in turn suggests another similarity between the two artists. Although he did not write fluently, as Van Gogh did, Bacon's catalogue statements and some of his letters are nevertheless remarkably perceptive. He had a wide range of interests and talked brilliantly, often with a memorable turn of phrase. And some of the many interviews that Bacon gave – notably his extensive conversations with Sylvester – rank, like Van Gogh's letters, among the most revealing documents ever recorded on the life and thoughts of an artist.

THE HAUNTED FIGURE

While Bacon's specific engagement with Van Gogh lasted a relatively short period of time (essentially 1956–7, then again in 1959–60), Van Gogh had long occupied a prominent place in the English painter's strictly chosen pantheon of artistic heroes. Bacon often said that it was to Van Gogh's early work, especially *The Potato Eaters* and the studies of worn-out shoes that he had been drawn.[12] The only clue as to why Bacon chose to make variations on Van Gogh's *The Painter on the Road to Tarascon* of 1888 comes in a remark to the art historian John Russell. Describing how he had worked on the series at top speed so that they would be ready for his show at the Hanover Gallery in London (which opened in March 1957), Bacon told Russell: 'I'd always loved that picture – the one that was burnt in Germany during the war – and as nothing else had gone right I thought I'd try to do something with it. Actually I've always liked early Van Gogh best, but that haunted figure on the road seemed just right at the time – like a phantom of the road, you could say.'[13]

This was not, of course, the first time that Bacon had become involved in making paraphrases of another artist. Most famously, over a period of some twenty years, he did no fewer than some fifty variations on Velázquez's *Portrait of Pope Innocent X*. With characteristic contrariness, Bacon repudiated the entire series later on; but during that period, the variation on the Velázquez amounted to an obsession – or what Bacon likened to the kind of crush that a young schoolboy might develop for an older boy or a master. Right through the 1950s, Bacon tended to work in series, whatever the subject. As mentioned earlier, he painted no fewer than seven versions of *Man in Blue*, as well as several *Sphinxes* and a number of studies after the life mask of William Blake. Bacon found that one image tended to spark off another one, as noted earlier, so that once he had found a richly suggestive theme he felt impelled to make several variations or paraphrases on it.

There seems little to connect the Velázquez image of the supreme pontiff (which Innocent X himself found '*troppo vero*') to Van Gogh's evocation of the painter setting out for a day's work in the fields of Provence. Where one represents absolute power, temporal as well as spiritual, in all its silken pomp, the Van Gogh self-portrait conjures up doggedness and frailty. Outlandish-looking, weighed down by all his painting paraphernalia (and often cruelly victimized, as we know, by local youths), Van Gogh moves towards his impossible task of capturing Nature, of fixing a fleeting sensation in paint; the landscape that he crosses seems relatively benign, but for us at least, it carries the shadow of what is to come in the other, more northern fields of Auvers. In fact, one might say that the two images are almost exactly opposed: the crushing papal authority, against which Bacon railed, and the artist in all his noble vulnerability, with whom Bacon identified passionately. There is one perfectly factual link between these two magnificent pictures, however. Bacon saw neither of them in the original. He had used reproductions of the Velázquez throughout his many variations on it; and, famously, when he visited Rome in 1954, he declined to go to the Palazzo Doria Pamphilj to see the work. With the Van Gogh, of course, the original no longer existed, so Bacon could very legitimately have as his unique source the one reproduction that had survived.

NORTHERNERS GONE SOUTH

By the time Bacon began his variations on this destroyed image, several other experiences had brought him psychologically closer to Van Gogh. Firstly, like Van Gogh, he had travelled south, not to Provence (which Bacon already knew), but to North Africa, and notably to Tangier and the country surrounding that exotic and seedy port. From the mid-1950s to the early 1960s, Bacon visited Tangier regularly, setting up a makeshift studio in various hotels and rented rooms – even though he knew, from past experiences on the French Riviera, that it was almost impossible for him to paint in bright sunlight. Nevertheless, the vivid colours of Morocco – clashing in the sunlight and recollected under a café awning or in the shade of the souk – made a lasting impact on his visual imagination. Like Van Gogh, he was a northerner who had gone south, and the experience jolted him out of the midnight blues and muted greens that, over the previous few years, had come to dominate his palette.

The other reason why Van Gogh had become so present in Bacon's mind – no doubt subconsciously at first – was the feeling of isolation, distress, and possibly even incipient madness that the English artist had experienced in Tangier. Van Gogh's sufferings are famous – indeed in some senses the most famous aspect of his life. Bacon's periods of extreme unhappiness have rarely been evoked, and never analysed, partly because (unlike Van Gogh's) they were never documented; and also because Bacon was formidably resilient and determined, in his steely, dandyish disdain, to laugh off the pain and suffering that befell him. Tangier, at all events, marked the nadir of his existence. Having fallen desperately in love with Peter Lacy, a former RAF fighter pilot turned bar pianist (whose nerves, Bacon believed, had been irreparably shattered by the war), Bacon followed him when the latter left London to set himself up in a rackety existence in Tangier.

The liaison between the two men had always been tumultuous, a great passion that flared up into terrifying, destructive rows. In Tangier, the tension between them grew worse, not least because both men were drinking heavily and having random affairs. As a result, Bacon was often found wandering the Tangier streets at night so badly beaten up that he was barely conscious. Lacy (whose sadistic tendencies had apparently been deliberately exacerbated by the masochistic Bacon) also regularly knifed whatever paintings of Bacon's he could get his hands on. Yet, even at the heights of their love and degradation together, Bacon was too self-aware not to know that the relationship with Lacy was danger-ous and doomed. But Bacon had been so powerfully drawn to its cycle of destruction that he could not break free. 'It was like that song', Bacon commented with wry detachment years later. 'I couldn't live with him, and I couldn't live without him.'[14]

UNDER A SCHIZOPHRENIC SUN

It seems very possible that the poignant image of Van Gogh engulfed by the Provençal landscape, its bright colours stained with the portent of Mistral and madness, came forcibly to Bacon as he himself struggled to keep a sense of his own identity while all around him, and all within him, was disintegrating. In his acute, highly dramatized sense of his own fate, Bacon had already identified before with Christ on the cross, as his many, highly personal representations of the theme appear to suggest.[15] Almost certainly, the thought of suicide haunted Bacon at this time; for all his exuberant attachment to life, he considered the possibility seriously more than once. What is certain is that his own precarious situation – caught in a homosexual *folie à deux* (at a time when homosexuality itself was still considered a crime), with no fixed address, no reliable income, and at best a *succès de scandale* as a painter – recalled the pathos of Van Gogh and his plight; perhaps, at this point, Bacon felt like another potential '*suicidé de la société*', as Antonin Artaud memorably described Van Gogh.

Concurrently – and this can hardly have been a coincidence for a man like Bacon who took in everything – a renewed wave of interest in Van Gogh's life had been generated by Vincente Minelli's film *Lust for Life*, based on Irving Stone's novel, with Kirk Douglas playing Van Gogh and Anthony Quinn as Gauguin. As the tensions grow and the rows flare up between the two men filmed living within the confines of the little 'yellow house' in Arles, Bacon must have been put vividly in mind of his own disastrous experiences, from Berkshire cottage to Moroccan hotel, with Peter Lacy. Bacon saw the film shortly after its release in London in 1956 – in other words, at almost exactly the time he painted his first picture on the Van Gogh theme.[16]

Bacon began the first picture of the series in the early spring of 1956. Painted almost entirely in dark blues and greens, with hatched brush-strokes of gold highlighting the artist's straw hat like a comic crown (a crown of thorns, certainly), this sombre portrait shows Van Gogh trudging through the darkness, with his face closed and his gaze intent, like a nocturnal apparition (Bacon's 'phantom of the road'). Bacon had at first been very enthusiastic about this painting, then quickly revised his opinion of it and nearly destroyed it – like so many other of his paintings, especially at this period.[17] Perhaps this abrupt change of mind was the reason why he then went no further with the theme until he took it up again, in a great frenzy of work, in March 1957, almost exactly a year later. *Study for Portrait of Van Gogh II* leaves its predecessor literally in the dark: Van Gogh is lifted out of Stygian gloom and placed against a background of charred brightness, as if a pitiless sun had reduced the landscape to slashes of primary reds, blues, and harsh, schizophrenic yellows. 'Under Van Gogh's nail,' Artaud wrote, 'landscapes show their hostile flesh'; in Bacon's picture, the skin of the Earth has been lifted back and the hostility flows out as surely and destructively as lava.[18] By comparison, with its warm greens and golden browns, Van Gogh's original image seems ordered and of an almost autumnal gentleness.

In the following study, now in the Hirshhorn Museum, the sensation of nightmarish brightness and isolation has grown even stronger. Van Gogh is shown as a battered silhouette against a landscape whose warring colours betoken nothing but menace, as if the planet, the sun, and the stars had slipped their moorings and were now careering toward eventual cosmic obliteration. The figure is a mere survivor: even its blue-black shadow (a motif Bacon returned to obsessively) lies fractured and dismembered on the rippling, flamelike ground.

The onslaught continues from one picture to another throughout the series. The last one, *Study for Portrait of Van Gogh VI*, shows a figure literally divided into two: the calcinated torso is split, as if filleted down to the backbone, with the body's substance pouring into a formless, liquid shadow on the ground. Bacon painted the whole series at high speed for the show that he had promised to the Hanover Gallery, which opened in the same month, March 1957. The last two of the six studies were delivered still wet, with the result that the more turbulent guests on the opening night (which included a contingent of drunk Teddy boys) had traces of Bacon's thick, slashed, and trowelled impasto branded on their backs.

The event appears to have had an electrifying impact, principally no doubt because in these pictures Bacon had expressed his own extreme personal crisis so forcefully. The wildness of the paint strokes, the menacing layers of discordant colour, the threat, in a word, of a famous suicide re-enacted in a world of murderous sunshine and Mediterranean colour could not go unnoticed. Bacon, it seems, was his usual urbane self, helping to staunch a wound when, according to a report of the time, something fell from the Hanover's mezzanine and cut open one of the guests' foreheads. But it seems evident, in retrospect, that Bacon was acting out the emotional impasse he had fallen into in front of the whole world.

Why had Bacon chosen Van Gogh on his way to work as a theme through which he could vent his own chaotic emotions? Because Van Gogh was doomed, by his own brilliance, his own contradictions, his own overwhelming fate to be an artist – all things that Bacon shared, and from which, under the pounding sunlight and clashing colours of Morocco, after the interminable alcohol-inflamed rows and vicious punishments from Lacy (who wanted in their life together to have Bacon literally chained, like an animal, to the wall), he had tried to get some distance by painting them. 'If I didn't have to live,' Bacon once claimed, 'I would never let any of this out.' But these paintings were the cries of a man at the end of his tether, painting wildly, painting as if his own sanity and survival depended on giving a voice to the mad contradictions of a deeply unhappy, deeply passionate love affair where one person is infatuated, captivated, by the unfailing accuracy of the harm another can do to him.

The whole series helped Bacon survive the affair, and in this strange sense Van Gogh died a second death as the surrogate for the victim in an extreme sadomasochistic homosexual love affair. Lacy died in 1962, and Bacon (who received news of his lover's death among the telegrams of congratulation during the opening of his triumphant retrospective at the Tate Gallery in the same year) was convinced that Lacy had deliberately killed himself with drink. But with the Van Gogh pictures, Bacon had to some extent already exorcized Lacy from his life. Before finishing with the theme, Bacon returned to it a couple of times, notably with a hallucinating *Head of Man – Study of a Drawing of Van Gogh*, where a cranium with black eye sockets rises out of a few sweeps of thickly loaded white, green, and red paint.

Bacon also executed a *Homage to Van Gogh* in 1960 to accompany a small gallery exhibition of Van Gogh self-portraits. This last homage was a deeply felt act of gratitude. Van Gogh had become a symbol of extremity and survival to Bacon as his life fell apart and his belief in himself as an artist foundered. For a time, racked by his own extreme contradictions, Bacon believed he was treading the same path over the abyss as his predecessor. As he painted the series of variations on the artist on his way against all odds to work, Bacon grew so close to Van Gogh as to imagine that he was Van Gogh, thereby creating one of the strangest cases of one painter identifying completely with another in the whole history of art.

1   Most accomplished artists over the last hundred years would acknowledge a debt to one or the other of these near-contemporaries (and occasionally to both). Chaïm Soutine, however fiercely he rejected the notion, owed a great deal not only to Van Gogh's highly personal and daring sense of colour, but also to his all-enveloping, flamelike application of paint. Other modern painters to have been directly affected by Van Gogh's example range from Joan Miró (notably in his early, emphatically delineated portraits) and Willem de Kooning, a fellow Dutchman by birth, whose extravagant 'Woman' series appears to take Van Gogh's freedom of colour and touch to a new extreme: figures held at the brink of a formless chaos.

2   Along with other works, the painting was taken from Magdeburg in 1942 and stored in the salt mines in Neustassfurt, where it was destroyed by a fire bomb in 1945. See Joseph J. Rishel with Katherine Sachs, 'The Modern Legacy of Van Gogh's Portraits' in *Van Gogh: Face to Face*, exhibition catalogue (Detroit: Detroit Institute of Fine Arts, 2000).

3   The plate in question had been published in Ludwig Goldscheider and Wilhelm Uhde, *Vincent van Gogh* (Oxford and London: Phaidon Press, 1945).

4   'I *would like* to do portraits which would look like apparitions to people a century later', Van Gogh wrote to his sister Willemien. 'By which I mean that I do not endeavour to achieve this by a photographic resemblance, but by means of our impassioned expressions.' (Letter 879, 5 June 1890; <https://vangoghletters.org/vg/letters/let879/letter.html>). In his book about Van Gogh and Gauguin in Arles, *The Yellow House* (London: Penguin, 2006), Martin Gayford suggests that Van Gogh may have been influenced here by Thomas Carlyle's contention that living people are no more than ghosts 'shaped into a body, an appearance, and that fade away again into air and invisibility. This is no metaphor, this is simple scientific *fact*.' This belief would have certainly struck a deep chord in Bacon, who set out to capture what he saw as the fleeting, insubstantial nature of all human appearance.

5   The letter and Leiris's reply to it are quoted in Michael Peppiatt, *L'Amitié Leiris Bacon: Une étrange fascination* (Paris: L'Échoppe, 2006). Bacon also explored the notion of realism (in French, once again) in an interesting interview published in *L'Express*: 'Whatever people say, I've got nothing of an expressionist', Bacon insists at one point. 'My painting isn't about expression, it's about instinct. I don't express. I try to remake the image of reality that is in my mind.... (I don't want) literal realism, illustration. To create realism without falling into illustration you have to invent a technique. Painters attempt from generation to generation to find ways of returning an image onto the nervous system. One by one, the techniques of the past wear out. Yet one still wants to paint the same things – a body or a face. So you have to reinvent technique in order to find a new way of conveying something, such as a chair, onto the nervous system.... All the painters who interest me have succeeded in doing this, and particularly Van Gogh, who did it in such an extraordinary way – a very simple but also a very mysterious way. After all, who can say how they work those little touches of colour with which he covered the canvas and which immediately convey – or, better still, recreate – a tree, a plant or grass?' (*L'Express*, 15–21 November 1971, pp. 98–100; the translation from the French is mine).

6 In 'Reality Conveyed by a Lie', an interview with Francis Bacon by Michael Peppiatt, *Art International*, no. 1 (new ed.), Autumn 1987, p. 30.

7 David Sylvester, *Interviews with Francis Bacon* (London: Thames & Hudson, 1993), pp. 172–3. Bacon read and scanned a huge variety of books and photographs. He almost certainly saw (not least because Brandt also took portrait photos of Bacon) 'Painter's Country: Van Gogh's Provence Photographed and Described by Bill Brandt', which the magazine *Lilliput* published in September 1948.

8 In conversation with the author. Antonin Artaud makes the perceptive comment in 'Van Gogh le suicidé de la société' that while Gauguin sought to raise aspects of life to the level of symbol and myth, Van Gogh derived the force of myth from the most ordinary things. I think Bacon shared that capacity: light bulbs had never been so malevolent, for instance, nor mirrors so nightmarish before.

9 Quoted by John Russell in *Francis Bacon* (London: Thames & Hudson, 1985), pp. 52–3. This appears to be a paraphrase of Van Gogh's statement in Letter 515, dated on or about 14 July 1885, <https://vangoghletters.org/vg/letters/let515/letter.html>. Van Gogh is reacting vigorously to a third-party criticism that Theo has relayed to him about 'certain faults in the structure of the figures in the *Potato Eaters*'.

10 Sylvester, op. cit., p. 172.

11 Conscious as he was of the ubiquity of death, I think Bacon saw grass above all as the endlessly renewed outcrop of buried flesh.

12 Bacon was categorical in his aesthetic judgments. I remember a discussion about Van Gogh in La Coupole in Paris between Bacon, the French painter René Strubel, and myself during which Bacon talked about the 'poignancy' of *The Potato Eaters*, ranking it insistently above all Van Gogh's other works. Once again, I think it was the direct and raw realism of the early picture that Bacon found so convincing.

13 John Russell, op. cit., p. 51.

14 Quoted in Michael Peppiatt, *Francis Bacon: Anatomy of an Enigma* (London: Weidenfeld & Nicolson, 1996), p. 151.

15 I have explored this theme in 'The Sacred and the Profane', the main essay in the catalogue to the exhibition of the same name published by the Musée Maillol, Paris, 2002.

16 In his 1964 monograph, Ronald Alley suggests that *Head* (1951), formerly owned by Lucian Freud and now in the Cleveland Museum of Art, started out as a *Pope* but changed, in Bacon's eyes, into a head of Van Gogh as he painted it. This seems unlikely in that the head retains several obvious *Pope* characteristics but nothing of the later Van Goghs. But it nevertheless seems to indicate that Bacon had been thinking of painting Van Gogh at least five years before he began his series of variations. John Rothenstein and Ronald Alley, *Francis Bacon* (London: Thames & Hudson, 1964).

17 Bacon was persuaded not to destroy the picture but to cut out the central part of the canvas by the collectors Robert and Lisa Sainsbury.

18 Antonin Artaud, 'Van Gogh le suicidé de la société', *Oeuvres complètes* (Paris: Gallimard, 1974), vol. 3, p. 170.

Originally published in the catalogue for the exhibition *Van Gogh and Expressionism*, Neue Galerie, New York, 2007

24

BACON / GIACOMETTI: PARALLEL VISIONS OF A TERRIBLE TRUTH

What incredible stroke of luck leads you, as a budding art critic aged twenty-one, to become involved with Europe's two greatest postwar artists? I have already touched on aspects of this story,[1] so here I will be as brief as a succinct account allows. At my father's insistence in early 1966, I accepted a job as junior editor on a magazine, not in London, which had become my cherished home after leaving Cambridge, but in Paris – a city I had always admired but found aloof and inhospitable on my brief stays there. The idea that I was about to work for a glossy magazine called *Réalités* should have filled me with satisfaction, but the sudden uprooting from a very agreeable, wayward style of life filled me with dread as I contemplated the one-way ticket that arrived in the post. Before I left, I had one last night out on the town with Bacon, which began with drinks in his Reece Mews studio.

'Now, who do you know in Paris?' Francis asked, as he eased the cork off another bottle of champagne. 'You should really get in touch with Giacometti. There's something terribly sympathetic about him.'

Alberto Giacometti's name had been returning more and more often to our conversations because Bacon had seen him several times during his trips to London to prepare for his big exhibition at the Tate Gallery in 1965, and he had been very impressed by both the range of the sculptor's work and his brilliant conversation. Although I realized that this was another artist I needed to come to terms with, I had missed the exhibition and had not even bothered to consult the catalogue. Thus I was woefully unprepared to meet a genius clearly so essential to an understanding of our times that even Bacon admired him. When I told Bacon this, he simply ripped out a double page from an issue of *Paris Match* that was lying on the floor and wrote me a letter of introduction to the great sculptor. Carefully folded into an anthology of Nietzsche's writings, the letter came with me on a stay in Paris that I thought would end within a year, but which actually lasted three decades.

For the first few weeks, Paris proved to be as unwelcoming as I had feared, but once I had got into an office routine and found myself a small flat, my life improved. Every evening after work, I explored my new area avidly, seeking out the best little shops and bistrots. One of the streets that crossed the one where I now lived sported the rather pompous name of 'rue Hippolyte-Maindron', which rung a faint bell. Then I noticed that on the door of one of the tumbledown buildings that lined the street someone had written 'GIACOMETTI' in small, white capitals. I went back to my flat, retrieved the letter of introduction that Bacon had written for me, then returned to Giacometti's studio. But as I raised my hand to knock on the door, a wave of shame swept through me. Who was I, an obscure newcomer to the city, to interrupt a great artist no doubt grappling with a new work that the whole art world was awaiting? My hand dropped and, flushing with embarrassment, I beat a hasty retreat in case an angry Giacometti pulled open the door to see who the intruder was. On several subsequent evenings, I went through the same motions but could never bring myself to actually knock on the door; the dilemma was solved shortly thereafter when I learnt that *Réalités* was planning a special issue on Giacometti, who had just died in hospital in his native Switzerland.

That, of course, might have been the end of the story, but the obscure sense of loss that I felt at Giacometti's disappearance continued to gnaw at me. Just as my life in London had been immeasurably enhanced by the whole aura of Bacon's work and personal presence, I realized I must have hoped that Paris would be transformed by getting to know Giacometti and participating, however tangentially, in his life and career. I felt that I had missed a unique opportunity, and that if my life in Paris were to go forward, I needed to compensate for that loss as best I could. Before long, prompted by my fascination for everything about Giacometti, I came across many of the people who had made up his world. Among the writers who had written memorably about him, I already knew Michel Leiris, Jacques Dupin,

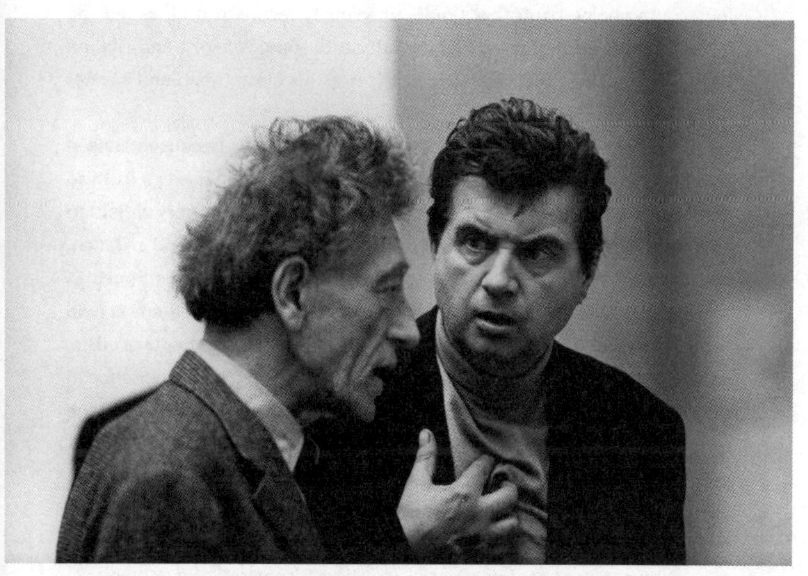

Alberto Giacometti and **Francis Bacon**, 1965,
photographed by Graham Keen

and David Sylvester from various evenings spent in London and Paris with Bacon. Other eminences, including James Lord, Gaëtan Picon, Jean Leymarie, and Yves Bonnefoy, swum into my ken from the ever-lengthening list of poets and critics whose imagination had been fired by the irreducible, human nobility that emanated from Giacometti's figures. A few of his sitters and family members, notably Annette, his widow, and his brother Diego, joined the choice band that I half-consciously reconstituted, as did the artist's main dealers, from Pierre Matisse to Aimé Maeght and Claude Bernard, as well as such éminences grises as his close friend and adviser Louis Clayeux.

If I plunged deeper into Giacometti's world, it was because I sensed that his art stemmed entirely from his obsession with conveying a truth so personal and powerful it had become universal – for me the very definition and prime purpose of great art, in whatever form, that I had found in Bacon, whose work and presence (he visited me regularly in Paris) continued to affect the core of my thinking and feeling. I came to consider them as twin tutelary deities since I referred to them both, above all in moments of crisis, knowing that each of them had confronted the extremes of experience in their work. It was not even about art as such, but about life, or the way the art of Bacon and Giacometti impacted directly on my life like beacons lighting my way across dark, stormy seas. No doubt this sounds overdramatic: but it indicates the importance these two artists had in the more fraught moments of my existence, when I would ask: how would Bacon react in these circumstances, or what strength can I draw from Giacometti's figures reduced to the bone, to their irreducible essence? How can they help me overcome a black depression or find my way through a situation gone badly awry?

Whenever the occasion arose to write about their art, I seized it as an opportunity to deepen and refine my growing expertise, first in reviews of specific exhibitions, then in more thematic essays and, eventually, in monographs on each artist. I also began to curate exhibitions of their work, first in group shows (notably, in the case of Bacon, as the key figure in the School of London), then in retrospectives that were shown in museums across Europe and America. Each book and each exhibition was of course a unique opportunity for me to look in depth at their work; and every time their genius appeared all the more clearly since I realized there were new depths to plumb, new enigmas and contradictions to analyse.

In this way, Bacon and Giacometti have accompanied me both emotionally and intellectually for more than fifty years, in other words, throughout my adult life. They have been not only a source of intellectual fascination, but mainstays of my existence. So when I was offered the chance to work on a Bacon / Giacometti exhibition at the Fondation Beyeler in Switzerland, I seized the opportunity with both hands.[2] It was an illuminating experience, and never more so than when every last detail of the installation was in place and the exhibition was about to open. I had feared at certain moments that one artist might overpower the other, but as I walked through the finished show, I sensed a balance between two points of view, two visions, that complemented one another in all kinds of unexpected ways.

The essay that I contributed to the catalogue, written under the inevitable pressures of deadline and word limit, seemed in retrospect to have missed certain essential points of comparison between the two artists that the exhibition itself suddenly indicated. I have considerably enlarged and rewritten it for the present publication.

In the postwar British art world, Giacometti enjoyed the status of a hero. Just as Paris itself seemed grittier, sexier, and more daring than London in that bleak era of privation, so its art appeared to delve more deeply into the 'human condition' and the philosophical problems that confronted a generation that, after years of destruction and debasement, now had to deal with the challenge of survival. Of all the artists across the Channel, none, not even Picasso or Matisse, could claim the aura of Giacometti as he toiled nightly in the solitude of his cavelike studio in search of a new image of man emerging, spectrelike, from the rubble of civilization.

That aura only increased for many British artists as the new wave of American abstraction began to unfurl over Europe and Giacometti stood out as the figurative tradition's prime defender. Francis Bacon and several of his contemporaries (not least Henry Moore[3]) had long been aware of Giacometti's importance both as an artist and as a figurehead in the complex struggle of figuration versus abstraction that was thenceforth to characterize modern art. The youngest British artists, who were just coming of age professionally, were also fascinated by the concept of Giacometti not only as the defining sculptor of their time, but as a leading exponent of the seductive new movement called existentialism (from which Giacometti later sought to distance himself). Consequently, no sooner had cross-Channel borders reopened than Eduardo Paolozzi, Lucian Freud, and William Turnbull beat a direct path to the revered sculptor's famously chaotic studio in Alésia, while other British artists, such as Frank Auerbach,[4] Leon Kossoff, Elisabeth Frink, and Bernard Meadows continued to admire him and his example from afar.

Partly as a result of their interest, Giacometti was also recognized by the official British art world. In 1949, the Tate Gallery acquired both a sculpture, *Pointing Man* (1947), and a painting, *Seated Man (Diego)* (1949).[5] A few adventurous private collectors, such as Peter Watson (who funded the influential literary review *Horizon*[6]) and Robert and Lisa Sainsbury (whose wealth derived from the eponymous grocery stores), also bought works of his. The Sainsburys, who collected Bacon as well, went on to establish a more personal relationship with Giacometti (having been introduced to him in 1949 by his first Parisian dealer, Pierre Loeb), and in 1955 they persuaded Giacometti to make portrait drawings of their two children. Characteristically, Giacometti deemed the drawings worthless and refused to accept money for them, until the Sainsburys solved the problem by sending a handsome Aquascutum raincoat from London as a present for his wife Annette.[7]

Gallery and museum exhibitions followed. Erica Brausen, whose Hanover Gallery had a reputation for choosing the most 'advanced' art from the Continent, showed Giacometti's work on several occasions, as indeed she regularly exhibited Bacon from 1949 onwards. Then, in 1955, the Arts Council dedicated an entire retrospective to Giacometti, with a catalogue introduction by Bacon's friend and commentator, the art critic David Sylvester.[8]

Thus Giacometti's reputation was already well established in Britain as Bacon began to come into his own in the late 1940s and early 1950s. Bacon avidly followed recent developments on the Paris art scene – which for him meant essentially Picasso and Giacometti's latest work – by consulting the appropriate catalogues, talking to Francophile friends and scanning the leading French art magazines, notably *Cahiers d'Art*, available at Zwemmer's international bookshop on Charing Cross Road. Bacon also made trips to Paris, the city he loved above all others, and he would have frequented the cafés and brasseries in Montparnasse and Saint-Germain-des-Prés that Giacometti patronized. Indeed, on at least one occasion, Bacon actually saw Giacometti and went over to introduce himself and tell Giacometti how much he admired him and his work.[9] We also know that as early as September 1955, when he was staying at the Hôtel Martinez in Cannes, Bacon suddenly realized that Giacometti was sitting at the table next to his at dinner in a restaurant beside the port, though it sounds unlikely that the two men actually spoke on this occasion.[10]

A personal relationship between the two artists did not really get under way, in fact, until the following decade, when each had a retrospective show at the Tate: Bacon in 1962 and Giacometti in 1965. Numerous factors promoted closer ties between them, as we will see. Not only were both men resolutely figurative in a period increasingly dominated by abstraction, they also drew inspiration directly from the history of Western art (a practice then much frowned upon as retrograde in 'forward-thinking' artistic circles). Moreover, and perhaps most importantly, they had several bosom friends in common. Here Isabel Rawsthorne, a hard-drinking, high-spirited artist and model, emerges as unquestionably the key figure. She first met Giacometti in the 1930s, when (having modelled for Jacob Epstein and André Derain) she was already acting as a vital link between the Paris and London art worlds. Having been portrayed several times by Giacometti and Bacon, with both of whom she established a close friendship, Isabel made it a point of honour to bring the two men together. The ideal occasion arose when Giacometti began visiting London in the run-up to his big show at the Tate, enabling Isabel to organize a series of dinners in Fitzrovia and Soho for the two men, while inviting such other mutual friends as Leiris, Sylvester (both significant commentators on the two artists), and Bacon's new boyfriend, George Dyer.[11]

These evenings tended to last late into the night, starting in restaurants like Wheeler's, famous for its Whitstable oysters and Dover sole, or L'Étoile in Charlotte Street, and continuing in clubs, such as the Gargoyle or Bacon's home-from-home, the Colony Room, where the barman was well used to the exuberant painter's habit of ordering prodigious amounts of champagne. The two artists thus had ample opportunity to discuss everything that interested them, from gossip about their friends through the relative merits of Paris and London to the highest aims of their art.

By now both men knew each other's work well, since Bacon had visited Giacometti's major retrospective at the Tate and Giacometti went out of his way to see the latest portraits Bacon had done of such close friends as Isabel herself, Dyer, and Lucian Freud. These latter paintings on exhibit at the Marlborough gallery[12] impressed Giacometti so strongly that he commented, with characteristic self-irony, that compared with Bacon's powerful, inventive portraits his own looked 'old-maidish'.

This remark in turn prompted Bacon to say that he thought Giacometti was indisputably the greatest living artist, to which Giacometti replied that, on the contrary, Bacon was the greatest living artist; and this refrain, this duet, was repeated at various intervals throughout the evenings the two artists spent together. But although he was deeply flattered, Bacon was well aware that the older artist (born eight years earlier than Bacon in 1901) could lay claim not only to have been exhibited far more widely than himself, but also to have been extensively commented on by such literary eminences as Jean-Paul Sartre, Jean Genet, and Leiris. Although Bacon might not have admitted it freely, he was also conscious of being indebted to Giacometti for various stylistic devices, notably the cagelike structure – or 'space frame' – that he clearly borrowed from Giacometti and employed regularly as a means of isolating and focusing attention on the central figures in his compositions, which otherwise would have lacked perspective. It might also be said that Bacon (who, as a budding young designer, had formerly worked in spotless, stylish interiors) derived the spectacular chaos of his studio, piled ankle high in paint-spattered books, photographs, and artist's materials, from the much-photographed (and highly photogenic) mess that Giacometti had built up in his 'cave' behind Montparnasse.

For Bacon as for Giacometti, one should emphasize here, the studio became the hub and carapace of existence, the very repository of their imagination, because it contained so many traces and reference points for their work that by merely being within its paint- or plaster-strewn chaos it triggered off potentially stimulating ideas and images. For both artists, the studio resembled an archive of their achievements, their failures and their aspirations: Giacometti and Bacon knew every splinter of plaster, every smear of paint, in their respective workplaces, and this familiarity acted as a spur, an incitement, to take their 'search for the absolute' (in Sartre's words) a stage further. So much so that, long after both men could have easily afforded larger, more commodious ateliers, neither ever moved out of the humble and inconvenient, if picturesque, lairs that served the needs of their art so well.

*

From what Bacon told me in some detail about the evenings he spent with Giacometti,[13] they were lively, even boisterous, although the story that James Lord tells in his Giacometti biography about Bacon sending all the plates and glasses on the restaurant table crashing to the floor to illustrate a philosophical point sounds out of character.[14] It seems likely, however (as Lord was quick to note), that Giacometti was intrigued by Bacon's new lover, the ill-fated Dyer,[15] to the point of saying, 'When I'm in London, I feel homosexual', and that he suggested that George came to see him in Paris so as to learn French and a trade like gilding or patinating; according to Bacon, Giacometti went so far as to follow George down to the toilets in one of the restaurants they visited.[16] The two artists would also have gossiped about their respective dealers (Pierre Matisse had come over especially for Giacometti's Tate show[17]), not least because Giacometti had recently broken with his Paris dealer, Aimé Maeght, and Bacon, who had recently signed up with the Marlborough, would have sympathized, reiterating his underlying conviction that 'all art dealers are crooks'.

After a few similar sallies, the two artists would nevertheless have settled down to try and define, both for themselves and for each other, the pressing problems and aims of their art. As numerous published interviews confirm, both men were consummate talkers, skilled dialecticians capable both of highly penetrating analysis and of finding the exact phrase, the *mot juste*, for a new concept or definition. In company, Bacon often complained that he had no one he could really talk to, whether about life or about art, and Giacometti went so far as to claim, in one of the absurd exaggerations that he enjoyed, that he would happily accept being reduced to a trunk, without arms or legs, and placed on a mantelpiece, so long as he could engage in interesting discourse with the people in the room before him. The conversations between these two nimble, unorthodox intellects about their artistic practice and convictions could only have been of the highest order, and it is a great pity (as Simone de Beauvoir said of Giacometti's voluminous conversations with Sartre) that their closely argued exchanges were not recorded for posterity.

Significantly, both artists had already gone on record as saying that they considered their art above all as 'realist'. Time and again, Giacometti emphasized that his only true goal was to try to reproduce things, whether a glass, a nose, or a tree, exactly as he saw them, whereas Bacon claimed that he only sought to convey the deepest 'sensations' about life that he felt as a convinced atheist (even if he had to use a 'Crucifixion' or a 'Pope' theme to achieve that aim); Bacon also replied to charges that his subject matter was 'horrific' by claiming that it was hardly more horrific than the news that the newspapers relayed every morning on their front page.

It would have soon become apparent to both artists that their notion of 'realism' differed, given that the notion itself is both highly subjective and ultimately indefinable.[18] But those very difficulties would have prompted a spirited exchange, all the more so because Giacometti had come to hate being pigeonholed as an 'existentialist' artist just as much Bacon loathed the 'expressionist' label so often applied to his work. ('I'm not expressionist at all', Bacon would attest airily. 'After all, I have nothing to express.') Having freed themselves of those crudely journalistic tags, however, they might well have agreed that, as younger men, they had both fallen under the spell of another '-ism' – namely that of Surrealism.

Giacometti had of course actually played a memorable role in the Surrealist movement, producing highly inventive sculpture for several years while he was caught squarely under its influence. If he later rejected the movement fiercely, it had nevertheless helped to form him at a crucial stage in his development. Bacon was also highly aware of Surrealism's potent lure, which he had first encountered during his early visit to Paris in 1927; he read the movement's declamatory tracts and followed its development for many years thereafter, adopting Surrealist attitudes and techniques that were to affect both his attitudes and his painting lastingly. In fact, possibly because he had never been so close to the movement's epicentre as Giacometti, Bacon rejected it less violently. Such strategies as bringing together two quite dissimilar objects (as in Lautréamont's famous 'chance meeting on a dissecting-table of a sewing-machine and an umbrella') stayed with him throughout most of his career, enabling him to create such haunting images as the screaming pope (the Velázquez portrait overlaid by the cry of Sergei Eisenstein's wounded nanny) or the bloodied bull alone in an arena dominated by a Nazi banner (*Study for Bullfight No. 1*, 1969).

Velázquez himself, the painter's painter, would certainly have been invoked in these epic exchanges as Bacon drank immoderately and Giacometti smoked immoderately through the night. Both artists had actually copied the masterful *Portrait of Pope Innocent X*,[19] housed then as now in the Doria Pamphilj collection in Rome, and both immediately acknowledged their overwhelming debt to the great art of the past, from the magnificent achievements of Egypt onwards. But here a difference in this similarity between the two artists becomes clear, for where Bacon had narrowed down his pantheon to a handful of great names (Michelangelo, Rembrandt, Velázquez, Degas, Manet, Van Gogh, Picasso), Giacometti was more inclusive in his choice, since his capacity for admiration ran wider. Indeed, in one remarkable phrase, Giacometti acknowledged that, 'All the art of the past rises up before me, the art of all ages and all civilizations, everything becomes simultaneous, as if space had replaced time.' And where Bacon paraphrased certain great images of the past, integrating them into his work, Giacometti copied them, as a delicate homage, in endless drawings, but without visibly incorporating them into the fine-spun stuff of his vision.

At some point in their intense discussions, Bacon would have brought up his central belief in the need to 'distort' appearance in order to give an image maximum intensity. Since both the great art of the past and photography had already 'cancelled out' (as he put it) so many of figurative painting's possibilities, he felt that only by distorting the figures he created could he give them the vitality they would need to renew tradition and survive. Only by twisting appearance radically, Bacon insisted, could a new truth be revealed; and here one might apply Sartre's description of Giacometti's forms as 'always mediating between nothingness and being' as revealingly to Bacon's near-deliquescent figures. Less obviously expansive than his English counterpart, Giacometti would no doubt have absorbed Bacon's credo with caution, since his own fundamental belief was that his entire activity consisted of attempting 'merely' to reproduce what he saw, and that he drew, painted, and sculpted above all to understand the world as he found it. But Giacometti was too subtle not to have realized that his patient search to capture a human presence had resulted in distortions as extreme, if more self-contained, as any of Bacon's wildly dislocated limbs and exuberantly pummelled flesh. One might indeed argue that distortion in three dimensions becomes even more subversive and disturbing than in two.

Another decisive element shared by both artists was their love of literature. Bacon and Giacometti were dedicated readers, although here, once again, Giacometti's tastes proved more diverse, since he read not only the great classics but also his contemporary poet friends, such as René Crevel and Georges Bataille, whose new books he illustrated (even as a boy, he had always done drawings inspired by the books that he read). Regular contact with a range of gifted writers, and notably Breton, encouraged Giacometti to write several significant texts himself, in French moreover rather than in his native Italian. Since he followed the intellectual discussions of the day closely, Giacometti also kept abreast of such leading literary and artistic reviews as *Documents* and *Cahiers d'Art*. Likewise, with his keen interest in current politics, Giacometti devoured the daily press, developing meanwhile an unexpected passion for military history and particularly such specialist themes as Napoleon's battlefield strategies.[20] The sculptor had a distinct taste for detective novels, too, such as the 'Série Noire' thrillers that Gallimard published, of which some sixty were found scattered around the studio at his death.

Bacon, on the other hand, focused more exclusively on the very highest dramatic and poetic achievements, from the Greek tragedies and Shakespeare through to such modern masters as Proust, Yeats, and Eliot; he also purported to have been directly affected by literature while painting such key works as *Triptych Inspired by T. S. Eliot's Poem 'Sweeney Agonistes'* (1967) and *Triptych Inspired by the 'Oresteia' of Aeschylus* (1981).[21] His own library, much of it strewn across the studio floor, nevertheless reveals a wide mix of interest, from Van Gogh's *Letters* and various classic novels (Honoré de Balzac and Charles Dickens, Joseph Conrad and Thomas Mann) to cookery books, which the artist read for relaxation, particularly when he was unable to sleep. Like Giacometti, Bacon was not limited by his native tongue, and he read French fluently, above all when one of his French writer friends such as Leiris or Dupin brought out a new book. The painter also consulted a range of language primers, since he longed to be able to speak Spanish and even modern Greek on his trips abroad.

Other similarities that bound Bacon and Giacometti together include the distinct, not to say anguished, isolation in space of the figures they created, notably by means of the cagelike device mentioned earlier. Both artists, too, tended to confine their subjects to the four walls of a room, to the extent that, while Giacometti broke out occasionally to produce the odd, desolate landscape, Bacon very rarely ventured beyond his tightly sealed, strangely airless, claustrophobic interiors. With the European landscape devastated by war, life had been driven indoors, with man all the more isolated within the empty banality of a modern interior. The two artists also shared a marked preference for portraying the same people, repeatedly and obsessively. If Bacon's inner circle chiefly comprised his lover Dyer and a handful of close friends (Lucian Freud, Isabel Rawsthorne, Henrietta Moraes, Muriel Belcher), then Giacometti's was even more restricted and focused above all on his brother Diego, his wife Annette, and, later, his lover Caroline. And of course, since neither artist, having set their sights so high, ever felt satisfied with anything that they had produced, they both abandoned or destroyed a substantial number of works throughout their careers – unlike Picasso, who appears to have rarely called into question the quality of what he created and consequently destroyed little.

*

If numerous beliefs and working habits draw Bacon and Giacometti together, there are – unsurprisingly – several polarizing differences between these two twentieth-century masters. Perhaps the most significant and divisive of these is the fact that whereas Giacometti based everything he did on drawing, Bacon at most did only very basic, notational sketches – virtual squiggles – and freely admitted that he could not draw, did not draw, and was moreover not even interested in drawing; at the same time, somewhat ambiguously, he declared that what he liked most in Giacometti's whole oeuvre were his drawings rather than his achievements as a sculptor or painter.[22] For Giacometti, on the other hand, only constant drawing, copying, erasing, and copying again, seemed eventually to enable him to reproduce what he saw, whether it was a chair, a tree, or a face. Bacon meanwhile – and here the difference between them takes on its full significance – felt that preliminary drawing would hamper the spontaneity that he sought: with only an outline of an image in mind, and uncertain how he might realize it technically, he wanted to attack the canvas directly and take advantage of whatever unforeseen shapes and suggestions the first fluent, loaded brush marks in oil paint made. This is what Bacon, the inveterate gambler, the devotee of roulette, called 'chance' or 'accident', and although (doubtless influenced by his early contact with Surrealism) he perhaps exaggerated its actual role in the making of a new image, he believed in it as a central tenet of his creativity. While Giacometti was amused by this profession of spontaneity, he nevertheless believed that Bacon's inability to draw was a severe handicap to making durable, worthwhile imagery.[23]

Another aspect of Bacon and Giacometti's respective practices that divided them sharply was the importance of models. In the earlier part of his career, Bacon had painted from sitters. We know, for instance, that Lisa Sainsbury sat for him regularly while he painted her portrait, as did the society photographer Cecil Beaton. The latter, however, was so horrified by the portrait that eventually emerged that Bacon, as soon as he heard of Beaton's alarm, destroyed the offending canvas without hesitation. But from about the time of this incident (and possibly because of it), Bacon would only paint portraits from photographs, which he asked his friend, the Soho photographer John Deakin, to take especially for him. Bacon explained away this new departure by saying, somewhat melodramatically, that he would not want to 'practise before them the injury that I do to them in my work'. He also came to prize the 'accidents' that happened to these photographs as they became splattered with paint and trodden, dented, and folded under foot into the mass of other images littering his studio floor.

For Giacometti, however, being able to work from a model immediately to hand was an article of faith: his entire artistic routine revolved around having Diego and Annette come every day to sit for him. During these sessions, he was so focused on capturing what he saw, tantalizingly, before him that he virtually forgot who his sitters were. Thus when he saw Annette one evening, after she had spent several hours patiently sitting for him, Giacometti remarked famously: 'I haven't seen you all day.' A few other sitters, such as the Japanese philosopher Yanaihara or James Lord, accepted the exacting conditions that sitting to Giacometti entailed, with their return tickets to Japan or the United States being constantly booked, then cancelled.

This fundamentally different approach between the two becomes all the more marked once one takes into account how deeply Bacon's art was indebted not only to photographs of his sitters but to photography in general. Whereas Giacometti's studio was filled with his own sculptures and drawings, as well as plaster shards and artist's paraphernalia, Bacon's was awash with photographs of every conceivable sort, from reproductions of famous paintings to birds in flight, war scenes, athletes in competition, Nazi leaders in full harangue, and monkeys in the zoo. All these images, moreover, were scattered across his studio floor, and as already noted, crumpled underfoot and laced over by endless skeins of dropped, dripped, or thrown paint. And of course many of these photographic images, whether taken from Eadweard Muybridge or from *Paris Match*, found their way into Bacon's painting. This certainly would have perplexed Giacometti, who required no more than a single, living model, or a glass on a table, in order to have the necessary stimulus to reconnect to his endless search for the single, inalterable truth.

Bacon, seen from this particular perspective, was much more of a showman than Giacometti was. While the latter had long established the narrow, if inexhaustibly demanding, limits of his field of enquiry, Bacon welcomed the chance to expand his universe with allusions to a wide variety of sources. If Giacometti's universe hangs on the knife-edge profile of a bronze head or the linear reverberations of an apple drawn on his studio's pitted wall, Bacon's opens up to the ambiguous connotations of a papal throne, a syringe, a Sphinx, a swastika on an arm. While Giacometti pursues his maniacal quest for an eye to represent all eyes, a figure to represent all figures who ever strode or stood stock still, Bacon opens the encyclopaedia of history, of events that happened or might still be conjured from the past. Thus the nurse's scream issues from the Velázquez pope, the bull charges under the

Nazi banner, and the chimp, baring its fangs, reappears as the business-man in the dark-blue suit.

The two artists whom we have mainly considered for their similarities nevertheless spring apart once again as their disparities come into consideration. Bacon bursts forth in vivid colour – blood reds, acid greens, voluptuous pinks – as Giacometti clings to the varieties of grey to which he is accustomed in his dusty reflections on the world. Giacometti hardly needs the operatic gesture, the full-blown conceits of Bacon since he is simply creeping up on hard-won purchases of a certain elusive truth. '*Ma grisaille*', 'my greyness', Caroline, his prostitute-mistress, called him fondly. But there was nothing grey and no lurking in the modest back-rooms of painstaking trial and error about Bacon: he exulted in large formats as well as acid bright colours and sharp tonal contrasts, which he encased under glass in lustrous gold frames. In the same way, where Giacometti's images remain mostly silent and withdrawn, as if folded back on themselves, Bacon's scream for attention.

*

Bacon was a born star, drawn to the limelight like a moth to the flame, and always ready to raise the stakes, gambling a whole painting on the final twist of the brush just as he gambled a fortune on the spin of a roulette wheel. He always managed effortlessly to be the centre of attention in whichever situation he happened to be, by his exuberant charm and wit, and he was particularly adulated in the restaurants and bars where he bought champagne for everyone in sight. Considerably less flamboyant, Giacometti also tended to hold court wherever he was, but less by an extravagant manner than by the unusualness of his presence, intellect, and garrulousness, as well as by his genuine fascination with all kinds of other people. If Bacon burst out of his studio to go on the town in the evening, it was not as a bedraggled artist with his hair and jacket still caked in paint and plaster, as Giacometti did when he made his modest way up to Montparnasse. Bacon wore a perfectly pressed, bespoke suit and a crisp, new shirt and he looked, if anything, like a slightly gangsterish banker. Rather than the democratic spaces of La Coupole and the other Left Bank brasseries that Giacometti favoured, Bacon went straight to the gastronomic top, with champagne at the Ritz, then dinner in another exclusive hotel or, if he deviated from Wheeler's classic fish menu, the latest, glamorous restaurant in Soho or Mayfair.

Politically, to come at them from a completely different angle, the two artists were poles apart. Giacometti had been aligned to the French Communist Party in the earlier part of his career and he never wavered thereafter from the left. Bacon, on the other hand, considered himself as an 'old-fashioned Liberal' and believed that the individual generally had more freedom and less 'interference' under a liberal, right-of-centre government. He was notably sceptical about those friends of his, like Leiris, who supported left-wing causes while leading lives of considerable comfort and privilege. In both artists, however, there was a deeply individualistic, anarchic streak that conditioned any political views they might have; and neither of them would have accepted that their art had any explicit political implication.

Another potential point of discord between the two artists might have been their respective attitudes towards Pablo Picasso, whom Bacon never met while Giacometti came to know him well. As a young painter, certainly, Bacon idolized Picasso, imitating and absorbing his extraordinary bold, formal inventiveness quite undisguisedly until he produced his first masterpiece, *Three Studies for Figures at the Base of a Crucifixion*, at the end of the war; and for ever thereafter Picasso's achievement remained Bacon's ultimate touchstone for his own art. What drew Bacon to Picasso above all were the highly suggestive beach scenes that Picasso produced at Dinard in 1928, when he was secretly carrying on an affair with Marie-Thérèse Walter. The erotic overtones of these images made an enduring impression on Bacon in his search for an imagery that would convey 'what it feels like to be a human being' – although in time he grew outspokenly critical of Picasso's late work. Giacometti had also originally conceived a distinct admiration for Picasso, and vice versa, so that for many years, from the 1930s on, the two met frequently in each other's studios. At one point, Giacometti actually began to make a bust of Picasso, and Picasso gifted him a drawing. Then, as Picasso became more and more a magnet for the media, Giacometti had one of those abrupt volte-faces that occasionally marked his relationships (he had a similar fall out with Sartre), and from that moment on he broke with Picasso for good.

*

It is only when one is confronted by Giacometti sculptures interwoven with Bacon paintings, however, that the deepest difference between the two artists is revealed, suddenly and unforgettably, and one realizes that whereas Bacon's art is a constant, furious struggle against death, Giacometti's not only accepts death but commemorates it as having already happened.[24] If Bacon's figures are contorted and deformed, it is by their desire to live. Bloodied and mutilated, they have been brought to the brink of destruction, where momentarily they survive. The odds have been stacked against them, as of course they are stacked against all mortals, yet Bacon's heroes and heroines hang on, brutally reduced, writhing in agony, shrieking out their pain and humiliation. Beneath this great wave of human distress, an extraordinary energy pulsates: the protagonists, fuelled by unquenchable indignation at their fate, throw themselves in picture after picture against insuperable forces in a tragic attempt to confront and defeat death.

Giacometti's figures, on the other hand, have long come through that struggle. Emaciated, whittled down to the bone, they are also survivors. But whatever they have endured lies in the past. Gaunt and spectral as they are, they are calm, secure in the knowledge that they cannot be attacked, humiliated, or reduced any further.[25] Rather than struggle with death, they have accepted, even incorporated, it. Their sightless gaze is trained now on infinity, and as one walks among them, Genet's beautiful description of them as 'guardians of the dead' comes back to mind as the most apposite. The figures now appear to safeguard the dead, as if they had once stood in early burial grounds or been retrieved from ancient tombs.

This fundamental difference is underlined at every point as one's eye flits between Bacon's fleshy bodies and Giacometti's shrunken silhouettes (one can indeed hardly talk of 'bodies' in Giacometti – only outlines, contours, residues, skeletons). It is echoed in the near-absolute contrast between Bacon's hot colours throbbing and clashing on the canvas and Giacometti's unearthly cold tones, where all the colours of the grave are played out in shades of black and grey. Even in the latter's painted plasters, the colour only serves to underline the pallor of death, like corpses that have been cosmetically enhanced. Bacon's vivid, luscious brushstrokes, on the contrary, reflect all the sensuality of life. However fiercely they appear to attack, they confer an aura of heroic vitality on his embattled figures. Even in the most extreme of his sadomasochistic scenarios, the richness of Bacon's impasto betrays his love of life.

The same difference comes to the fore when one looks from Giacometti's preternaturally immobile figures, radiating the stillness of ancient Egyptian sculpture, to Bacon's protagonists, who in their exaggerated contortions seem to have come straight out of the Baroque, or even the Mannerist, period. Glimpsing their two worlds intertwined from various angles in the same space produces a bewildering kaleidoscope of forms. Giacometti's figures no longer move: they are either stock still (his women in particular) or held in permanent stasis, frozen in an arrested stride. They do not move because in death they have already arrived; all their becoming is now behind them. Bacon's figures meanwhile thresh furiously around the black hole of mortality, seeking at all costs to retain life, to go on becoming. Theirs is literally a fight to the death, and whereas Giacometti's mankind is uniformly and forbiddingly silent, Bacon's screams out its pain, its panic, and its fear.

Bacon puts on a play in every canvas in which man is shown battling his fate. Giacometti has no such story to tell. He has accepted the end in order to describe and record it more accurately. In Giacometti, the worst has already occurred. In Bacon, the worst is yet to come. There can hardly be a more fundamental difference, either in temperament or in artistic vision.

*

Yet once again, no sooner does one focus on the more mundane – however fascinating and revealing – details of the way the two artists behaved in their everyday lives, than the similarities between Giacometti and Bacon turn out to be significantly more numerous and convincing than their differences. Both artists loved big cities and their nocturnal attractions, carrying large amounts of cash on them (as, incidentally, did Sartre) wherever they went, ordering countless restaurant meals with expensive wines and tipping extravagantly, as if money were of no importance. Neither Bacon nor Giacometti had any truck with the official honours that were periodically pressed on them (Bacon, for instance, officially turned down a knighthood, and Giacometti appeared to shun fame and fortune assiduously). Both also showed not only a gentlemanly deference towards the people who served them, like waiters, but also a distinct taste for what's called 'low life'. Prostitutes, petty gangsters, chancers of every stripe appealed equally to Giacometti and Bacon, possibly because it occurred to them that they, as artists, were also operating at a level which challenged society – questioning dearly held beliefs, subverting basic convictions, and suggesting transgressive alternatives.

At all events, Bacon's homosexuality, which put him automatically on the wrong side of the law for much of his life, tended to lead him into compromising situations and distinctly dubious circles (which included notorious East End gangsters like the Kray twins), while Giacometti's passion for Caroline brought him into contact with various underworld characters who extorted significant sums of money from him (which he appears to have handed over with voluptuous alacrity). Both artists actually found the company of such low-lifers more stimulating than the art-world dignitaries and bourgeois collectors with whom they were professionally obliged to spend much of their time.

*

Had Giacometti lived longer, the friendship that he had begun with Bacon would undoubtedly have deepened, particularly since he developed a distinct taste for London during his Tate retrospective, and Bacon began to visit Paris more frequently in the years following Giacometti's death in 1966. Later that very year, for instance, Bacon had a show of new paintings at Galerie Maeght, Giacometti's own former gallery, and its success paved the way for his major retrospective at the Grand Palais in 1971–2, during which he made regular stays in the French capital. Bacon remained influenced and impressed by Giacometti the man and the artist, confiding to one of his biographers, Daniel Farson, that, 'Giacometti has influenced me more than any other living artist.'[26] As soon as he heard of Giacometti's death, Bacon wrote to Leiris, saying, 'I know that the death of Giacometti has shattered his friends as well as people he barely knew. I wanted to write to Annette but I did not know what to say. When you see Annette would you give her all my best wishes and love.'[27]

Later on, at the request of the Parisian dealer Claude Bernard,[28] who had organized an exhibition of Giacometti's drawings, Bacon wrote a brief tribute to Giacometti the draughtsman: 'For me Giacometti is not only the greatest draughtsman of our time but also one of the greatest of all time.'[29]

What Bacon did not say here, although he occasionally referred to it in conversation, was how much of Giacometti he himself had absorbed, both from his art and his way of life. But then Bacon, who once compared himself to a 'grinding machine' into which everything he had ever seen was 'ground up very fine', assimilated everything that came within his voracious gaze, from a lover's tortured face or a sports photo to a dripping tap or a crumpled reproduction of an Old Master, that might at some point serve his composite image-making. He built up a whole personal dictionary of visual experience on which he drew obliquely, folding one heavily loaded reference into another. Giacometti was on the whole more selective, feeding his imagination as directly as possible with both the art of the past and nature.

But each artist had absorbed so much of the period through which they both lived that it was woven into the fabric of their art: the sense of alienation to which postwar man was condemned, the unrelenting awareness that life is played out in a godless void, the need to distort the human image in order to communicate these terrible new truths. This created the strongest bond between them, and this in the end is what emanates most powerfully from every comparison of their work.

1 See, for instance, the memoir describing my friendship with Francis Bacon: *Francis Bacon in Your Blood* (London: Bloomsbury, 2015).

2 Here I should like to thank Sam Keller, director of the Fondation Beyeler, and my two co-curators, Catherine Grenier and Ulf Küster, for making this exhibition possible.

3 Moore, like Ben Nicholson and Barbara Hepworth, first visited Giacometti in Paris in the early 1930s.

4 Auerbach has said that in the 1950s 'an artist like Giacometti offered hope, to continue to give everything for a truthful art without any compromises'. Quoted in *London Calling*, exhibition catalogue (Los Angeles: J. Paul Getty Museum, 2016), p. 17.

5 In recognition of this early gesture of support, Giacometti allowed the Tate to acquire a body of his work (eight sculptures and two paintings) at a very reasonable cost, £8000, when his retrospective opened there in 1965.

6 *Horizon*, edited by the keenly Francophile Cyril Connolly, published an article on Giacometti by Michel Leiris in its June 1949 issue. Peter Watson also co-founded the Institute of Contemporary Arts (ICA), where Giacometti and Bacon were exhibited in the course of 1955.

7 The Sainsburys thus acquired three drawings of their son for £27.6d. It may be worth noting here that several other prominent collectors, such as the Goulandris family and Esther Grete, have made a point of collecting both Bacon and Giacometti.

8 According to Sylvester, Giacometti saw a painting by Bacon (*Study for Figure II*, 1953) for the first time at an exhibition at Erica Brausen's Hanover Gallery in London in 1955, and his reaction then was that he found it 'too expressionistic' (see David Sylvester, *Looking Back at Francis Bacon* [London: Thames & Hudson, 2000], p. 204). Sylvester, it is worth noting here, wrote an essay entitled 'Bacon and Giacometti: Likeness and Difference' to accompany a small exhibition of portraits by the two artists in the Robert and Lisa Sainsbury Collection held at the Sainsbury Centre for Visual Arts just outside Norwich in 1996.

9 Bacon himself mentioned this to me without giving any precise date.

10 In a letter to David Sylvester dated 9 September 1955, Bacon recounts this chance encounter with Giacometti in detail (David Sylvester Papers, Tate Britain Archives).

11 Other guests probably included Lucian Freud (who at one point had modelled for Giacometti) and Sonia Orwell, the widow of writer George Orwell, well known for regularly bringing together French and British writers and artists at dinner parties in her house in London.

12 Giacometti had already visited the Marlborough with Bacon in 1964 to see the first ever exhibition of Egon Schiele in Britain, as noted by the exhibition's organizer, the Austrian dealer and writer Wolfgang Fischer, in his diary. (See *Alberto Giacometti: Pionier der Moderne*, Leopold Museum, Vienna, 2014.)

13 I first met Bacon in June 1963 to do an interview with him for an issue on 'Modern Art in Britain' that I was editing for the student magazine *Cambridge Opinion*.

14 However drunk, Bacon usually retained self-control and avoided 'scenes' in public. According to the James Lord papers held at the Beinecke Rare Book & Manuscript Library, New Haven, Lord interviewed Bacon about Giacometti on three occasions in London in 1970. No further information about these interviews appears to exist.

15 Bacon was already anxious about Dyer, who, having retired as a cat burglar, was doing nothing but drink heavily. As is well known, Dyer committed suicide just before Bacon's retrospective opened at the Grand Palais in 1971.

16 This information came directly from Bacon, who was convinced that all men were fundamentally homosexual. It is also likely that Giacometti wanted to show that he was at ease in homosexual company; he had already had some practice at this, notably during his close friendship with the poet René Crevel.

17 Interestingly, Matisse later wrote to Bacon to inquire whether he might exhibit at his by then already famous gallery in New York (letter from Pierre Matisse to Bacon, January 1967. Pierre Matisse Gallery Archive, Morgan Library and Museum, New York).

18 As Michel Leiris noted pertinently in his *Journal* in 1966: 'Many artists of our time claim they are realists (Giacometti and Bacon, for example). If that were objectively true, wouldn't they be bound to reach similar results? And yet that is absolutely not the case. One must therefore conclude that their realism is of a subjective sort! Yes, they are realists, but each in his own way.'

19 Giacometti made a single pencil drawing of the head only, while Bacon executed numerous variations on the entire image.

20 I owe this information to the poet and gallerist Jacques Dupin (1927–2012), who became a close friend of Giacometti's and wrote the first monograph on him. Dupin also got to know Bacon well when the latter exhibited at Galerie Maeght in Paris. He wrote about the artist, who later painted a portrait of him.

21 Bacon later claimed that his gallery had suggested at least the first of these literary allusions rather than he himself.

22 In 1974, Bacon remarked to David Sylvester: 'My own feeling about Giacometti is that he never had any necessity either to do sculpture or to paint, that he was able to do everything in his marvellous drawings. I always feel that his sculptures and his paintings were other aspects of the drawings, and for me not as satisfactory.' (See Sylvester, op. cit., p. 245)

23 Jacques Dupin told me Giacometti had mentioned that he thought Bacon's inability to draw represented a major weakness in his work. Similarly, Bacon once stigmatized Giacometti's sculpture as 'arty'. Worth mentioning in this context is Bacon's own interest during the 1970s in producing sculpture, which he took as far as discussing certain technical solutions before abandoning the project entirely.

24 These reflections were sparked off by seeing the recent *Bacon/Giacometti* exhibition in its final juxtaposition just before the official opening at Fondation Beyeler – but as if for the very first time. I should like to thank Dr Jill Lloyd for the stimulating conversation we had as we walked round it together, discussing the profound contrast between the two artists, which, once defined, became increasingly dramatic.

25 A notable exception to this general rule is *Woman with her Throat Cut* (1932), in which erotic violence, outstripping Picasso's, has an intensity that only Bacon would later achieve. In the outspread legs of this work, there is even a hint of Bacon's voluptuousness – not a quality that one usually associates with Giacometti. I am grateful to Patrice Cotensin for having drawn my attention to this significant comparison.

26 Daniel Farson, *The Gilded Gutter Life of Francis Bacon* (London: Penguin, 1994).

27 Letter to Michel Leiris, dated 25 January 1966.

28 It is interesting to note that Giacometti left Galerie Maeght when his influential gallerist friend, Louis Clayeux, left after a disagreement; later Clayeux organized a posthumous exhibition of Giacometti's drawings at Galerie Claude Bernard. Bacon had a similar trajectory, exhibiting at Galerie Maeght, then at Galerie Claude Bernard, before returning to the first gallery, rebaptized as Galerie Lelong, in 1987.

29 This tribute was reproduced in Bacon's handwriting and dated '8/10/75' by him.

This essay is a considerably enlarged and revised version of the text that I published in the catalogue for the *Bacon/Giacometti* exhibition that took place at the Fondation Beyeler in Switzerland in 2018. A similar version was first published, in a translation into French by Patrice Cotensin, by L'Échoppe in Paris in 2019.

25

LUCIAN FREUD'S
LARGE INTERIOR, W11
(AFTER WATTEAU)

What a difference a couple of decades makes! The art-world 'event' described below took place in 1984 in London. It seemed an unusual and significant occurrence at the time – and one that pleased the fairly conservative tastes of the people then running *Connaissance des Arts*, the Paris-based magazine that commissioned the article in question as a review of the show. Lucian Freud, a painter then still relatively unknown in France,[1] was exhibiting his latest work, entitled *Large Interior, W11 (after Watteau)*, in a gallery on Bond Street. Part of the 'frisson' that this exhibit produced stemmed from the aura that Freud had managed to create around himself and his work – different, but not unlike, the cloak of scandal and enigma that his erstwhile friend, and in certain respects mentor, Francis Bacon had wrapped around himself. Another ingredient in this nevertheless relatively modest occasion (the art world itself being then notably smaller and more low-key than it is today) was the fact that an internationally well-known Old Master dealer, Agnew's, was staging the event with only one painting by the artist. The pairing of a contemporary painter with a venerable, wood-panelled, top-lit gallery (operating since 1817) specializing in traditional art and exuding a semi-museum atmosphere of established taste and value sent out distinct shock waves. At that time, a clear, uncrossable line separated the art of the past from the art of the moment. On the one hand, there was Agnew's, Colnaghi (which dates back to 1760), and a few other well-established galleries deeply intertwined with the history of art – as, in the museum

266

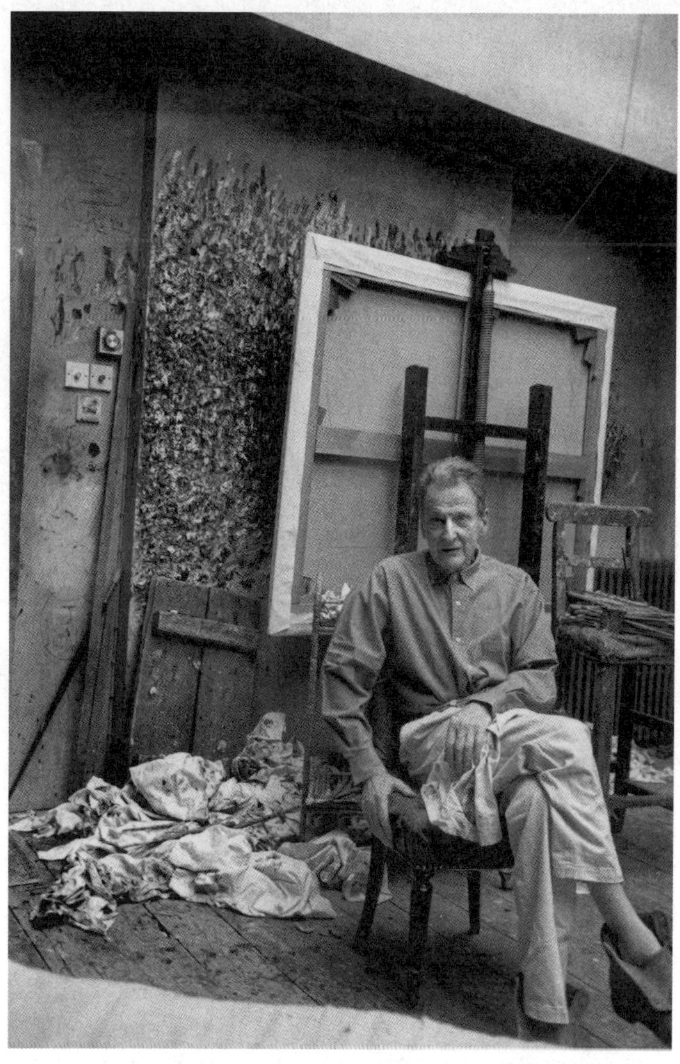

Lucian Freud, London, 1997, photographed by Henri Cartier-Bresson

sphere, was the National Gallery; on the other stood the relatively recent establishments of contemporary art, such as Waddington or Anthony d'Offay galleries – and, of course, the Tate Gallery – which dealt in the art of the living or, at least, the recently dead. The idea that a venerable Old Master gallery would exhibit a contemporary artist – and a subversively challenging one at that – seemed unprecedented.[2]

Another sign of the extent to which times and taste have changed came recently when, in a public-relations coup, Damien Hirst unveiled his new Bacon-inspired paintings at London's Wallace Collection: there was little shock but considerable embarrassment that contemporary art should look so sketchily insubstantial when exhibited in an art-historical context. On the other hand, there was a real visual jolt, it seems to me, when Bacon himself was shown during the autumn of 2009 with Caravaggio and other Old Masters at the Galleria Borghese in Rome. There, a current of near-hysterical, twentieth-century anxiety was unleashed, shaking and inflecting the solemnly settled scenes and portraits of the great European tradition. Only painters of Bacon's originality and intensity, one might conclude, can withstand the scrutiny of the past.

A further jostling of convention came from the very content of Freud's new picture, which had taken some two years to complete (1981–3). The air of '*misérabilisme*' that came off both its peeling, disinherited interior, underscored by an insistently dripping tap, and its huddle of slightly freakish, forlorn-looking characters became all the more striking for being exhibited in the plush and hushed surroundings of the Bond Street gallery. An aura of mystery and secrecy enshrouded the people Freud painted in those days, since their identity was kept strictly confidential. Thus we could not have known (as we have subsequently found out) how intimately connected the sitters were to Freud.[3] Gathered together in his grimly bare studio, they are from left to right: the painter Celia Paul (the artist's mistress at the time), Freud's daughter Bella (holding the mandolin), a stepson of his called Kai (as the modern-day 'Pierrot content', apparently overwhelmed by being hemmed in by so much femininity), and the boy's mother, Suzy Boyt (mother of four of Freud's children), while in the foreground lies a little girl whose sole purpose, according to Freud, was to 'break' the unity of Watteau's original composition.[4] As Freud has commented on the otherwise seemingly disparate group: 'I'm the connection. The link is me.'[5]

What we might have found out, however, was that Watteau's *Pierrot content*, painted around 1712, belonged to Baron Thyssen-Bornemisza, the well-known collector. And Freud's interest in the painting – a light-hearted evocation of Pierrot's happiness as he sits between two young women in a forest glade – was already apparent in one of the portraits that he painted of Thyssen, in which a detail of the Watteau appears in the background. Freud had also taken the central image of Pierrot flanked by two desirable companions and transformed it into a play about the complex entanglements of his own private life.

I myself met Freud in the early 1960s when I was a student and editing an issue of a university magazine, *Cambridge Opinion*, on 'Modern Art in Britain'. Having spent some time interviewing Bacon, I saw Freud – as well as Auerbach, Kitaj, and Hockney – quite frequently. Bacon and Freud were boon companions during those years, and at many of the memorable meals that I shared with Bacon, Freud was present. He gave off an impression of lightness and deftness, like a bird, as ready to pounce as to disappear, suddenly, without trace. At one point, Freud gave me a lift in his elegant Bentley that I have never forgotten because he literally charged through the streets of Soho, up pavements and down one-ways, as if he were giving free rein to a huge, runaway horse. I was so taken by his expert recklessness that I forgot to be afraid. We also did an interview together one afternoon, in a large room at the top of someone else's grand house in Knightsbridge. As night fell, Freud made no attempt to turn on a light so that soon there was nothing but our disembodied voices (above all, with its Germanic overtones, his) floating spookily around in the dark. In the end, this did not become the interview. Freud telephoned later on, from Scotland, and dictated a very brief text, which at the time seemed to him to encapsulate what he felt about life and about art. The text has never been quoted since then, as far as I know, so I will reproduce it here, in all its admirable terseness:

'When man finally sealed his destiny by inventing his own inevitable destruction, he also gave art absolute gravity by adding a new dimension: this new dimension, having the end in sight, can give the artist supreme control, daring and such awareness of his bearings in existence that he will (in Nietzsche's words) create conditions under which "a thousand secrets of the past crawl out of their hideouts – into his sun".'

Much has changed dramatically since the chronicle below was painstakingly hammered out on my trusty Olivetti portable. Freud is now recognized as one of the masters of our age, and indeed before his death in 2011, he was hailed as the world's greatest living 'realist' painter, as well as the 'greatest living painter' tout court. Exhibitions of his work have become more frequent, above all in Britain, the United States, and Germany, as have books and catalogues on his art. Not surprisingly, the prices paid for his paintings have more than kept pace with the vertiginous rise of his reputation. In 1998, *Large Interior, W11 (after Watteau)* itself, for which Sotheby's produced a separate, lavishly illustrated, 44-page catalogue, sold at auction in New York for more than $5.8 million. In 2008, *Benefits Supervisor Sleeping*, an impressive mound of female flesh painted in 1995, was carried off by the Russian oligarch Roman Abramovich, for no less than $33.6 million.

When the lines below were written, none of this had come to pass. Freud was still to some extent waiting in the wings. The premier English painter was at that point Bacon, who was to die in 1992. He had carved out an almost prophetic role for himself, as the artist who had defied abstraction during its mid-century heyday and spearheaded a return to figuration and to the values – however subverted and distorted – of the great European tradition. Freud, while more interested in purely painterly values, subscribed to many of the same beliefs, and when Bacon disappeared into the night the mantle of great British artist fell virtually without question on him (although he has never acceded to the higher ranks of my pantheon). Now, one might say, other London painters, notably Frank Auerbach and Leon Kossoff, both prominent members of the School of London, wait in the wings. I do not think this kind of situation obtains anywhere else in the world, and it is curious that it should happen in a country not best known for its visual talent. One is reminded, at however different a level, of the kind of competitive hierarchy that evolved out of the great centres of the Italian Renaissance, as recorded by Vasari in his *Lives*. But I digress! Dear reader, travel back in time now to an event that sent out a few shock waves in the then far smaller and more hermetic art world of London in the early 1980s.

An unusual event polarized the London art world recently: a solitary painting, albeit a large one, by a living artist, albeit a well-established one, was put on exhibition in a gallery best known for its dealings in

Old Masters and nineteenth-century art. I use the word 'event' advisedly, not only because the British press reported it at length but because the artist in question, Lucian Freud, has a devoted following and a myth-encircled reputation (comparable in kind, if not in extent, to the legends that surround Alberto Giacometti and Balthus). A correspondingly large number of people flocked to the gallery in question, Agnew's of Bond Street, where a spacious enclave had been set aside to present *Large Interior, W11 (after Watteau)*, Freud's most recent and most ambitious painting to date. There, between plush-covered walls and under the best top light in London, chairs had been provided for the public to view what one leading British daily had headlined, in a burst of cautious audacity, as 'Perhaps a masterpiece'.

The event was, of course, in the best nineteenth-century tradition. Single pictures, from Théodore Géricault's *Raft of the Medusa* to large works by once immensely revered artists, such as Rosa Bonheur and Frederic Edwin Church, travelled far and wide, sometimes throughout the Western world, as exhibitions in themselves. They had something of the impact on their age that popular films do nowadays, and they provoked spirited debate. Although the Freud picture was presented with considerably less razzmatazz than its nineteenth-century predecessors,[6] it has engendered both controversy and a certain bewilderment, not least by the open acknowledgment in its title to a master of the past: '*after Watteau*'.

Were one not already informed of this debt as one confronts *Large Interior, W11* for the first time, Watteau would surely be one of the last sources to come to mind. My immediate – and indeed lasting – impression (as the artist indubitably intended) is of pure Freud, on a scale and at a degree of mastery hitherto unparalleled. The initial impression, though 'shock' might be the more accurate word, does not come only from the powerful realism and sense of desolation that permeate the work, but also from the resolutely traditional means it employs to convey a scene of absolute contemporaneity. For whatever the picture takes from Watteau in the grouping of its five figures, it speaks entirely and authoritatively about the younger generations of today.

Figures painted with such conviction have a spectral presence, and the eye needs to absorb some of their strangeness before it can begin to work out the way they have been made. This subsequent scrutiny reveals to what extent the images have evolved, as if organically, through layer after layer of dry, crumbly looking oil paint. The ghostliness, it turns out, is not merely an art critic's conceit, but a physical fact: the product of numerous *pentimenti*, of previous figures walled up behind the final paint surface. Standing close to the canvas, one grows acutely conscious of the mass of short brushstrokes creating a thatch of tightly connected colour. Everything in this picture is expressed through the grain of the paint, with difficulty and at times clumsily, as if the artist were struggling with a half-forgotten language (which, in our unstructured, technically ignorant, 'postmodernist' age, he certainly is). Being the sum of past failures, like most serious works of art, these images take on a curious density; they establish their own, very specific equivalencies between the paint and the thing represented – whether knuckle, veined leaf, or shoe. In this other register, the paint does not approximate the thing in question, but *is* it, according to its own laws. That Freud himself sees his work in this light is confirmed by one of his rare statements about his aims as an artist. 'I would wish my portraits to be *of* the people, not like them', he has said. 'Not having a look of the sitter, *being* them ... As far as I am concerned, the paint *is* the person.'[7] These hauntingly mournful figures are thus paint-flesh and, in their lingering dependence on their creator, echo Gerard Manley Hopkins' line, 'Thou hast bound bones and veins in me, fastened me flesh.' By the same token, there is also a paint-fabric, a paint-foliage, and a paint-floor, each with an internal coherence that the painter has orchestrated into the whole.

By the time one is this far into the painting, it becomes obvious that Freud has used Watteau's *Pierrot content* above all as a point of departure, much as Bacon used Velázquez's *Innocent X* for his series of popes. But beyond the general compositional borrowing, one may perhaps detect Watteau's influence on the carefully modulated effects of light with which Freud has touched the skin and fabric, iron and enamel of his picture. The space portrayed is in fact the painter's new, large studio in Notting Hill (London, W11) and although the source is not shown, quite clearly the light falls from an overhead opening (as in the gallery where the painting was exhibited). From this traditional studio top light, a cool muted luminosity pours into the room, creating a subtle pattern of highlights that binds the various parts of the picture more closely together. But the light not only binds, marbling the walls so that even their roughness has a discreet kind of splendour, it also emphasizes, bringing a painful rawness to certain areas of flesh, or isolating by its cold evenness the sense of despair that pervades the scene.

Several elements combine to suggest this atmosphere of doom. First, the flesh itself, the most naturally eloquent substance in the painting, is filled with pathos; one cannot look at it without being made sharply aware of its mortality, the 'thousand natural shocks' it is heir to. But the pathos is a subdued one, and notably more controlled than in certain of Freud's earlier portraits, above all during the 1960s, where the paint-flesh seems to have been deliberately whipped up into red rawness to produce a dramatic effect. Particularly evocative here are the attitudes and expressions of the figures themselves, for although they are seated close together (far more so than in the Watteau), each appears trapped in a world of private sorrow – as if each were reacting in his or her particular way to a tragic truth. Even the child, with her strangely aged face, gazes with dull-eyed disillusionment (like an abandoned toy) from her position on the floor. A memory of Watteau's tender melancholy may be found in the comforting hand that the woman on the far left rests on the young girl's thigh.

Having heard Freud talk about his painting and about art in general on several occasions, I suspect that he would resist any 'interpretation' of this kind, preferring at best comment of a purely technical kind on the formal relationships between the figures and the space they occupy. He has however admitted that the people he portrays tend to be those he has known closely, often over a long period of time – and therefore the people most likely to engage his most personal emotions. 'My work is purely autobiographical', he has said. 'It is about myself and my surroundings. It is an attempt at a record. I work from the people that interest me, and that I care about and think about, in rooms that I live in and know. I use the people to invent my pictures with, and I can work more freely when they are there.' On further research, one finds that all three women portrayed in *Large Interior, W11* have been painted by Freud on previous occasions, and that the haunted-looking Columbina with the mandolin is in fact the artist's own daughter.

Much of what passed for art appreciation at a certain point in the nineteenth century consisted of guessing hidden meanings in pictures, most of which did in fact set out to illustrate a moral or tell a story. This encouraged superficial talents and introduced so much trivia into painting that, in the twentieth century, 'storytelling' or narrative has become synonymous with bad art. Yet having been deprived for so long of content of this kind (a staple of painting at all other periods in history), the eye now begins to hunger for it. One day soon, no doubt, the notion of narrative in painting will lose its stigma. In the meantime, any work containing several figures is almost bound to say something about the relationships that exist between them (the most obvious exception being Picasso's *Les Demoiselles d'Avignon*, where the relationship is exclusively one of form). And only the most blinkered modernist could be insensible to the atmosphere of anxiety that creeps round Freud's group of loved individuals like a poison gas.

Several means have been used here to suggest threat and unease. Unlike the Watteau, where the players are set squarely in the middle of the picture space, Freud's figures are concentrated into the right-hand half, which immediately strikes a note of imbalance, of precariousness. The slightly plunging point of view from which the spectator looks at them also adds to their vulnerability. But what gives the scene its most vertiginous sense of doom is the perspective created by the floorboards, which appear to rush beneath the figures' feet like road beneath a fast-moving car and to force the huddled group to recede ever faster. Beyond the damp-stained, fissured studio walls, the glimpse we get of the city ripples disquietingly out of true, amplifying the anxiety that dominates the room and cutting off all thought of escape. A tap running aimlessly counterpoints the picture's central theme of time, hope, life running out.

Yet this undeniably disturbing vision is conveyed with a greater gentleness than is usual in Freud's work. Gone, certainly, are the rhetorical, not to say melodramatic, devices that the artist has used in the past, such as a nude with prominent nipples lying beside a dish containing two fried eggs or, more notoriously, a naked man fondling a rat within marked proximity to his genitals. Without any such obvious efforts to impress or alarm, the new picture conveys a profound impression of the transience of life. Though the figures portrayed are undoubtedly children of the nuclear age, their sadness appears to be more universal as if they were mourning the human condition as a whole. Convincingly elegiac in tone and admirably accomplished in execution, *Large Interior, W11* not only confirms Freud's reputation as one of the outstanding figure painters of our time but indicates that his best painting may still be to come.

At this point, the French reader might well feel the need for some background information about the artist, since Freud has never been exhibited in France – and only very rarely elsewhere outside England. In London, however, where he has shown regularly in a succession of prominent galleries, his gifts have long been recognized (in 1940, when Freud was only seventeen, for instance, the influential literary review *Horizon* published a self portrait drawing by him). Born in Berlin in 1922, son of an architect and grandson of Sigmund Freud, the artist arrived in England as a boy of ten. Although he has remained distinctly un-English in his cultural inheritance and stylistic attitudes, no painter has been more London-bound in his life and work.[8] He has concentrated from the beginning on a handful of close friends and family, as well as occasional scenes of the London he knows best. With certain notable exceptions (such as those mentioned above), Freud's pictures eschew extraneous detail and address themselves to the particularly difficult task of 'straightforward' representation. Consequently, although he often adopts unusual perspectives, Freud depends first and foremost on the expressive qualities of his brushwork. If he has made little attempt at formal invention, there is no doubt that his abiding interest has been to convey observed life as directly and persuasively as he can – without what his London-based colleague R. B. Kitaj has called 'modernist intervention'.

Freud's lengthy and arduous development as a painter has gone through three main stages. In the first, he was clearly indebted to a highly linear, near-satirical tradition (much of his early work has a Grosz-like cast). From about 1950, the artist concentrated more and more exclusively on portraits, and his style, while remaining predominantly linear, grew to depend on direct observation of his models. (Freud has emphasized how important the model is to his work: 'I am never inhibited by working from life. On the contrary, I feel more free; and I can take liberties which the tyranny of memory would not allow.' The flesh in these pictures has a clear-contoured translucence more reminiscent of the great Flemish masters, and the atmosphere is of extreme human vulnerability. Then, from the late 1950s onwards, Freud's paint became as loose as before it had been tightly controlled, and his brushwork both freer and more deliberately expressive. This last major change was perhaps connected to his deep admiration of Bacon's work. Since that radical transformation (comparable to a sonneteer deciding to write in blank verse), Freud has followed a course of uncompromising individuality and dedication to his art.

Large Interior, W11 is certainly the magnum opus of Freud's maturity as a painter so far. Several external reasons prompted him to undertake a work of this scale (the painting is 185 centimetres by 198 centimetres, and took three years). One was the Courbet exhibition at the Grand Palais in Paris in 1977, which revived Freud's long-standing ambition to attempt a composition with several figures. Another was the simple fact that he had recently moved to a new studio (the 'large interior' in question) that could accommodate bigger canvases. A third reason cropped up while Freud was engaged on a portrait of Baron Thyssen-Bornemisza, whose collection contains Watteau's *Pierrot content*. Freud was sufficiently captivated by the picture that he used part of it as a background to his portrait. 'At first I intended to make a copy of the Watteau', he says. 'Then I thought: why don't I make one of my own?'

Once he had decided on the models that he wanted, Freud began on his picture without benefit of preliminary sketches; a number of related drawings were in fact done *after* the completed painting. From what one can glean from sources close to the artist, he worked piecemeal, first on one figure, then on another, at whatever time of day or night the models were available. The differences between the finished picture and its original inspiration are manifestly greater than the similarities. The twilit sylvan glade has given way to a seedy, urban interior, from which all hope of graceful pleasure *à la dix-huitième* has been banished. A little of the lustrous clothing remains, but where an almost childlike content united Watteau's smiling actors, Freud's people are bound by a joint sense of loss and foreboding. It is just that pitch of anguish – the particular blend of silk dresses and bare feet, of mandolins played in decaying places – that gives the painting its urgent contemporaneity, compelling us to look into it as into a secret, elusive mirror of our time.

1 Freud's first and – as far as I am aware – only solo exhibition in Paris was held at the Galerie Berggruen in 1990. The show, for which I wrote the preface, consisted of engravings ('*l'oeuvre gravé*'). Five years later, the Fondation Maeght put on *Bacon–Freud: Expressions* in Saint-Paul de Vence, for which Jean-Louis Prat wrote the introductory text. Freud's next – and thus far, I believe, last significant – appearance in France was in *L'École de Londres, de Bacon à Bevan*, the exhibition that I curated in 1998, which included eight major canvases by Freud alongside works by Bacon, Auerbach, Kossoff, Kitaj, Andrews, and others. This selection of works by London-based figurative painters, all of whom knew each other and had followed each other's progress closely throughout their career, was shown first at the Musée Maillol in Paris, before travelling to Santiago da Compostela and finally Vienna (although Freud expressly insisted, through his London lawyers, that his works be withdrawn from this show, held in the birthplace of his famous grandfather).

2 This was not in fact the case, of course. In Victorian times, Agnew's, Colnaghi, and the Belgian-born dealer Ernest Gambart dominated the contemporary art market of the period, selling new pictures to new money. And earlier art dealers, such as Watteau's supporter, Edmé François Gersaint, would have mixed new and old art in their displays without a qualm.

3 In his book *Lucian Freud*, published in 1982, the painter and teacher Lawrence Gowing constantly emphasizes that Freud's sitters cannot – indeed, should not – be named, insisting that the paintings' innate qualities can be better appreciated as a result. However, in his own text, the issue of whom they are predominates so much that their namelessness becomes more of an obstacle than an aid to appreciation.

4 This kind of detail about his paintings, which Freud had tended to suppress, became available once his retrospective exhibition opened at the Tate in 2002 and William Feaver's catalogue essay was published.

5 Quoted in Starr Figura, *Lucian Freud: The Painter's Etchings* (New York: Museum of Modern Art, 2008), p. 20.

6 Special effects, such as gas jets flickering in silver reflectors, as well as evocative accessories and furnishings, were stock-in-trade at many such single-painting exhibitions.

7 Quoted by John Russell in his preface to the catalogue for Hayward Gallery exhibition, *Lucian Freud*, London, 1974.

8 The notion of London as a key centre – even *the* key centre – of significant contemporary art is beginning to gain credence. Of the most important figurative artists to be deeply connected with the city, only Francis Bacon and David Hockney have been widely exhibited abroad. In the coming years, I believe, the exemplary achievement of the others – such as Freud, Auerbach, Kitaj, Kossoff, Andrews, etc. – will be increasingly acclaimed.

Originally published in *Connaissance des Arts*, Paris, March 1984; republished in French with a new introduction by L'Échoppe, Paris, 2010

26

RAYMOND MASON CONFRONTS THE TORRENT OF LIFE

The sculptor and painter Raymond Mason remains unclassifiable, and that in part explains why his work is not better known. He was born in Birmingham but lived for his entire career in Paris, where he got to know Picasso and Giacometti and became friendly with other leading personalities, such as the poet Yves Bonnefoy and the photographer Henri Cartier-Bresson. Hugely talented, he attracted attention early on with his bronze relief *Barcelona Tram* (1953), and other works that focused deliberately on ordinary people in ordinary city scenes. He then began a series of monumental reliefs in epoxy resin that he painted in bright, even garish colours – on subjects such as the closing-down of the Les Halles marketplace in Paris or grape-picking in Provence – maintaining that they brought an extra degree of realism that would interest the public at large and not merely the rarefied art world. He also continued to produce watercolours of great delicacy that contrasted strongly with his controversial polychrome sculpture.

I organized two exhibitions of Mason's work, one at the Serpentine Gallery in 1982 and another at Musée Maillol in 2000. I also included him in a travelling School of London show because his work was so staunchly figurative and he had exhibited with the other London artists at Helen Lessore's Beaux-Arts gallery in London. Mason himself was highly articulate and had evolved a robust theory in support of his approach to sculpture. I felt that it would be interesting to find out more about the life of this highly individual artist, which had begun not in the heady existentialist

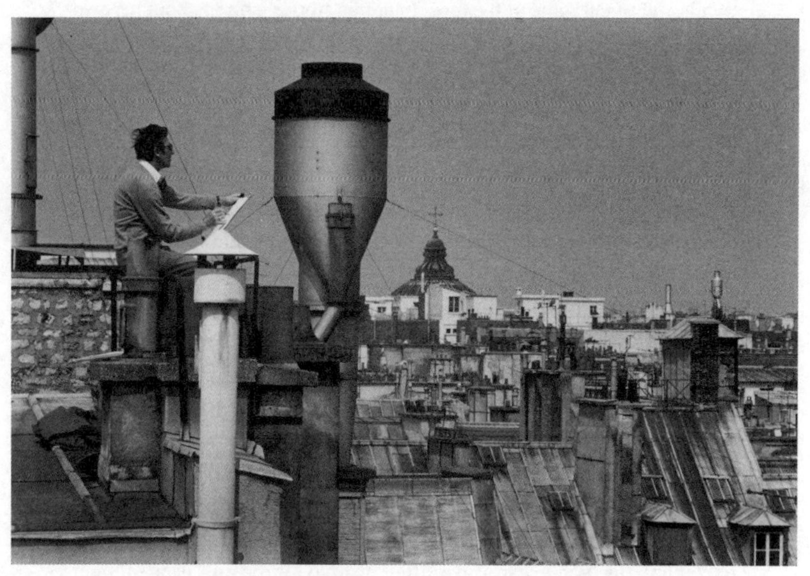

Raymond Mason, Paris, 1976, photographed by Henri Cartier-Bresson

atmosphere that he encountered in Paris when he arrived in 1946, but in the backstreets of industrial Birmingham. Mason, who had a prickly personality and was highly protective of his reputation, wanted me to present him and his work in a certain way, so it took some time before he accepted this introduction to the latter show. The whole experience became fraught, while mercifully leavened by Mason's capacity to see the funny side of things and to tell some of the most hilarious stories – often about his own gaffes – I have ever heard.

As a child, Raymond Mason spent his mornings not at school but at home, struggling with chronic asthma. He dutifully inhaled the vapours from the asthma powder that his mother left burning by his side, but his attention was totally fixed on what he could see from the window. It looked out onto a narrow street of small houses in a working-class area of Birmingham: there was a grocer's and a sweet shop at one end, a pub at the other. Opposite, looming over the terraced houses, stood a red-brick factory whose massive presence the little boy found both mysterious and reassuring, and which he was later to refer to as his 'Mont Sainte-Victoire'. Very little happened in the street. Neighbours met from time to time on their way out, and very occasionally a car or a horse-drawn van would trundle past. But from his enforced seclusion, fighting for breath, the child was entranced by the slowly changing spectacle: the women bent against the wind clutching their shopping bags, the kids playing on the pavement, the men in cap and muffler headed for the pub, each of them sharply delineated against the factory's rain-darkened facade.

This was Mason's window on the world. It gave him everything that he needed to awaken his enormous visual curiosity, and essentially it has stayed with him ever since. Some seventy years later, Mason is still confined to a room, avidly absorbing the spectacle of people going about their lives in the street outside. The room where he spends so many solitary hours every day is, of course, his studio near the Luxembourg Gardens, and the street is usually one of those that run closest to his front door. Mason continues to observe and record his immediate environment with the same painstaking passion that he had when he began to draw as a boy, marvelling at the richness, the ordinary extraordinariness, of daily existence.

But, as the present retrospective of his work amply reveals, Mason's window has never ceased to grow, to vary, and to deepen. Mason is essentially a city-dweller, having moved from Birmingham via Oxford and London to Paris, which he has made his home since he first arrived in 1946. But although Paris has been by far and away the main theatre for his art, Mason has also found time to paint and sculpt several other large cities, notably London, New York, Rome, and Hong Kong. Man in the city, poignantly alone or swept up in a crowd, has always been the most constant theme in Mason's work; but he has also brought his powers of observation, like a huge headlight, to bear on the city itself, devoid of inhabitants and revealed as pure architecture, a mass of colour and form all the more evocative for being empty. Similarly, Mason's window has often opened onto landscape, above all a low-lying mountain in Provence called the Luberon, where he used to spend his summers. Like his cityscapes, the landscapes are always meticulously topographical, often with no sign of human life beyond a deserted farmhouse. Yet even here, man is occasionally accorded a place, and, in the large sculpture called *The Grape Pickers* (1982), takes on a dramatic, dominant role.

The scale of Mason's work is as varied as its subjects. There are small initial sketches, executed with admirable immediacy and vigour, as well as fully worked-up drawings in black ink, watercolour, or gouache. There are painted studies for the sculpture, and maquettes, then the full-scale sculpture itself. Every major theme in Mason's development has been subjected to this rigorous examination: it has been studied from various angles, in various media, in various sizes, and finally in three dimensions. If there is a notable variety in the scale, there is even more in the treatment. What strikes me as especially revealing in this exhibition is that it shows the artist at his most intimate as well as in his most public guise. At one extreme, there are the astonishingly delicate watercolour studies of fruit or plant life, and at the other, the overwhelming, almost brutal forcefulness of the large polychrome sculptures. The distance between the two extremes in Mason's work is as great as between a lyric fragment and an epic drama, and it can come as a shock to realize that both derive from the same author — that the sensitive watercolourist devoted to nuance coexists with the impassioned dramatist seeking maximum popular impact by every plastic means. Similarly, the spontaneity that characterizes Mason's drawings – surely among the most evocative drawings of any artist alive – is replaced in the sculptures by the most carefully rehearsed and deliberately executed composition. Where, in many of the preparatory drawings, everything appears to be still in flux, undecided as to its final form, the sculptures have been defined down to the last detail from whatever viewpoint the spectator cares to look at them.

The spectator plays an absolutely essential role in Mason's view. Indeed, he believes that the whole purpose of making a work of art is to communicate with as many people, on as many levels, as possible. Everything Mason does is thus projected from the start towards the outside world. His sculpture, in a nutshell, is about people, for people. Mason himself frequently reiterates this theme, which forms the core of his artistic credo. 'As far as I'm concerned, the only movement of an artist is towards life, towards others', he has stated. 'I seek to express and, if possible, to exalt the world immediately surrounding me and which I know.... I have been occupied specifically with the human theme and with the doings of humble folk. This is clear and simple. What is decidedly less so, in an epoch of declining beliefs, is the choice of a subject of universal nature capable of interesting and speaking out to the general public, to the entire world. For what matters to me is not only the subject of the work, but the public comprehension of it.'[1] Moreover, Mason writes, gives interviews, and talks to the media about different aspects of his sculpture, since he believes it is an artist's duty to give his work every chance of being recognized and understood before it is sent out into the world.

It follows that Mason is not primarily concerned with self-expression. Yet his development as an artist has followed such an individual course that his work can be read as an autobiography, at least on the creative and intellectual level. His daily existence and his work are in fact so interdependent that the most radical changes in his style, marking an altogether new phase, have undoubtedly transformed his life. These radical changes have always come about in Mason's career with the creation of a key work. Mason believes that the artist's abiding concern should be to make masterpieces, and certainly his own course has been determined by a handful of extremely ambitious sculptures, which have summed up the works that preceded them and which, by creating so definitive a watershed, have obliged the artist thereafter to seek a fresh subject and a new compositional challenge. Four large sculptures, in particular, can be seen as defining stages in Mason's development, and since this retrospective is to a large extent articulated around them, I should like to consider them in detail here.

Mason started out at the very beginning of his career as a painter; and later, when he was firmly established as a sculptor, he nevertheless characterized himself as a 'painter in three dimensions'. When he arrived in Paris, he began by experimenting with abstract sculpture. Then he came into contact with Giacometti, falling under the spell of both the man and the work. Recalling that decisive encounter, Mason says that 'Giacometti was the saviour, the only rallying-point possible in the luxurious art world of Paris. He was the example for the young man who felt that the image of the world had to be worshipped. He showed that it was possible.' *Man in a Street* (1952), a bronze relief in which the bust of a young man set against an anonymous building stares out at the spectator from hollow eye sockets, shows Giacometti's influence most clearly; and by the following year, when Mason completed *Place Saint-Germain-des-Prés*, with its more complex organization of contrasting planes, that influence had been sufficiently absorbed to allow the young sculptor to start exploring the theme of figures in an architectural setting that was to occupy him throughout the 1950s.

It was with *Barcelona Tram*, however, that Mason came unmistakably into his own. Although it dates from the same year as *Place Saint-Germain-des-Prés* (1953), the young sculptor gives full proof here of technical prowess and stylistic independence – the traditional requirements for a 'masterpiece'. As often in Mason's work, *Barcelona Tram* grew out of a specific experience: of being struck, as he drew in the Catalan capital, by how rounded and sculptural figures, especially female figures, appeared standing bathed in strong sunlight on the street. Mason was also fascinated by the fact that the Barcelona trams had no glass in their windows, which allowed passengers to sit as in a box at the theatre, watching the world go by, and in turn being watched by the people on the street. As if in direct reaction to the powerful visual impression that the crowded, open-windowed tram had left on him, Mason made his first high relief, working the plaster to create some figures in the round and accentuating the recesses in the imposing Estacíon de Francia, the gateway from

Barcelona to Paris, which looms up behind – much, one imagines, as the factory had loomed over the street where the artist grew up. While Mason's previous low-relief bronzes had radiated stasis, a suspension in time and place, this composition was alive with movement: the figure jumping onto the departing tram, the breeze catching the woman's skirt, even the waves of sunlight one can sense beating down in front of the cavernous gloom of the city's main railway station, all capture a moment of everyday life – the street life that was to become Mason's main theme – with a poetic vividness.

While clearly indicating the power and originality of the young sculptor's talent, *Barcelona Tram* also brought him to the notice of Picasso, Balthus, and Bacon, who all remarked on the work and who were, with Giacometti, the twentieth-century artists whom Mason has always admired most; and from this time on, Mason became keenly aware of the compositional mastery of Balthus's large pictures, above all *La Rue* and *Le Passage du Commerce Saint-André*. For the following ten years, the young English artist concentrated on a series of Parisian street scenes that were essentially developments on the themes contained in *Barcelona Tram*. They explored the influences that Mason was still assimilating of Giacometti and Balthus, as well as Honoré Daumier and (a sculptor Mason had revered since boyhood) Michelangelo, culminating in an outstandingly ambitious, major work entitled *The Crowd*, which took the sculptor five years, from 1963 to 1968, to complete.

The best way to approach *The Crowd* may be to follow in Mason's footsteps and look at the many preparatory studies that he made – in ink on paper as well as plaster – in the run-up to the final massive sculpture. The maquettes, in particular, demonstrate the daring and the difficulty of the undertaking. Up until this point, Mason's figures had always been conceived within an architectural context: buildings, receding streets, and even a bronze sky contained them, situating their everyday actions and gestures against a specific background. But the very raison d'être of Mason's new sculpture was to present a crowd in its most abstract essence: humanity, set outside any concept of time and place, a mass of figures dependent only on each other for their meaning. The idea for the works had grown out of Mason's fascination with the phenomenon of large groups of people moving along, rising and falling like waves, full of internal contradictions and personal idiosyncrasies yet nevertheless held together by their sameness, one man multiplied into many men, impelled in a single, general direction. What impresses most in the finished work, now permanently installed in the Tuileries Gardens, is how fluid the great mass of bronze appears. Wherever the eye alights – on a hat, an ear, an arm – it is led detail by detail from one side of the composition to the other. Movement flickers across the whole, like a flame or sunlight on the sea. An almost threatening restlessness is released from this dark, seething mass of heads, some fully formed, others still featureless knobs, that piles up and tumbles down on the spectator like a lava flow of human forms. *The Crowd* might equally well have been called 'The Source', since this seething multiplicity of figures looks above all like a well out of which successive generations of human beings are pouring forth.

The casting of *The Crowd*, during a hot summer in a foundry in Rome, left Mason so exhausted that he vowed never to work in bronze again. But another, more significant reason underlay this decision, prompting both a crisis and a turning point in his career. Since coming under Giacometti's influence, Mason had banished colour from his work. Yet he had begun his artistic life as a painter, and colour remained a vital component in his desire to intensify and recreate his feelings about life through art. Having bought a house opposite the Luberon in Provence, Mason abandoned himself once again to the pleasures of painting by executing a series of watercolour landscapes of his new Provençal environment. Mindful that landscape, with genre painting, came at the bottom of the traditional hierarchy of subjects, Mason cast around for a way of uniting his love of colour with his true métier as a sculptor. The breakthrough came when he chanced upon a technique for moulding sculpture in epoxy resin that Dubuffet had been using for some time. Mason had a small plaster moulded and was delighted by the lightness and durability of the cast. To recapture the expressive intensity of his original, the sculptor added a few touches of paint to the dead-white resin; then he realized that, as if by chance, he had found his ideal medium, since it brought together his love of colour with his love of three-dimensional form.

After the strain of *The Crowd*, Mason decided that his next subject would have to be something that he was sure he could work on with pleasure. He had always been fond of markets, with their interaction of colourful characters, the sensuous beauty of the great piles of produce and the general commotion. (Later, in a memorable phrase, he was to sum up his aim as an artist by saying: 'The commotion, the emotion, the torrent of life, that's what I'm after.'[2]) Mason, the great chronicler of ordinary events, had always regarded Les Halles as one of the magic, not to say sacred, places of Paris. Since he enjoyed spending time there, he roamed the area, rubbing elbows with the locals – the porters, the prostitutes, the fruit-sellers, and the tramps – and making sheaves of drawings of the nightly spectacle of the flowers and the fruit, the sides of meat, and the cartloads of vegetables arriving in the heart of Paris. He had not worked out precisely what his new project might be, but when President Pompidou gave the order to raze Les Halles, Mason realized that he had an urgent task: to devise a sculpture that would commemorate the passing of an irreplaceable part of Parisian history stretching back to the Middle Ages, with all its popular pageant and its deeply human connotations, before it was swept away for ever.

It took Mason some two years, living like a recluse in his studio, to conceive, mould, cast, and finally paint the monumental sculpture that he entitled *The Departure of Fruits and Vegetables from the Heart of Paris, 28 February 1969* (1969–71). Strikingly different from his previous works, the vast, fresco-like relief showed a procession of market folk ceremoniously taking their leave, and their produce, from what had long been known as the '*ventre de Paris*' (the belly of Paris). The colourful figures, each one highly individualized, were flanked on either side by the late Gothic facade of Saint-Eustache on one side, and the metal-and-glass pavilions of Baltard on the other. When the new work was first exhibited, even some of Mason's staunchest supporters were perplexed. They appreciated the powerful formal qualities of the piece: the way the wheel on the vegetable cart was exactly echoed by the rose window of Saint-Eustache, whose tracery was in turn recalled in the veining of the humble cabbage leaves, left no one in doubt as to the compositional brilliance of the work. But the acrylic colours, deliberately chosen to contrast violently with each other and so reinforce the illusion of space, provoked general consternation. Yet, some thirty years later, the vivid tones of the sculpture, muted by time and the solemn gloom of Saint-Eustache where it now stands, have come to seem both natural and necessary.[3]

Mason compares himself to a novelist whose work will expand to include as much content – as many facts and observations – as possible (as opposed to a poet, whose aim tends to be reduction and concision). One day, as he read in the newspaper about a mining disaster that had occurred in northern France, his whole Birmingham past seemed to well up before him. He immediately set to work on a small low-relief based on the newspaper photograph, and later went to visit the site of the accident. With its groups of huddled figures, its muted colours, and generalized sense of calamity, *A Tragedy in Northern France. Winter, Rain and Tears* (1975–7) forms an exact counterpoint in shock and suffering to the jaunty, life-affirming cortège of the Les Halles sculpture. The deployment of the large cast of figures against their red-brick background (once again instantly reminiscent of Birmingham) is so effective that it combines the immediacy of a photograph with the permanence of a three-dimensional structure that opens up new perspectives from whichever angle one comes at it. There is an implacable visual logic in Mason's work that has foreseen the spectator's every move and set up a maximum amount of form and colour, light and shade, for the eye to feed on.

This strategy – of providing an almost kaleidoscopic interplay of form and colour to retain the spectator's attention – is used to brilliant effect in *The Grape Pickers* (1982). Mason clearly felt the need to return not only to a more joyful theme, but also to first-hand experience. The sculpture represents a plot of land and a group of figures he knew by heart: the rows of vines, growing in the field beside Mason's summer house in Provence, were tended by his next-door neighbours. Having devised an overall composition that would bring a maximum of visual drama to this otherwise ordinary harvesting scene, Mason made numerous studies in situ to work out every detail, from the exact tilt of the grape picker's hat to the autumnal tones of the vine leaves and the shadows cast by the October afternoon sun. What Mason aimed at, through all his painstaking research as a 'novelist', was to impart such a sum of verifiable information to the image that he was creating that it would take on the fullest possible density – and hence, he hoped, longevity.

Before the hanging of this exhibition got under way, Mason made tiny maquettes of all his works, which, with customary meticulousness, he placed to what he considered their best advantage round the walls of a tiny scale model of the Musée Maillol's rooms. Looking at these maquettes, rapidly fashioned for the occasion yet somehow perfect in themselves, brought home to me in an unexpected way the almost uncanny vitality that Mason's art communicates. Although rather smaller than a matchbox, *The Grape Pickers*, for instance, radiated a warm, Provençal light, while the minuscule *Tragedy* struck dismal notes of grief. However straightforwardly representational Mason's sculptures appear at first, their sheer formal ingenuity and coherence lift them onto another plane. They possess a kind of surcharge of realism, which makes them both like and quite unlike the daily reality that they claim to portray, elevating ordinary life to the mythical realm of art, where its enduring significance is gradually revealed.

1 'Responses by Raymond Mason to Questions by Michael Peppiatt', in the catalogue
   to Raymond Mason's first retrospective at the Serpentine Gallery, London, 1982.
2 'The Torrent of Life', a conversation between Richard Cork and Raymond Mason for
   BBC Radio 3, reproduced in the catalogue for the exhibition *Raymond Mason: Sculptures
   and Drawings*, Birmingham City Museum and Art Gallery, 1989.
3 Since 2001, the work has been held in the Tate's collection.

Originally published in the catalogue for the exhibition *Raymond Mason*, Musée Maillol, Paris, 2000

27

R. B. KITAJ: PAINTINGS AS NOVELS

It is still difficult to get the measure of Ronald Brooks Kitaj. He was one of those artists (like Raymond Mason) whose vigorous presence and appetite for debate and controversy gave wings to his paintings: his work seemed part of a larger 'life-programme' that included paying homage to the poets and painters whom he most admired and exploring his own identity as an American-born Jewish intellectual permeated with European culture. I knew him well, and we worked on a couple of projects together, notably a travelling School of London exhibition that took Kitaj's original concept of the theme as its starting point while narrowing the number of painters down to a 'hard core' of six.[1]

There was something about Kitaj that reminded me of a highly skilled sports coach, someone who had specialist knowledge and a huge enthusiasm for the game without being quite a 'player'. I have not had the opportunity to look at his paintings for many years, but as I look at illustrations of them, I sense that in themselves they now appear more and more as that: 'illustrative', illustrating a wide range of concepts and ideas, some of them immediately recognizable, others more covert and subtle, not existing as works of art in and of themselves as much as manifestos of the artist's preoccupations and allegiances. This is a difficult concept to explore in a few lines, but surely a sign of great art is that it exists entirely on its own terms and, while it may well include all kinds of references to other elements and sources (one thinks of T. S. Eliot, one of Kitaj's heroes), it absorbs them so entirely into its own unique language that it references itself above all. This does not quite happen in Kitaj, as it did not in Mason, since the story seems always to talk louder than the paint, never unleashing the full force of the medium that they are using which, in the end, is what fully convinces and satisfies the eye.

We look so easily and frequently at images that we are tempted to forget what strange things they are. Yet the magically potent pieces of canvas and stone to which we return again and again are as full of enigma and revelation as oracles were for the ancients. We go to them to clarify our perceptions, to deepen our insight into the nature of things; and, after a certain absence, to gauge the way our taste and thinking have changed. However much this complex and secret process is turned into part of the daily round (as it often is, of course, for critics and curators), it remains essentially a mystery: analysed from every side for centuries, but never explained.

One outstanding quality of R.B. Kitaj's work, to my mind, is that it persistently recalls the inherent strangeness of images. By a whole array of distancing devices, buried references, and other disruptions operating at a barely conscious level, his pictures keep in view, as it were, the intricate artifice of their own making. They do not merge into the mind as a purely aesthetic experience (an exact harmony in which image and spectator are one); rather they state that they are there to be interpreted, that the eye has to go and get them through a maze of personal and learned allusion. Thus Kitaj's paintings stand apart, intrigue, puzzle, even irritate, because no sooner has the initial impact been made than the spectator is confronted by a resolute elusiveness, an otherness that has to be tracked down.

'Otherness' appears to have characterized Kitaj from the very start. He was born, in 1932, in Cleveland, Ohio, to what he calls 'enlightened working-class' parents of Russian Jewish origin. As a small boy, he became entranced by the treasures of the great Cleveland Museum, where he attended children's art classes and made drawings of classical sculpture. At sixteen, he went to an art school in New York where 'everyone was working with house-painter's brushes in the first flush of "action painting"'.[2] But love of museums had fired the young Kitaj to want to paint like Hans Memling, so that such gestural spontaneity ran exactly counter to his aims. Inevitably, he left the New York school; and for the next

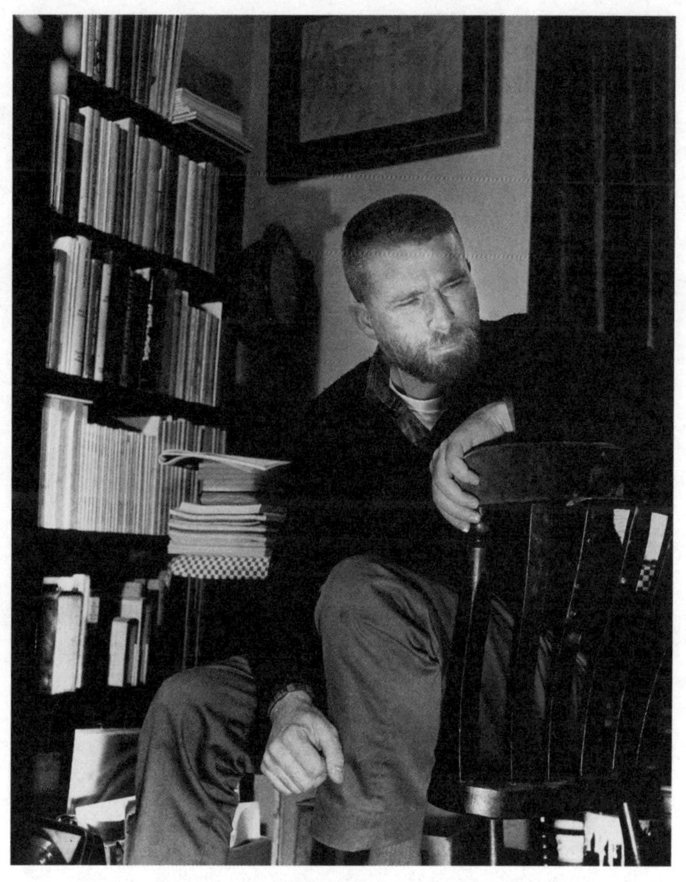

R. B. Kitaj, 1963, photographed by Jorge Lewinski

couple of years, with a sketchbook to hand, he travelled, mostly as a merchant seaman, and began to develop an extraordinarily varied store of knowledge about the world.

When Kitaj came to Europe, half student, half mariner, in 1951, the city that first claimed him was Vienna, where several of his forebears had lived. Following in Schiele's footsteps, he enrolled at the Viennese Art Academy and received a training that had barely changed in a century. At the same time, the war-torn cosmopolitan capital, haunted by the grandeur of its political and intellectual past, deeply impressed the young American. 'I read a lot in cafés that are now gone in the wind', he reminisces, 'and ran in a louche pack of students who lived and loved in romantic attics. Kafka and Joycean exile meant more to me than the gorgeous Breughels and Velázquezes in the great Hapsburg collection. But I was drawing every day from models, rosy with cold, who were meticulously placed early in the morning – even to the placement of the joints of the fingers.'[3] When the Academy course came to an end, Kitaj moved to another ravaged, imperial city, London, and began classes at the Royal College of Art at exactly the same moment as David Hockney, a close friend ever since. The sense of artistic comradeship, of working in a place marked by so many gifted painters – from Francis Bacon to Frank Auerbach, Lucian Freud to Michael Andrews – was one of the main reasons Kitaj made London his permanent home.

By the time Kitaj's lengthy academic apprenticeship was completed, several of his lasting preoccupations as an artist had come to the fore. Given his background and his travels, he found himself deeply versed in three cultures – American, Jewish, and European – without belonging specifically to any one. Naturally enough, he was drawn towards an art of synthesis, an imagery in which quite disparate sources might be fused. His pictures would be as kaleidoscopic and conflicting as his experience of the world had been.

A parallel concern was that his painting should have some social relevance. Kitaj had grown up in an atmosphere of 'compassionate idealistic socialism' (several of his mother's leftist, intellectual friends had fought in the Spanish Civil War, for instance), and he aspired to create an art that would make an effective moral statement. The hope remains, though the artist – who is most mindful of such phrases as Theodor Adorno's

'No poetry after Auschwitz' – has considerably refined its implications. 'I've been mulling for years the possibility of representing the Jewish tragedy under the Nazis', he remarked recently. 'Formalists will laugh at that, but the ancients believed in what has been called the *type-coining power* of art, and so do I. Types, figures were invented which embodied emotional states saturated with "reality".... Artists *can* coin examples of social well-being – Matisse wanted that. If artists can apotheosize persons, principles and practices, they should also have the power to bear witness to unhappiness by coining a remembrance to it.'

Though perhaps the most manifest, these concerns were not the only ones affecting the young artist. In his earlier works, the whole world presses in on him to be painted. Enigmatic compositions, with no less enigmatic titles, such as *Apotheosis of Groundlessness* (a mysterious shedlike image) or the better-known *Where the Railroad Leaves the Sea*, hinted at many different areas of troubled, and troubling, experience. Whether complex allegories with several figures, single portraits, or half-abstract inventions, these canvases brought together disparate elements that worked like riddles, or conflicting court evidence, in the mind. The station roof, the unspecified lateral constructs, the couple kissing, and the tableware that make up *Where the Railroad Leaves the Sea* produce a hauntingly dislocated poetry not unlike lines of early Eliot or snatches of certain pre-war German cabaret songs.

The result is a diffuse anxiety. We look at these bright, iconographically lively pictures and, for all their apparent suggestiveness, we are not at all sure what they say. The particular mixtures of images appear to communicate at an intuitive or semi-conscious level, generating sensations as elusive and difficult to describe as a sound or a smell. Yet Kitaj's paintings are planned with the deliberation of a well-constructed novel. Like a novel, they have characters and a story, both of which are generally personal or learned references. A simple example can be found in *Bill at Sunset*.

The painting was sparked off by a graffito of a tramp that the artist saw on a boxcar; this put him in mind of his own adventures when he roamed America, like a whole army of youths and hobos, by jumping trains and never paying. Thus Bill is suffused with a slightly ironic nostalgia for a period (just after the Second World War) that was both grim and insouciant.

A more complex example, such as *If Not, Not*, shows how Kitaj weaves quite separate themes and allusions into a single composition. The overall look of the picture, Kitaj says, was 'conditioned by my first look at Giorgione's *Tempesta* in Venice, of which the little pool at the heart of my canvas is a reminder'. But several other sources were brought into play. The picture is alive, for instance, with references to Eliot's *The Waste Land*. As one penetrates the surface lushness of the scene, it turns into a landscape of nightmare strewn with the 'stony rubbish' and 'broken images' evoked in the poem (the subject, incidentally, for the important mural that Kitaj has been commissioned to make for the new British Library). Like Eliot, Kitaj was also influenced by Joseph Conrad, who inspired the dying figures among the trees to the right of the painting. The strew of objects in the middle also owes something to a Jacopo Bassano picture illustrating the aftermath of battle, but the work's main, pervasive theme is the massacre of European Jews. Dominating this lurid desolation of the painting's middle ground is that most sinister of modern landmarks: the gatehouse to Auschwitz.[4]

The genesis of each picture cannot of course be reduced to a simple cross-fertilization of references. It is an altogether more fascinating and more mysterious process, creating images, to use a phrase of Kitaj's, that 'sit in the unconscious'. In a more recent work, *The Jewish School*, the artist returns to the subject he has been 'mulling for years'. Kitaj was taken by a nineteenth-century engraving that mockingly evokes a Jewish classroom in chaos. The references prove to be direct and oblique in turn: the overturned inkpot in front of the anxious-looking teacher spills blood (the 'blood accusation' traditionally levelled against Jews); the youth at the board is drawing a golem – which will not come alive in time to save the Jews from their impending doom; the child in the centre is a semi-autobiographical figure, a kind of personal witness (named after a man, Joe Singer, who nearly married the artist's mother) who recurs in Kitaj's work; and the strangely compacted boy banging his head against a brick wall (an image that Hieronymous Bosch utilized is the rebellious Jewish child who might, or might not, survive the holocaust).

Little of this would be apparent to the uninitiated spectator, but Kitaj is in no way troubled by the fact that the narrative aspect of his painting will fail to reach most people. 'We go on being fascinated by all kinds of pictures that contain stories we no longer understand', he says. 'Just think of all the allegorical pictures of the Renaissance.' He himself is fascinated by the idea of inventing characters as in fiction, which he considers as a great, barely tapped source of imagery. One day, Kitaj has suggested, it might not seem out of the question that Tolstoy or Dickens are more helpful and pertinent to painting than Malevich or Duchamp; and he is in no doubt that, 'every painter of real interest I know is deeply imbued with literature'.

Kitaj's own sources are by no means limited to the museums or his own spectacularly well-filled bookshelves but can also be traced back as well to sailor's port and brothel, family and friends, London suburb, or landscape of the mind. He is particularly aware of the 'strictures of the modernist aesthetic – of allowing oneself to be boxed in by style', and by reaction he welcomes all experience as potential matter for art. This catholicity has provided him with so much material that now, he says, 'I have enough themes to last me the rest of my life.' Given the profusion of subjects and the artist's long-drawn-out, meticulous working methods, as many as a score of canvases may be in progress at any one moment. 'The longer I can hold onto them,' Kitaj admits, 'the better I can make them come out. And I also love the idea that a painting can go on and on, like a novel being developed.'

Like so many characters waiting to become independent of their creator, nearly finished portraits and other compositions in pastel, charcoal, and oil line Kitaj's handsome studio on the ground floor of his house in Chelsea. As one might expect from having studied the paintings, the studio itself contains a well-stocked archive of visual and literary material. Besides Kitaj's own works (of which he keeps his favourite examples) are paintings by friends – notably Auerbach and Hockney; and, among other things, a collection of Manet etchings. Row after long, tantalizing row of books fill the remaining wall space and continue in other rooms. More books stand in piles amid stacked papers on the studio tables, while several easels and some artist's materials round out the impression of a well-ordered abundance of things for the mind and the eye.

Kitaj's reaction to the not undaunting prospect of a large retrospective of his work is that he is 'just beginning – just spreading my wings'. He is particularly anxious to develop both his themes and his techniques, like the 'great Protean masters, Degas, Matisse, and Picasso', whose achievements have become second nature to him. In his latest works, he has been experimenting with the consistency of his paint: after years of using very thin colour, to the point of staining his canvas with paint-dipped rags, he has been trying the effects of impasto, notably in *The Jewish School*. He has also performed something of a volte-face within his own stylistic terms by concentrating on a 'straightforward' rendering of things. As a preparation for this, he has returned to drawing directly from professional models who come (as they did to all traditional artists' studios throughout the nineteenth century) to pose every week. These sessions have proved valuable to Kitaj, who believes that 'when you get a face or body right, you get the whole world in'.

The artist's current ambition – after what he calls 'half a digressive lifetime' – is to do a series of pictures of the sea. They will all be inspired by the Mediterranean seen from the Catalan village where he spends much of the summer; and some of them will no doubt contain figures. But, above all, they will represent a 'direct confrontation with Nature', and thus a fresh approach, for Kitaj intends them to be quite free of the allusiveness of his earlier work. At the same time, he does not intend to 'deny the passions of my youth'. One suspects that, in the end, Kitaj's gift for synthesis will prevail and that what seemed irreconcilable will merge into an unexpected accord, opening a new chapter in the restless narrative of his art.

1 Bacon, Freud, Michael Andrews, Auerbach, Kossoff, and Kitaj himself. The exhibition was entitled *A School of London: Six Figurative Painters* and was shown at four venues in 1987/8: Kunstnernes Hus, Oslo; Louisiana Museum of Modern Art, Humlebaek; Museo d'Arte Moderna, Ca' Pesaro, Venice; and Kunstmuseum, Düsseldorf.

2 From the preface to the catalogue for the exhibition *The Artist's Eye*, curated by R.B. Kitaj at the National Gallery, London, in 1980.

3 From 'A return to London', an interview with R.B. Kitaj by Timothy Hyman in the *London Magazine*, February 1980.

4 I am indebted, here and at several other points in this article, to Timothy Hyman's excellent preface to Kitaj's exhibition at the Marlborough gallery, New York, in April 1979.

Originally published in *Connaissance des Arts*, Paris, September 1981

PICTURE CREDITS

ACKNOWLEDGMENTS

I am particularly grateful to my publisher, Sophy Thompson, my commissioning editor, Philip Watson, my editor, Andrew Brown, the designer, Karolina Prymaka, and all at Thames & Hudson who have helped to bring out *Artists' Lives*. Special thanks to my research assistant, Michael Kurtz, for enriching and correcting the text, as well as for his encouragement and unfailing good humour.

My wife, the art historian and exhibition curator Jill Lloyd, has not only contributed her invaluable knowledge and skills to this book, as she does to everything I write, she has also given me ideal conditions in which to write it.

For their advice, support and friendship, I should also like to record my gratitude to Fiamma Arditi, Katharine Arnold, Charles Asprey, Alice Bellony, Philippe Bern, Thérèse Tigretti Berthoud, David Blow, Anne and Yves Bonavero, Miel de Botton, Majid Boustany, Viscount and Viscountess Bridgman, Adam Brown, Ben and Louisa Brown, Richard Bucht, Marlene Burston, Charles and Natasha Campbell, Rebecca Carter, Guillaume Cerruti, Neil and Narisa Chakra Thompson, Charles Cholmondeley, Patrice and Mala Cotensin, Sir Howard and Lady Davies, Hugh Marlais Davies, Adrian and Jamie Dicks, Manos Dimitrakopoulos, Christopher Eykyn, Michael Fishwick, Lord Norman and Lady Elena Foster, Colin and Sophie Gleadell, John Gordon, Nicholas Goulandris, Claude-Bernard Haïm, Nadine Haïm, Andrew Hochhauser, David Hockney, Max Hollein, Catherine Howe, Henry and Alison Meyric Hughes, Mark Inglefield, Christina and Richard Ives, Bill and Janet Jacklin, Sam Keller, Toby Kidd, Alastair King, Ulf Küster, Andrew Lambirth, Mingwei Lee, Mark and Lucy Lefanu, Alan and Christina Macdonald, Nicholas Maclean, Gillian Malpass, the late Sandro Manzo, Graham Marchant, Tim Marlow, Thérèse Meier, Lucy Mitchell-Innes, Bona Colonna Montagu, Serena Morton, David Nash, Hughie and Clare O'Donoghue, Francis Outred, Alex Peppiatt, Ann Peppiatt, Clio Peppiatt, Elliott Power, Renée Price, Lesley Ramos, John Rivett, Christopher and Carmel Shirley, Frank and Pauline Slattery, Michel Soskine, Alex Stavrakas, Arturo di Stefano, Sir Ian and Lady Stoutzker, Stanley Tucci, Ortrud Westheider, Thomas Williams, Clive and Catherine Wilson, and Michael Ziegert.

INDEX OF NAMES

MICHAEL PEPPIATT

ARTISTS' LIVES

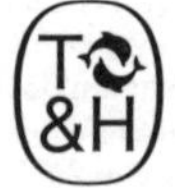